B Joh

3/11/11

WITS AND WIVES

BY THE SAME AUTHOR

Fanny Burney: Her Life

Wits and Wives

Dr Johnson in the Company of Women

Kate Chisholm

Chatto & Windus
LONDON

Published by Chatto & Windus 2011

2 4 6 8 10 9 7 5 3 1

First published in Great Britain in 2011 by
Chatto & Windus
Random House, 20 Vauxhall Bridge Road,
London SW1V 2SA

www.rbooks.co.uk

Addresses for companies within The Random House Group Limited can be found at:
www.randomhouse.co.uk/offices.htm

The Random House Group Limited Reg. No. 954009

A CIP catalogue record for this book
is available from the British Library

ISBN 9780701169046

The Random House Group Limited supports The Forest Stewardship Council (FSC®), the
leading international forest certification organisation. Our books carrying the FSC label are
printed on FSC® certified paper. FSC is the only forest certification scheme endorsed by
the leading environmental organisations, including Greenpeace. Our paper procurement policy
can be found at www.randomhouse.co.uk/environment

MIX
Paper from
responsible sources
FSC® C016897

Typeset by Palimpsest Book Production Limited, Falkirk, Stirlingshire
Printed and bound in Great Britain by
CPI Group (UK) Ltd, Croydon, CR0 4YY

To my father, a parish priest
who argued against the ordination of women
but encouraged many women in their ministry

Contents

1 *Intimations*   1
   In which we discover Johnson's empathy with women, his concern
   for the plight of prostitutes, his belief that women should be educated
   enough to converse with their husbands, his desire to act as 'a neutral
   being' between the sexes, and his influence on Mary Wollstonecraft.

2 *Here's a Brave Mother*   14
   Sarah Johnson, aged forty, gives birth to her firstborn son Samuel;
   has to cope with his sickly childhood and her melancholic husband;
   runs the bookshop after Samuel leaves for London to make his name
   as a writer; does not see him for twenty years, not even when he is
   told that she is dying.

3 *Love and Death*   40
   Samuel Johnson marries Elizabeth ('Tetty') Porter, a woman old
   enough to be his mother, in 1735. He declares it is 'a love match on
   both sides'. But she loses everything when she marries him – even
   her children. She's thought of as 'a painted poppet', a woman who
   drank cheap spirits and lounged around reading romantic novels, but
   when she dies Johnson is devastated.

4   *An Equal Mind*   68
     Elizabeth Carter comes to London to find employment as a writer,
     encouraged by her scholarly father. She works alongside Johnson on
     the *Gentleman's Magazine*, but she establishes her reputation long
     before him. Her translation of the Stoic philosopher Epictetus is a
     huge success. She is also renowned for the excellence of her puddings.

5   *Miss Sainthill and the Female Quixote*   97
     Not long after Tetty dies, Johnson begins writing to Hill Boothby in
     search of spiritual guidance and consolation. Is she a potential second
     wife? In the meantime, he nurtures the talent of the precocious
     Charlotte Lennox, who arrives in London from New York and in 1747
     makes her name with a poem entitled 'The Art of Coquetry'.

6   *A Stifled Sigh*   132
     The newly wed Hester Thrale invites the celebrated Mr Johnson to
     dinner in 1763. He enjoys her sharp, witty conversation; she values
     his literary celebrity. While she gives birth to twelve children in
     fourteen years, Johnson is rescued from his morbid melancholy by his
     part-time life with the Thrales. He confesses his secret thoughts to
     Hester; she relishes the opportunity to flex her ever-inventive mind.

7   *'Renny Dear'*   172
     Frances Reynolds, like her brother, Sir Joshua, is a keen portraitist.
     She paints her friends in an unorthodox, pared-down, homely style.
     When she quarrels with Sir Joshua, Johnson intervenes on her behalf,
     trying to reconcile the siblings. Her unpublished 'Recollections' disclose
     the beady-eyed insights of an artist.

8   *The Taming of a Female Wit*   200
     Hannah More arrives in London in 1774, is befriended by David
     Garrick and has a huge success on the West End stage with her
     tragedy *Percy*. She also adopts the cause of the Abolitionists,
     publishing *Slavery: A poem* in 1788. But London life soon palls and
     she retreats to Somerset to do good works.

9 *Resolutions?*   232

After Richard Samuel's acknowledgement of female achievement in
his *Nine Living Muses*, women begin to retreat from the public stage.
Johnson's attempt to place himself as 'a neutral being between' the
sexes is not repeated; Mary Wollstonecraft's debt to him is ignored.
Where next for the female wits?

Acknowledgements   243

List of Illustrations   245

Chapter Notes   247

Index   279

1

Intimations

One afternoon in early spring 1784, a young schoolmistress sets off to walk the three and a half miles from her home in Newington Green on the outskirts of London into the heart of the City. She is about to call on a man whose writing she has long admired. Rarely a week goes by without his name being mentioned in the newspapers – Mr J. is unwell, has spent the evening at Ranelagh Gardens, is about to marry the widow of the Streatham brewer. He is not too grand, though, to have forgotten his origins as a bookseller's son from Lichfield who arrived in London with no money, a 'rustick tongue' and nothing to commend him except an unusual degree of sense and a persevering constitution. The young woman is hoping he will advise her on how to begin her own career as a writer. How can she find an outlet for the thoughts and ideas that unsettle her peace of mind, but also make enough money to support herself and her sisters?

She hesitates for a moment before turning down the dark cobbled lane off Fleet Street where she has been told she will find his lodgings. This grimy, dirt-filled passage appears such an unlikely home for the hard-working scholar and contemplative writer she knows him to be. The tenements on either side are scruffy, uncared-for, their windows narrow and covered with sooty dust. The street beyond is bustling with farmers driving cattle on their way to market, the carriages of the rich, and the cries of women selling fish, milk, and nosegays of lavender and orange peel against the stench. Are these bleak surroundings all that the great Mr J. can afford?

The young woman herself could be mistaken for a poor washerwoman in her plain brown woollen skirt and paisley shawl, a cotton scarf tied round her unruly hair. Few would guess that her name would soon be known not just within London's literary circles but also in Dublin, Paris, Vienna and Venice. From her homespun clothes it is obvious she is struggling with hard times, but still she cuts a striking figure, her cheeks flushed pink from her long walk in the chilly wind, her deep-set eyes shining brightly, reflecting her eager, inquiring mind.

To her surprise, when she knocks at No. 8 Bolt Court the door is opened not by a pert maid but by a black man in middle age who takes her straight upstairs to meet his employer. Mr J. is sitting uncomfortably on a broken chair in his chaotic, paper-strewn parlour, his wig askew, his cuffs and necktie spattered with tea stains. A heavy, ungainly man, he is almost bent double in his discomfort, his legs swollen like an elephant's, his every movement clumsy with pain. But he welcomes his unexpected visitor with enthusiasm. Here at last is the prospect of a conversation which might distract him for the afternoon from his malignant fears.

'Frank,' he bellows downstairs, a characterful strength in his voice in spite of his infirmities. 'Be so kind as to bring us some fresh tea.'

Mr J. might have been less welcoming if he had suspected that his visitor, Mary Wollstonecraft, would in just a few years publish her provocative *Vindication of the Rights of Woman*. Or would he?

Otherwise known as Dr Samuel Johnson, Mr J. has often been depicted as a man's man. The writer and creator of the *Dictionary of the English Language* is reputed to have had little patience or sympathy for women who voiced their opinions too stridently. Almost from the moment of his death in December 1784 (just a few months after Mary Wollstonecraft called on him at Bolt Court), his published and private thoughts were being endlessly retailed in collections of his 'table talk', his wise words, his 'beauties'. Mr J. soon became, like the Bible and Shakespeare, a source of endless quotation, mostly derived from his friend James Boswell's *Life of Samuel Johnson, LLD*, which is an unusually personal study and stuffed full of his clever remarks.

Johnson was never afraid to express his opinions, or to flex his journalist's knack for hitting upon an unforgettable phrase. Boswell took care to note down as many of these observations and maxims as he could, and to include them in his biography. 'It is so far from being natural for a man and woman to live in a state of marriage,' we are warned in the *Life*, 'that we find all the motives which they have for remaining in that connection, and the restraints which civilised society imposes to prevent separation, are hardly sufficient to keep them together.' But on another occasion Johnson is reported to have declared, 'Even ill assorted marriages were preferable to cheerless celibacy.' How then should we live? Especially if, as he wrote in his dystopian tale *The History of Rasselas, Prince of Abyssinia*, 'Human life is everywhere a state in which much is to be endured, and little to be enjoyed.'

Taken out of context, Johnson's often witty, always perceptive comments on domestic life and the business of being human might persuade us that he was a misanthropic whinger with a low opinion of women. In *The Beauties of Samuel Johnson*, a collection of aphorisms taken from his essays and published even before he had died, there's a section entitled 'Weakness, female'. Needless to say, there's nothing about 'Weakness, male'. By the late 1840s this image of Johnson was so familiar that when the artist James Doyle portrayed Johnson at dinner with a group of friends, he surrounded him with men. Not a single woman graces the painting, which was later engraved and reprinted many times; even the servant is a young black man.

Mary Wollstonecraft, though, had read many of Johnson's works, and she thought of him rather differently. She knew that in 1750 he had written an essay in which he confesses, 'The reproach for making the world miserable has been always thrown upon the women.' And why is this? Because, says Johnson, most published writers (and their publishers, too) are male, and they have always viewed the world from their own rather narrow perspective. He instead promises to 'divest my heart of all partiality' and attempt an extraordinary transformation, becoming 'a neutral being between the sexes', neither male nor female. This, he hopes, will enable him to adjudicate with 'equal regard' between husbands and wives. Maybe then he will better understand the peculiar difficulties experienced by women? The originality of Johnson's promise, his independence of mind, becomes even clearer if we remember that he was writing at a time when divorce had to be negotiated by an Act of Parliament and married women had no rights of ownership over property.

Bored wives, angry teenagers and miserable prostitutes often make an appearance in Johnson's essays. 'How frequently have the gay and thoughtless, in their evening frolicks, seen a band of these miserable females, covered with rags, shivering with cold, and pining with hunger,' he writes about the women of the night who accosted him as he walked across town on his way home from an evening of conversation in a cosy tavern. 'And, without either pitying their calamities, or reflecting upon the cruelty of those who perhaps first seduced them by caresses of fondness, or magnificence of promises, go on to reduce others to the same wretchedness by the same means.'

These were not the casual words of a paid journalist, a commentator on the affairs of men and women. Johnson took direct action to help those he came across who had been reduced to a life of poverty and distress. He could not walk past a beggar without emptying his pockets – and the streets of London in those years were filled with those who had no money even for food. Late one night, he stumbled upon the prostitute Poll Carmichael, who was lying in the street after collapsing from exhaustion and malnutrition. Shocked by her condition, instead of walking on past her almost lifeless body, or just throwing her some loose farthings, he picked her up and carried her home across his broad shoulders.

He was not idealistic about his actions in trying to help her, or about Poll herself, talking of her as 'that surly slut'. He was simply trying to make amends, in his own way, for the endemic injustices of society. Infuriated by Poll, and her slovenly ways, he told his friend Hester Thrale, 'I had some hopes of her at first, but when I talked to her tightly and closely, I could make nothing of her; she was wiggle-waggle.' Yet Poll stayed on in his household for several months until she was able to take care of herself without resorting to the street.

Mary Wollstonecraft was driven by the same abhorrence of inequalities, and especially of misplaced domestic and sexual power, having as a child watched her mother being abused by her violent and incompetent father. When she read in Johnson's *Rambler* essay that women should be free *not* to marry, since marriage was a condition of life not always conducive to their health or happiness, she was surprised to discover a male writer who knew how she felt. 'The custom of the world seems to have been formed in a kind of conspiracy against [women],' Johnson writes, as this 'neutral being' he has promised to turn himself into. Whether women marry, or choose to remain single, they are 'exposed to sickness, misery, and death'. Why, he wonders, do young women agree to marry at all? After all, 'Marriage . . . is much more necessary to a man than to a woman; for he is much less able to supply himself with domestic comforts.' Mary relished what she read; here at last was a writer who could see into her own mind.

4

Not long before her visit to Bolt Court, a new edition of *The History of Rasselas* was published. Mary would have been surprised to read its unconventional conclusion 'in which nothing is concluded', and to discover that Johnson allows his hero, Prince Rasselas, to be outshone by the two female characters, Princess Nekayah and her maid Pekuyah. While the Prince prevaricates, not sure of the best path to follow at the end of his journey of self-discovery beyond the Happy Valley of his childhood, his sister Nekayah decides she will set up 'a college of learned women, in which she would preside, that, by conversing with the old, and educating the young, she might divide her time between the acquisition and communication of wisdom, and raise up for the next age models of prudence and patterns of piety'. Education of the mind, implies Johnson, should be our priority, and this is just as important for young girls as it is for their brothers, using words that Mary Wollstonecraft was soon to echo in her *Thoughts on the Education of Daughters*.

Many of the fathers and husbands even in Johnson's enlightened circle would have disagreed with his views on expanding the opportunities for education to women. When he offered to teach the novelist Frances (or 'Fanny') Burney the Latin and Greek languages so that she could read the literary classics, many of which were still unavailable because not yet translated, her father, the musician and writer Dr Charles Burney, refused to give his permission – even though his daughter was by then in her late twenties. Dr Burney was trying to protect Frances, believing that it was dangerous for women to be too clever, and especially women with no fortune. An appearance of learning might ruin her chances of a fortuitous marriage.

Johnson, who spent his life analysing and attempting to understand the impulses and responses that shaped his own character, recognised where these prejudices came from. He once admitted to Hester Thrale, 'it is a Paltry Trick indeed to deny Women the Cultivation of their mental Powers, and I think it is partly a proof we are afraid of them – if we endeavour to keep them unarmed'. Johnson was too honest with himself not to admit that the reason why he was sometimes uneasy when in the company of women with sharp minds was because he disliked the sensation of being outwitted.

His meeting with the young schoolteacher from Newington Green was brief and not repeated. On the surface there can have been little in common between the independent-minded young woman, whose life experiences would turn out to be so unconventional, and the elderly founder of the all-male

Literary Club. Yet in the letters and published works of Mary Wollstonecraft (born in 1759) there are often unexpected echoes of Johnson (born fifty years earlier in 1709). What were these connections and affinities? And why does Wollstonecraft's biographer, her husband William Godwin, make special reference to their brief and single meeting as if it had meant something to her?

Perhaps it is time for us to take a closer look at Johnson's relations with women, and especially with his mother and his wife as well as with his colleagues and rivals as writers, his protégées and spiritual mentors. Perhaps, if we did, we would discover a different Johnson, or rather gain access to a truer, richer, deeper portrait of the man these women knew as a friend, a correspondent, a conversational sparring partner. We might also find out something about the lives of these women. Who were they? How did they overcome the contradictions of being wives, wits and writers? What compromises did they make to reconcile their private, secret ambitions with their domestic duties, or in some cases the chance of a professional life with the demands of marriage and family? Perhaps, too, if we adopted Johnson's suggestion and placed ourselves as 'neutral beings' between the sexes we might discover something about ourselves, and about the gender pressures that still have influence within our superficially more enlightened society.

A few weeks after his conversation with Mary Wollstonecraft, Johnson was invited to dinner by Eva-Marie Garrick, widow of the great actor. The only other guests were three women: the scholar Elizabeth Carter, the playwright Hannah More and the novelist Frances Burney. Johnson was the solitary male among a group of clever, witty women. This was not uncommon. In his broad circle of friends, there were as many as eighty-five women, who sought his company because his conversation, like their own, ranged so widely from 'the common affairs of life', such as his love of gooseberry tart or his dislike of cucumber ('it should be well sliced, and dressed with pepper and vinegar, and then thrown out'), to affairs of state, the vices of Voltaire, or the extraordinary sight of a hot-air balloon over St George's Fields in Lambeth.

Wollstonecraft would not have been surprised to find Johnson in such company. 'In former times,' he had written in 1753, 'the pen like the sword was considered as consigned by nature to the hands of men . . . The revolution of years has now produced a generation of Amazons of the pen, who with the spirit of their predecessors have set masculine tyranny at defiance.'

Cheaper paper and the relaxation of many of the government's taxes on paper, printing ink and advertisements had made possible the rise of the daily newspaper and monthly magazine. By the 1730s, the guild of printers, the Stationers' Company, no longer controlled the rights to printing and publishing, and every large provincial town had its own newspaper. In London, there were as many as seventy-five master printers at work, hungry for manuscripts to keep their presses working, that number increasing to more than 120 by 1760. Women writers rose to the challenge, supplying collections of poetry, translations, essays, histories and novels.

When Charlotte Lennox arrived in London in 1747, penniless and friendless, she at first tried to make a living as an actress but soon turned to writing as a more lucrative source of income. With remarkable speed she succeeded in meeting the leading figures in London's literary scene, as well as the printers and publishers she would need to convince of her talent. In 1751 Johnson hosted an all-night party of his Literary Club to celebrate her debut as a novelist, and for the next thirty years he often helped her out with introductions and professional advice.

Johnson's friendship with Lennox reflects his attitude to the women of his acquaintance, which was often both paternal and professional. 'I hope you take great care to observe the Doctor's prescriptions and take your physick regularly,' he wrote to her in a letter, which could be thought of as a little patronising. But then he added, 'I should be sorry to lose Criticism in her bloom . . . When Shakespeare is demolished your wings will be full summed, and I will fly you at Milton; for you are a bird of prey, but the Bird of Jupiter.' Lennox had just published three volumes on Shakespeare's plays; Johnson was now inviting her to apply her wit, her gift for incisive criticism, to the nation's great poet.

Another guest at that dinner, Hannah More, celebrated Johnson's 'Amazons of the pen' in her hugely popular satirical poem *The Bas Bleu*, (The Bluestockings), which begins:

> Long was Society o'er-run
> By Whist, that desolating Hun;
> Long did Quadrille despotic sit,
> That Vandal of colloquial wit;

and goes on to explain why it is the women wits, the bluestockings, who have saved us from this deadly boredom. As she was writing the poem, the artist Richard Samuel was creating his unusual group portrait, *The Nine Living Muses*, which portrays the artist Angelica Kauffmann and singer Elizabeth Linley at the centre of a classically posed posse of women writers: Hannah More, Elizabeth Carter and Charlotte Lennox, along with Elizabeth Montagu, Elizabeth Griffith, Catherine Macaulay and Anna Laetitia Barbauld. It's not a very good painting (Carter complained that it was impossible to tell the women apart since Samuel had painted them with so little attention to their individual characteristics), but *The Nine Living Muses* records a rare moment when women were allowed a degree of intellectual prowess and could even be dressed up as the classical muses.

The 'wit' which More, Carter, Lennox and the other 'muses' aspired to was not the sharp sallies of the comedian, but a capacity of mind and flexibility of thought. Their conversation, their industry had a precise function: the pursuit of virtue and understanding. 'It is really quite provoking,' remarked Catherine Talbot to her friend Elizabeth Carter in June 1746, 'to see wit thrown away upon people who discover their total want of taste by such ill placed marks of approbation, as one sees are thrown in, out of mere civility.' 'Wit' was a mark of intelligence; those gifted with it were obliged to use it wisely. It had nothing to do with posing, posturing, playing with ideas. For the educated women of the mid-eighteenth century, wit, or rather intelligence, was only valued if it was directed towards enlightenment and self-improvement.

In these years to be thought of as 'a bluestocking' was a compliment that applied equally to men and women. Johnson was often in their company but was never really thought of as one; Mary Wollstonecraft was too young, and not well-born enough. Who, then, were they?

The bluestockings emerged in the 1750s, taking their name from the gentleman-scholar Benjamin Stillingfleet, known for the brilliance of his conversation, who persisted in wearing his cheap, workaday blue woollen stockings when out in company instead of changing into the fine cream silk stockings of the drawing room or ballroom. 'We can do nothing without the blue stockings,' guests would tease their hostess on discovering that Stillingfleet had failed to turn up at an evening tea party or morning breakfast. But soon anyone who attended the drawing-room parties of the wealthy widow Elizabeth Montagu, and of her friends and rivals Elizabeth Vesey and Frances Boscawen, was thought of as a bluestocking; someone who preferred tea and conversation to playing whist or canasta. By the time Hannah More published *The Bas Bleu* in 1786, only women were thought of as bluestock-ings, but the moniker had not yet become as derogatory as we think of it today.

The bluestockings of the eighteenth century had a mission: to effect a moral reformation through the power of conversation. As More writes:

> Hail, Conversation, heav'nly fair,
> Thou bliss of life, and balm of care!
> Call forth the long-forgotten knowledge
> Of school, of travel, and of college!
> For thee, best solace of his toil!
> The sage consumes his midnight oil;
> And keeps late vigils, to produce
> Materials for thy future use . . .
> . . . Let taste her curious touchstone hold,
> To try if standard be the gold;
> But 'tis thy commerce, Conversation,
> Must give it use by circulation;
> That noblest commerce of mankind,
> Whose precious merchandise is MIND!

The flavour and the substance of these salon conversations were continued in the frequent letters these friends wrote to each other. Elizabeth Carter often sent off as many as twelve letters in an afternoon, posted within London for the price of one penny a letter (unless she could send a messenger). Postage was much more expensive from her home in Deal, costing twopence for a single sheet of paper, but sixpence for a double sheet (unless she could arrange for a franked letter, dispensed only by members of parliament). Her correspondents included Catherine Talbot, Elizabeth Vesey and Elizabeth Montagu, who was often described as the Queen of the Bluestockings because she was rich, which gave added lustre to her gather-ings and also allowed her to act as a patron, subsidising the publications of her women friends.

The letters between these clever, thoughtful women are full of life, of intellectual curiosity, of feeling, response and understanding. In a single letter, Elizabeth Carter recommends the benefits of exercise in combating 'nervous disorders' before, without a pause, moving on to the difficulty of translating Pliny, along the way delighting in a production of *Much Ado About Nothing* and the 'powerful magic of Mr Handel'. She asks Catherine Talbot for an account of the dress she wore to a masquerade; and then writes a critique of perhaps the greatest novel of the mid-eighteenth century, Samuel Richardson's *Clarissa*:

> Richardson has no doubt a very good hand at painting excellence, but there is a strange awkwardness and extravagance in his vicious characters. To be sure, poor man, he had read in a book, or heard some one say, there was such a thing in the world as wickedness, but being totally ignorant in what manner the said wickedness operates upon the human heart, and what checks and restraints it meets with to prevent its ever being perfectly uniform and consistent in any one character, he has drawn such a monster, as I hope never existed in mortal shape . . .

Carter was an astute critic, and not afraid of reputation. She appreciated Richardson's writerly skill but wondered about his intuition; after all, he was just a 'poor man'.

Johnson shared with the bluestockings their passion for letter-writing, because in such a communication he could exercise his mind *and* exorcise those difficult thoughts which kept him awake at night. Wollstonecraft was also a prolific letter-writer. In April 1787 she tells the Revd Henry Dyson Gabell:

> How can the mind govern the body if it is not exercised? Dr Johnson, has said, that the most trivial occupations, such as collecting shells, &c &c are of use, and even, promote the cause of virtue, as some time is stolen from sensual pursuits. I agree with him—and think if we were more perfect the *single* desire of pleasing the Author of all good might be sufficient to make us virtuous—but we are so framed that we want continual variety—and the appetites will rule if the mind is *vacant*.

Not only does she quote from Johnson, but she has come to know his writings so well that it's almost as if he is writing the letter, so close is what she writes to his epigrammatic style.

Mary Wollstonecraft echoes his thoughts, too. In several of his essays Johnson extols the virtues of true friendship, writing that 'Life has no pleasure higher or nobler than that of friendship.' We should, he urges, keep our friendships in constant repair. Wollstonecraft describes friendship as 'the medicine, the *cordial* of life'.

Rare, though, are the friendships that endure. 'The most fatal disease of friendship is gradual decay, or dislike hourly encreased by causes too slender for complaint, and too numerous for removal,' Johnson warns. In an *Idler* essay, he imagines 'Lonelove' and 'Ranger' retreating to the country 'to enjoy the company of each other', but they return after six weeks 'cold and petulant'. Johnson tries to work out the reason for their falling out with each other. He concludes that this was not so much because Ranger enjoyed walking in the fields while Lonelove's pleasure was 'to sit in a bower', but rather because, 'Each had complied with the other in his turn, and each was angry that compliance had been exacted.' Honesty is the essential ingredient of long-term friendships, taking us through the ups and downs of life.

Johnson's friendships with the women of his acquaintance depended on this mutual give-and-take, this frank exchange of need. When Frances Reynolds quarrelled with her brother, the fashionable artist Sir Joshua, it was to Johnson she looked for advice on how to repair their fractious relationship. Johnson, too, encouraged her in her ambition to paint, sitting for her on a number of occasions. But she, in turn, reassured and comforted him, understanding that the oddness of his physical appearance and his nervous tics were an ever-present affliction. Like Johnson, she saw through a glass darkly to what lies behind.

He once wrote that you can tell more about a man from the way he behaves at home among his family and servants than when he is out and about in the world doing great things, refining something that he had learnt from the women of his acquaintance. Johnson trusted the domestic experience, recognising that we only reveal our true selves when behind closed doors. If you want to test a person, to accurately portray their character in a biographical study, then you must discover something about their private life. Often it was a person's servant, without education or power, who knew his or her employer best.

Servants were a constant, shadowy presence in Johnson's time, waiting on table, tending to the drawing-room fire, and even in the bedroom, lighting candles, bringing hot water up several flights of stairs and taking away the slops. They were witnesses to the most intimate secrets of those whom they served. Johnson took an interest in their lives, just as much as in those of his friends and colleagues. He knew their worth.

In his study of Alexander Pope, for his *Lives of the Poets*, his ambitious round-up of the nation's great poets, Johnson wrote with unusual detail about Pope's private circumstances, information that could only have been derived from his servants. He quotes from a 'female domestick' who waited on Pope and who reported how intensely the acerbic writer and critic felt the cold and how 'His legs were so slender, that he enlarged their bulk with three pairs of stockings, which were drawn on and off by the maid; for he was not able to dress or undress himself, and neither went to bed nor rose without help.' Pope's weakness, Johnson adds, 'made it very difficult for [him] to be clean', which perhaps explains his irascibility and vicious criticism of other writers. Johnson understood that details which might seem trivial to a study of Pope as a poet were in fact crucial to his portrait of the man behind the phrase, 'Most women have no characters at all.'

Johnson often infuriated his wife Tetty by failing to appreciate the dinner she had cooked for him, and leaving behind him a trail of papers and dirty washing. But he did also value the domestic arts – at least in print – as a means to improving a person's character. In his creation of Lady Bustle in his *Rambler* essays, a woman who bores and infuriates her daughters by insisting they spend all their time fluffing up cushions or making preserves, he appears to be spoofing the kind of housewife who takes pride in having the best jam cupboard in the district. But in the process he betrays an intimate knowledge of culinary science and 'the art of scalding damascenes without bursting them, and preserving the whiteness of pickled mushrooms'. Where else did Johnson imbibe this appreciation of life's more prosaic virtues if not from his mother, whose struggles as the wife of Michael Johnson, too bookish to make a success of his trade in books, are hinted at by her son?

Lady Bustle is perhaps the personification of Sarah Johnson, who was affronted by her husband's niggardly habits and who cared too much about what the neighbours might think. Yet after Michael Johnson's death, she proved her resilience and her resourcefulness by taking over her husband's bookshop and keeping it going for twenty-six years.

This investigation into the lives of the women who knew Johnson will take us from Lichfield, where he grew up, to London and his life among the bluestockings. We shall look into his troubled marriage to Tetty and reinstate her as a key figure in his life, his 'dear Tetty'. When she died he was left 'in the gloom of solitude', without anyone to share the triumph of his *Dictionary*.

She could not be thought of as a wit, but she gave him the consolations of a wife.

Tetty would have been uncomfortable in the company of Elizabeth Carter, who, like Johnson, worked on the *Gentleman's Magazine*. Even he was sometimes wary of her, conscious that her intellect was sharper, her knowledge broader, her understanding deeper than his own. Carter's professional success illustrates that fleeting period in mid-century when women took to the public stage, exercising a degree of independence and revealing their capabilities.

The contrasting life experiences of Hill Boothby and Charlotte Lennox are reflected in their very different friendships with Johnson. He sought out Hill Boothby after the death of Tetty in 1752. Deeply religious, Boothby lived in genteel comfort in rural Derbyshire, from where she wrote letters fuelled by her faith, her spiritual connection. Johnson thought of her as 'My sweet Angel', and looked to her for comfort in his desolation. Lennox, in contrast, had no family connections and no money, arriving in London as a young woman in need of a husband. What she achieved was entirely through her own talent, as a writer and networker, meeting Johnson just as he was at last establishing his authority as a literary lion. He treated her like a daughter; she sought his advice and encouragement.

The talent of Frances Reynolds was also nurtured by Johnson, although in a different sphere. Her portraits of him, both on canvas and in words, give us an alternative Johnson, not the man we read about in James Boswell's biography. Her Johnson is old and weak, troubled and odd, yet exceptional because of his humanity, his empathy, his honest appraisal of himself and others. Frances Reynolds introduced him to Hannah More, who like herself had come to the capital from the West Country in search of professional opportunities. More's career as a writer, from the success of her play *Percy* in 1777 to her death in 1833, reflects the changing cultural atmosphere as the revolutionary events across the Channel began to have an impact upon attitudes to women who sought to live by the pen. By 1815, the caricaturist Thomas Rowlandson would depict the bluestockings in retreat, bounced off the pedestals they had stood upon in mid-century.

But we shall begin with Johnson's mother, a semi-educated woman from the county squirearchy whose determination ensured her son's survival as a weak and sickly child. Sarah Johnson (née Ford) was no wit, but she provided the right kind of emotional and intellectual ballast for her son, until he was ready to launch himself as a writer in the capital.

2

Here's a Brave Mother

'Mother' is given nine alternative definitions by Johnson in his *Dictionary of the English Language* – from the straightforward 'A woman that has born a child' to 'That which requires reverence and obedience'. As an illustration of his meaning, Johnson quotes from the scene in Shakespeare's *A Midsummer Night's Dream* where Quince is assembling his cast of mechanicals:

> Come sit down every mother's son,
> And rehearse your parts

Johnson was always keenly aware of his mother's presence in his life, writing in the week of her death, 'The life which made my own life pleasant is at an end, and the gates of death are shut upon my prospects.' Yet we know surprisingly little about Sarah Johnson. This son's mother has been forgotten by history. In Johnson's voluminous surviving correspondence, there are only four letters from him to her, and these were all written in January 1759 as she lay dying in Lichfield. We have no letters written by her.

Sarah Johnson has no voice in the story of her son. There is no surviving portrait of her, and James Boswell says very little about her in his vast *Life of Samuel Johnson*. She remains a shadowy, inconsequential figure. In the shelfloads of books about her son, she rarely merits more than a passing paragraph. When she does make an appearance, she is sketched in hastily as a small-minded woman who made her husband unhappy with her petty

14

complaints about money, and who exasperated her son by her obsession with trivia. Her incompatibility with her husband and their quarrels are often blamed for the jaundiced view of marriage essayed by Johnson.

The American critic Walter Jackson Bate in the 1970s did become interested in Johnson's relationship with his mother, taking a post-Freudian approach to familial relationships. In his view Sarah was responsible for the emotional troubles of her son. Bate suggests that Sarah and Sam were engaged in an Oedipal power conflict, and this explains Johnson's neurotic tics and his personal difficulties on leaving Lichfield. It is a fascinating and sometimes revelatory portrayal, but perhaps tells us more about the critic and his time than his subject, as is often the way with biography.

There was nevertheless something very fraught about Johnson's relationship with his mother. In his *Dictionary* Johnson adds another, more expressive quotation to his definition of 'mother', from Exeter's speech on the battlefield in Shakespeare's *Henry V*:

> I had not so much of man in me,
> But all my mother came into mine eyes
> And gave me up to tears.

Exeter is moved to tears by the gruesome sight of all the dead soldiers. The upsurge of feeling, his emotional response, leads him to think of his mother. Johnson, via Shakespeare, thus associates 'motherhood' in the *Dictionary* with our capacity for empathy.

Exeter's tears also represent something more complicated – his guilt about leaving, about his absence from home. In a letter Johnson wrote in May 1777 to console his friend Mary Cholmondeley (younger sister of the celebrated actress Peg Woffington) after the death of her son, Johnson reflects on mothers and sons, 'We all live on this condition that the ties of every endearment must at last be broken. The Mother must lose her Son, or the son his Mother.' Johnson, though, never quite lost the feeling that his mother was watching over him, which he found encouraging but also entangling, knotting him up in a complex web of feelings. Johnson was, after all, the prodigal son who *never* returned home.

Johnson made no effort to travel back to Lichfield in January 1759, after receiving letters warning him that his mother was close to death – even though he had not seen her since the winter of 1740. For many years, his excuse was pressure of work, the illness of his wife, his lack of money. But in May 1755, a month after the two vast volumes of the *Dictionary of the English Language* had at last been published, and to great acclaim, Johnson wrote to Bennet Langton, 'I have a Mother more than eighty years old, who has counted the days to the publication of my book in hopes of seeing me, and to her, if I can disengage myself here, I resolve to go.' But he didn't go.

In late July 1755 he travelled as far as Oxford to study in the Bodleian Library and to visit his friends among the academics, but still made no trip to see his mother. In October, he told an old friend from his youth, Richard Congreve, who lived close to Lichfield, that he expected to visit him soon. 'I fully persuade myself that I shall pass some of the winter months with my mother, I would have come sooner but could not break my Shackles . . .' But he never made the journey to see either Congreve or his mother. A year later, he was still insisting, 'I have been thinking every month of coming down into the country, but every Month has brought its hindrances.'

'As we come forward into life we naturally turn back now and then upon the past,' he admitted to his former schoolfriend Edmund Hector in November 1756. 'I now think more upon my Schooldays than I did when I had just broken loose from a Master.' He then declared, 'Happy is he that can look back upon the past with pleasure.' But he added, 'Of those happy Beings have you known many?' – as if he himself did not dare to look back. He didn't even make the effort to attend his mother's funeral. 'It is not of any use for me now to come down, nor can I bear the place,' he told his step-daughter Lucy (his wife Tetty's child), who looked after Mrs Johnson into her old age.

This reluctance to go back to the scenes of his childhood is perhaps easier to understand than his return two years later, during the winter of 1761–62, when travelling would have been difficult and uncomfortable in the gloomy, freezing weather. Johnson spent five days wandering about the old haunts he had not seen for more than twenty years. The streets, he noted, were 'much narrower and shorter than I thought I had left them, inhabited by a new race of people, to whom I was very little known'. Johnson was always too honest, too self-lacerating not to realise that it is impossible to retrace the steps that have led us away from our former lives. Yet, in spite of this sense of no longer belonging, this discomfort, unease, the loss of all his family, apart from Lucy, he began returning almost every year to Lichfield, even in the summer of 1784 just a few months before his death when his poor health must have made the journey very arduous. Why, then, did he not travel back while his mother was alive?

Until the spring of 1755 and the completion of the *Dictionary*, Johnson was always conscious that he had yet to fulfil the potential his mother had discerned in him and which had driven him away from Lichfield. He was also under incredible pressure of work – the *Dictionary* had taken him six years longer than planned, partly because he decided halfway through to change his working methods. He had begun by collecting quotations as illustrations for his definitions, but soon there were too many and there was no way they could be fitted into his manuscript lists of word definitions. After six years he had to begin again. It's not surprising he could not find the time, or money, to visit his elderly mother. But once that Herculean task was over, and his critics had been trounced, his life was transformed.

Johnson boasted, with some justification, that he had single-handedly tamed the English language, collecting 42,773 words and writing more than 114,000 definitions in his efforts to pin down their meanings. In France, he loved to claim, it took forty Academicians forty years to do the same for the French language. With the publication of the *Dictionary* his reputation was assured; he was *the* dictionary-maker, whose written definitions were of such quality and originality that he was hailed as 'one of the best writers of his age'. Johnson had surpassed any hopes that his mother might have had for him, and also his own ambition to make his name as a writer.

Financial security still eluded him. For this Johnson had to wait until 1762, when he was granted an annual pension of £300 (worth about £20,000 in today's money) by George III. Nevertheless, if he had really wished to see his mother again, he could surely have found the necessary cash for the cheapest wagon ride, some twelve shillings.

Johnson's relationship with his mother was beset by contradictions. In her *Anecdotes of the Late Samuel Johnson*, written as a memorial of her friendship with Johnson, Hester Thrale says about his mother, 'Nor could any one pay more willing homage to such a character than did Dr Johnson on every occasion that offered.' For the last twenty years of his life, Hester knew Johnson better than anyone. He often stayed with her and her family, either at the Southwark brewery owned by her husband or at their Streatham Park estate, just outside London. Her *Anecdotes* give us an insight into their frank conversations as she sat up with him late into the night while Johnson delayed going to bed until the candles had burnt down to the wick. 'So excellent was her character,' she wrote about Sarah Johnson, 'and so blameless her life, that when an oppressive neighbour once endeavoured to take from her a little field she possessed, he could persuade no attorney to undertake the cause against a woman so beloved.' She never knew Johnson's mother, so these reflections on Sarah's character must have come directly from his confidences.

A few days after his mother's death Johnson published an essay in his *Idler* series of weekly columns in which the narrator grieves for a dear friend. The narrator is not intended to be thought of as himself, but surely he had his mother in mind when he wrote, 'The blameless life, the artless tenderness, the pious simplicity, the modest resignation, the patient sickness, and the quiet death, are remembered only to add value to the loss.' A few years earlier, he had expressed similar thoughts to his friend James Elphinston, whose mother had just died. 'Dear Sir,' he begins his letter, 'You have as I find by every kind of evidence lost an excellent Mother; and I hope you will not think me incapable of partaking of your grief. I have a Mother now Eighty-two years of age, whom therefore I must soon lose . . .'

He advises his friend to write down 'minutely what you remember' of his mother before he has time to forget:

> . . . you will read it with great pleasure, and receive from it many hints
> of pleasing recollection, when time shall remove her yet farther from
> you and your grief shall be matured to veneration. To this however
> painfull for the present I cannot but advise you, as to a source of comfort
> and satisfaction in the time to come . . .

Yet Johnson never did this for his own mother (or perhaps he did, but such a memoir has never been found).

For many years Sarah's grave in St Michael's Church, Lichfield, was left unmarked. Only when Johnson was himself close to death did he think about arranging for a memorial stone to be erected over her tomb (as well as for those of his father and his younger brother, Nathaniel). On 2 December 1784, he told his agent in Lichfield, the surgeon and apothecary Richard Greene, 'The first care must be to find the exact place of interment, that the stone may protect the bodies. Then let the stone be deep, massy, and hard; and do not let the difference of ten pounds, or more, defeat our purpose . . . I beg that all possible haste may be made, for I wish to have it done while I am yet alive.' But he died eleven days later, before the job could be completed.

Sarah's epitaph, in Johnson's translation from his Latin original, reads with unusual richness of characterisation:

> Near to him [Johnson's father Michael] lies Sarah, his wife; of the ancient family of Ford; she was industrious at home, little known abroad, troublesome to no one, remarkable for quickness of understanding and accuracy of judgment; very indulgent to the errors of others—little to her own; always mindful of immortality—she was commended by almost every description of virtue. Born at Kings Norton, in Warwickshire, in 1669, and died in 1759.

'Troublesome to no one', though, is an oddly bathetic way to describe your closest relation. 'Very indulgent to the errors of others'? These aspects of Sarah's personality have not usually been observed in biographical studies of her son. Nor have her 'quickness of understanding and accuracy of judgment'. Her image has been distorted through the perspectives of time.

Sarah, daughter of Cornelius Ford, wife of Michael Johnson, mother of Samuel and Nathaniel, was born on 6 April 1669, just nine years after the Restoration of Charles II as King and the end of Cromwell's Puritan Commonwealth. Her father described himself as 'a gentleman', sending his four sons to Oxford and ensuring that his three daughters could read and write enough to study the Bible and books of devotional prayers. But while Sarah was growing up the family moved several times to other towns and villages in the vicinity. This was perhaps because of Cornelius's friendship with the recalcitrant priest, Thomas Hall. In 1661, Hall was expelled from his parish for refusing to swear allegiance to the Thirty-Nine Articles of the Church of England, a declaration of faith that was taken on oath (and which was still being printed in the *Book of Common Prayer* in 1980, although no longer legally binding). Those who refused to sign up to the Articles were no longer allowed to preach, and by the Five-Mile Act of 1665 they were even forbidden to live within five miles of their old parish. Sarah, along with her family, would have been regarded with suspicion because of her association with this Dissenting priest and her Puritan sympathies.

Her father owned a small library of Puritan texts, such as *The Saints Everlasting Rest*, a book of meditations compiled by a former chaplain to the Parliamentary army, Richard Baxter. The chapters have such alarming titles as 'The aggravations of the wicked's loss of Heaven'. Cornelius also had a copy of *The Whole Duty of Man*, first printed in 1657, which was designed to give 'a short and Plain Direction to the very meanest Readers'. Divided into seventeen sections, one lesson was to be read each Sunday on a continuous round-the-year basis so that each lesson would be repeated three times in every year. Repetition, it was believed, would imprint the book's religious teachings on the minds of the weak and faithless. Diligence and 'Temperance in sleep' were extolled in opposition to the 'Mischiefs of Sloth'.

These were the books that formed Sarah's childhood reading; texts that emphasised the individual's responsibility to care for his (or her) own soul and to be constantly aware of the ever-present dangers of sin. 'But we live in the midst of Thieves,' says the preface to *The Whole Duty of Man*, 'and therefore must look for them every Hour; and yet who is there among us, that hath that common Providence for this precious Part of him, his *Soul*, which he hath for his House . . . ?' Who are our enemies? How can we shield ourselves from sin, unless we are constantly on our guard, protecting ourselves from the sins that we might commit without knowing we have committed them? There is no safe place, no place in which we can hide away our thoughts.

Another popular devotional book by the Bishop of Ely, William Fleetwood, warned its readers, 'Short life is the punishment of disobedient children.' Sarah, and her son too, had read Fleetwood's *An Essay upon Miracles*. His threatening language was entirely believable at a time when a mild fever could bring on death in a matter of hours for a strong and fit adult let alone a small child. Infant mortality rates in the early eighteenth century were very high: about one in seven children would die before they reached the age of five. Life was lived with the fear of death as a real and immediate prospect. The Day of Judgment could be tomorrow.

Three times a year, every year, Sarah read in *The Whole Duty of Man* that God's vengeance, 'reaches even beyond Death itself, to the eternal Misery both of Body and Soul in Hell'. She trembled when she heard the words, believing them to be true. As also the warning, 'It is possible we may transgress against Men, and they not know it . . . But this we cannot do with God; he knows all Things, even the most secret Thoughts of our Hearts, and therefore, tho' we commit a Sin never so closely, he is sure to find us, and will as surely, if we do not timely repent, punish eternally for it.' Such teachings had a profound resonance for those who had lived through the years of Puritan control when a thoughtless word, a casual comment overheard even by a member of your family, could lead to betrayal and death.

They had a startling impact on those, like Johnson, with imaginative, deep-thinking, obsessional minds. Almost at the end of his life, when his reputation was secured, his talents fully employed, Johnson unnerved his scholarly friends on a visit to Oxford by vehemently declaring that he might well be among the damned. 'As I cannot be *sure* that I have fulfilled the conditions on which salvation is granted, I am afraid I may be one of those who shall be damned,' he told them. What do you mean by this? they asked him, shocked by such a confession. 'Sent to Hell, Sir, and punished everlastingly!' His friends were profoundly disturbed. How could Johnson, with his rigorous, rational mind, at the same time be held in the grip of these illogical religious convictions?

Sarah was thirty-seven when she married Michael Johnson of Lichfield on 19 June 1706, in the church at Packwood where her father was then living, just a few miles from King's Norton. The match surprised everyone. Michael was more than a decade older than Sarah and a confirmed bachelor. 'It is dangerous for a man and woman to suspend their fate upon each other at a time when opinions are fixed and habits are established,' declares Princess Nekayah in *Rasselas*, which Johnson wrote in the week following his mother's death in January 1759, when thoughts of Lichfield and his early life were uppermost in his mind. He had already published in the *Rambler*, 'Wives and husbands are, indeed, incessantly complaining of each other; and there would be reason for imagining that almost every house was infested with perverseness or oppression beyond human sufferance, did we not know upon how small occasions some minds burst out into lamentations and reproaches, and how naturally every animal revenges his pain upon those who happen to be near, without any nice examination of its cause.'

Was Johnson writing from his experience as a child watching his parents? Or making more general observations about human nature? 'We are always willing to fancy ourselves within a little of happiness,' he continues, 'and when, with repeated efforts, we cannot reach it, persuade ourselves that it is intercepted by an ill-paired mate, since, if we could find any other obstacle, it would be our own fault that it was not removed.'

Michael Johnson was from much humbler origins than his future wife, but by 1706 he had established a profitable business selling books on a stall in the busy cathedral city and market town of Lichfield as well as in nearby Uttoxeter. His work involved touring the countryside on horseback, carrying saddlebags filled with the latest volumes and pamphlets from London – essays by Dryden, political satires by Defoe and Swift, translations from Latin, Greek and French. Michael was not just a trader in books, he was also a typesetter and printer, preparing for sale small editions of those pamphlets and sermons he deemed were likely to interest his clients. He soon became thought of as a source of learning throughout the community: 'All the clergy here are his pupils, and suck all they have from him.' He also busied himself in the life of the city, serving as a magistrate and member of the council.

He was, though, a controversial figure; someone who was gossiped about, perhaps because he was a bit of a loner and almost fifty before he decided to marry. Many years later when James Boswell visited Lichfield while researching his biography of Michael's son, he was told by Anna Seward, a local bigwig with literary ambitions and a caustic tongue, that Michael had once been jilted by a woman called Mary Neild. He in turn had abandoned Elizabeth Blaney, who had conceived a 'violent passion' for him and died of heartbreak. (Her tombstone can still be seen in the cathedral, bearing an enigmatic epitaph, 'Here lies the body of Mrs Elizabeth Blaney, a stranger. She departed this life the 2nd of September 1694.') Whether or not these stories were true, it is curious that they were still being peddled about the town more than two generations later. (Seward had heard the stories from her mother.)

Johnson, looking back on his childhood, suggested that his parents' marriage was less than happy. 'My father and my mother . . . seldom conversed,' reads an entry in the *Annals*, an incomplete memoir of his early life published many years after his death. His mother, he says, did not care for books, an assessment of her character which he could only have made after leaving Lichfield, once he had met and befriended many women who were far better educated than Sarah. He concludes his account, 'Had she been more literate, they had been better companions.' Yet it was Sarah who taught her son to read and trained his mind in those first, impressionable years. His mother may not have been given a formal education, beyond basic lessons in reading, writing and religion – and she had little understanding of, or interest in, the world beyond the narrow confines of her Midlands upbringing – but she gave her most bookish son just what he needed as a child.

She perhaps met Michael while browsing through the books on his market stall on a visit to Lichfield to stay with her sister Phoebe, who was married to a local saddler, John Harrison. At first their marriage had all the signs of being happy and fulfilling. Sarah gave her husband a new confidence and burst of enthusiasm for his business. He acquired his own shop on the corner of the market square, converting two houses into an imposing residence. The ground floor, with its large windows designed to attract customers, was given over to Michael's bookselling business. He also had dreams of expansion, branching out into book-binding and creating a tannery so that he could himself prepare the leather used for the bindings. Books, then, were printed as sheets of uncut paper, which were folded and stitched together but without a jacket. Enterprising booksellers made an additional profit by offering to bind with fine leather these stitched bundles of paper for customers with the money to pay for them. The bindings were then custom-made, monogrammed and decorated to order, creating the matching, personalised shelves of books beloved of gentleman-scholars.

In the late spring of 1709 Michael was elected as that year's Sheriff of Lichfield. This obliged him to lead on Rogation Sunday the annual custom of riding around the borders of the cathedral city, inspecting and asserting its boundaries. Michael took to his role with the extravagant exuberance of a self-made man, hiring a superb white horse for the ride and entertaining his fellow aldermen with a sumptuous dinner. For years the Riding of 1709, and Michael's role in its organisation, was talked about as being of 'uncommon magnificence'.

A few months later, on the afternoon of 7 September, Sarah gave birth to their first child, named Samuel after the Temple prophet. Sarah was forty. She was of slight build and 'rather below than above the common size'. Her labour would have been long, painful and very dangerous to her as well as to her unborn child. When, eventually, young Samuel was pulled unwillingly into the world, he was limp and lifeless; a long, thin, straggly baby with huge hands and feet.

As Sarah lay in bed exhausted by her ordeal, having had nothing to mask the pain, she feared that her baby had been born dead. He made no sound. She was too weak to move and could only watch helplessly while George Hector, the male midwife who had been specially hired by Michael (no expense spared) to assist with the birth, frantically pummelled her baby's chest, willing him into life. Several more anxious minutes elapsed before Sarah at last heard her baby beginning to wail. 'Here is a brave boy!' declared Hector. (He perhaps should have said, 'Here's a brave mother!') That evening Sarah was so frightened her baby would die she called for the priest to baptise him.

Amazingly, young Samuel did survive those first traumatic hours. It was a mild September, the Johnsons' house was large and airy, and no infectious diseases were coursing through the town. After just a few weeks, though, Sarah sent her still fragile baby away to be fed by a wet-nurse. In those years fewer than half the mothers from the educated classes breastfed their babies, in spite of the stern teaching of *The Whole Duty of Man*: 'This [the nourishment of children] is a Duty which Nature teaches; even the savage Beasts have a great Care and Tenderness in nourishing their Young, and therefore may serve to reproach and condemn all Parents, who shall be so unnatural as to neglect this.' The anonymous author advises, 'Where no Impediment of Sickness, Weakness, or the like, doth happen, 'tis surely best for the Mother her self to perform this Office, there being many Advantages to the Child by it, which a good Mother ought so far to consider, as not to sell them to her own Sloth and Niceness, or any such unworthy Motive.'

Whether or not to breastfeed has always been a contentious issue. Mary Wollstonecraft was so disturbed by the 'unnatural' divorce of mothers from their newborn infants that she began *Thoughts on the Education of Daughters* by insisting that mothers should suckle their own children. It is, she asserts, the beginning of everything: 'Children who are left to the care of ignorant nurses, have their stomachs overloaded with improper food, which turns acid, and renders them very uncomfortable.' In a striking attack on her own sex, Wollstonecraft argues that it is the indolence, the vanity and self-love of women which persuades them not to breastfeed.

Johnson knew, though, that it was not his mother's decision to send him away to a wet-nurse. In the *Annals* he records that it was his father who persuaded Sarah to give her baby to the wife of John Marklew, a brickmaker who had done some work for Michael. Marklew's wife was just about to wean their eighteen-month-old son and so had milk to spare.

Sarah missed her newborn son desperately. She visited him every day and usually timed her arrival so she could be there while he was being breastfed. Wollstonecraft (writing in 1787 some years before she had herself given birth to a child) writes:

> The suckling of a child also excites the warmest glow of tenderness—Its
> dependant, helpless state produces an affection, which may properly

24

be termed maternal. I have even felt it, when I have seen a mother perform the office; and am of opinion, that maternal tenderness arises quite as much from habit as instinct . . . It is necessary, therefore, for a mother to perform the office of one, in order to produce in herself a rational affection for her offspring.

Anxious not to appear soft or over-sentimental in front of her neighbours, Sarah would leave behind a glove or a handkerchief so that she would have an excuse to visit again. Her subterfuge did not fool anyone, or so Johnson tells us in the *Annals*, and Sarah was teased for being so attached to her son.

How strange for a child to be told continually that his mother was too fond of him. But Johnson could only have known this story from his infancy if his parents had harped on about it when he was old enough to know what they meant. In a footnote to this passage in the *Annals*, one Victorian editor commented that the adverse reaction to Sarah's over-concern for her child's well-being was 'a curious instance of the brutality of the age', which in turn reads oddly to us, who like to believe that our own attitudes to child-rearing are more enlightened than those of the Victorians.

Sarah was right to be anxious about her son. Young Sam, who entered the world with such difficulty, refused to thrive and after only ten weeks was fetched home again by his mother as 'a poor, diseased infant, almost blind'. Samuel was probably suffering from conjunctivitis, which at that time could not be treated. The infection compromised the sight in Johnson's left eye, which was already very short-sighted.

Samuel may also have caught something far worse from the Marklews. He did not improve, and continued to lose weight. Swellings began to appear on his neck and upper arms, the telltale sign that he was suffering from tuberculosis of the lymph glands, also known as 'scrofula'. Sarah had been forced to wean her son early at just three months, having stopped feeding him herself and then taken him away from his wet-nurse. She did not know it, but untreated cow's milk is dangerous for young children, if the milk is taken from a tubercular cow. The source of Sam's infection, though, was most probably at the Marklews' home, for their young son was also suffering from the disease. Sarah could only worry it was all her own fault as she watched her infant son scratching the itchy boils on his arms and neck until they bled, releasing a foul-smelling pus.

This went on for months. Sarah dared not visit anyone with her new baby because Samuel looked such an unsightly mess, covered by weeping sores. No one called on her at home. Even her sister Phoebe refused to pick up the child to comfort him, frightened that she might be tainted by whatever was wrong with him. No wonder tensions crept in between Sarah and her husband.

Tuberculosis of the lymph glands was relatively common in Britain until the beginning of the twentieth century when milk began to be pasteurised, and it is still endemic in areas of poor hygiene and untreated milk. Although it is not often fatal it was very difficult to cure before the discovery of penicillin. The recommended treatment when Samuel was a child was to cut away the flesh so that the infected 'humours' could be drained out of the body. But how could you use a young baby in this way?

Sarah was told repeatedly by the doctors that nothing could be done to help Samuel, until finally she insisted they must try to cure her son by any means possible. With the ingenuity born of a mother's desperation, she prepared a bowl of custard and allowed it to cool before persuading her young son to put his hands into it. She hoped the thick, gooey liquid would soothe away his pain and prevent him from fidgeting while the doctor sliced open Sam's baby-thin arms and neck and peeled back the skin, releasing the pus. Afterwards, Sarah had to ensure the cuts were kept open so that the infected fluids could continue to drain away out of Sam's lymph glands. To do this, she inserted a small bead in the cut before wrapping his upper arms and neck tightly in bandages.

The cure was drastic, but did not take effect, at least not at first. Sam would be six years old before the bandaging was removed and the cuts allowed to heal. How did Sarah prevent him from scratching at his sores? How did Sam put up with the pain and discomfort of having his arms so tightly bound in bandages he could not move them freely? The wounds were deep. The scars they left on Johnson's neck were remarked upon by those who met him as an adult and can still be seen on the mask that was cast from his head and chest after his death in 1784.

In the meantime, applying her resourceful mind and following her belief in divine solutions, Sarah attempted to hasten the cure by trying out an 'alternative' therapy. Scrofula in pre-industrial England was not simply an unpleasant illness; it carried with it intimations of something much deeper even than young Sam's wounds. When Johnson came to write his *Dictionary*, he defined 'scrofula' as 'a depravation of the humours of the body, which breaks out in sores'. This is a surprisingly imprecise medical description, given that Johnson knew the disease so intimately. He added that it was 'commonly called the King's Evil'.

Since the days of Edward the Confessor, scrofula had been closely linked to the rituals and mystique of the royal family. Edward, who was acknowledged as a saint even before his death, was believed to have cured a young woman who was suffering from the illness simply by touching her infected sores. Thereafter scrofula was regarded as a special illness through which God's plan for humankind could be discerned. Those who were invested with royal power were also given powers of healing; it was a sign of their divine right to rule. Ceremonies were held either at St James's Palace or on a rotating circuit in the cathedral cities, when those suffering from the illness were brought before the King (or Queen) to be cured.

An elaborate ritual was developed over time, culminating in the royal person 'touching' the forehead of the sick invalid. These 'healing' services conflated the desire for strong leadership with the atavistic longing for another dimension of experience beyond the everyday. This desire for the supernatural, though suppressed by the Puritan revolution, was never eradicated and when the monarchy was restored in 1660 Charles II reintroduced the custom of 'Touching for the Evil'.

In the spring of 1712 Sarah took her ailing son to London to be 'touched' by Queen Anne, choosing her time carefully. She left home just before Good Friday (which in that year fell on 30 March) because she believed the connection between royal power and the divine will was more potent during the Easter festival, and especially on Good Friday, the day on which God's salvation was made manifest on earth through the crucifixion of his only son. Sarah carried in her pocket a letter of recommendation from the Lichfield physician, Sir John Floyer, who had encouraged her to make the journey. This letter confirmed that Samuel was indeed suffering from scrofula and was written for the palace officials who would need to be convinced that Samuel was an appropriate person to receive royal healing. The potency of the ritual was preserved by ensuring that only genuine sufferers from the illness gained access to the Queen's miraculous powers.

Sarah travelled the hundred or so miles to London by the cheapest stage wagon, taking almost three days in a carriage that jostled and swayed continually as it bumped along the muddy, potholed roads. Samuel, who was then aged two and a half, never forgot the discomforts of the journey: 'I was sick; one woman fondled me, the other was disgusted.'

Sarah was two months' pregnant with her second son, Nathaniel, born in late September 1712. That she made the journey alone without the company or patronage of her husband gives us insights into her strength of character not always appreciated by the biographers of her son. To embark on such a trip, she must have been determined and courageous, driven by maternal love and the desire to take action rather than watch helplessly as her son grew sicker and sicker. She could see that his health was deteriorating because of those deep and painful wounds. She resolved to do all she could to find a cure, even if this meant travelling while suffering the discomforts of early pregnancy.

On their arrival in the capital, Sarah made her way from the coach stop at the Three Chickens on Cheapside to Little Britain, behind St Paul's, where her husband had arranged for her to stay with a bookseller friend, John Nicholson. The contrast with Lichfield was daunting. Little Britain (which still exists as a winding lane) was in the heart of the City, and very close to the great meat market at Smithfield. Johnson in the *Annals* tells us that his mother sewed two guineas into a pocket which she inserted in her petticoat, 'lest she be robbed' while walking through the foetid streets, carrying her sick child in her arms to protect him from being kicked by an ox or stray sheep, or stumbling into a pile of animal dung.

Samuel's first impressions of the city with which he was to become so closely identified were so vivid that many years later he could still describe in precise detail the room from which John Nicholson sold his books, the cat with a white collar which he teased, and the dog called Chops who had been trained to leap over a stick. Of the ceremony at St James's Palace he had only a 'confused, but somehow a sort of solemn recollection'; a vague memory of 'a lady in diamonds, and a long black hood'. He thought that he heard 'another boy crying in the palace'.

The royal ceremony followed a ritual laid down for centuries. The Queen sat in regal state on a red velvet throne, her voluminous black brocade gown dripping with jewels and edged with fox fur. The service began as one of the priests delivered the special collect or prayer for healing, followed by a reading from the Gospel of St Mark, Chapter Three, in which the twelve apostles are sent out to continue Christ's healing mission. One by one, the petitioners were then led up to the Queen, old and young, rich and poor, from all parts of her kingdom, their social differences dissipating in the presence of the reigning monarch. Sarah, carrying Sam in her arms, knelt down before the Queen, who laid both her hands on Samuel's forehead before touching his wounds and slipping a thin white ribbon round his neck on which was threaded a specially minted gold amulet.

Johnson was born into a world in which evil spirits were thought to exist in the dark hours between dusk and dawn, and unbelief was feared as the gateway to chaos. Was he that 'crying boy' embedded in his memory? The crying of an unwilling child, bewildered by the artificial ceremonial, this man-made divinity.

Queen Anne, who died in 1714, was the last English monarch to 'touch' for the Evil. Ideas and beliefs were changing very quickly in these years, as medical knowledge developed. Sir John Floyer (who had sent them to London) was a pioneering doctor, one of the first to provide tabulated results of his researches on asthma and the workings of the pulse; his books were published by Michael Johnson. Yet he was still willing to recommend an alternative branch of healing whose agency was based purely on a superstitious belief in the existence of powers beyond our understanding.

As a child, Johnson was treated by a modernising doctor but also by superstitious practice. In the span of his life, beliefs in the mystery of the universe and that the world was governed by a celestial hierarchy diminished. Rational, scientific explanations for the concrete and abstract worlds were sought. By the time Johnson reached maturity any residual belief in the potency of royal power was, according to the atheist philosopher David Hume, 'attended with ridicule in the eyes of all men of understanding'. James Boswell, too, was bemused to discover that the 'hero' of his biography was a living example of such an outmoded ritual, writing in the *Life* that 'it is wonderful to think' that such 'a superstitious notion' should have 'prevailed so long in this country'. Yet Johnson never removed the chain from his neck on which was threaded the amulet, or 'touchpiece', that he received from the Queen on the day he was 'touched'. It can still be seen in the British Museum – a small gold coin, slightly larger than an old sixpence, with the impress of St Michael the Archangel on one side and a ship in full sail on the other.

Johnson was a man of his enlightening times but also in touch with another way of explaining the world around and beyond us. For him, reason had not yet been isolated from its irrational roots. His struggle to reconcile these divergent impulses gives to his writing, even to a supposedly factual work such as the *Dictionary*, the humanity that resonates with us still; in his life experiences, and in his writings, we can see the struggle personified, embodied, realised.

He once told a young woman who was thinking of converting to Quakerism, 'We ought not, without very strong conviction indeed, to desert the religion in which we have been educated. That is the religion given you, the religion in which it may be said, Providence has placed you. If you live conscientiously in that religion, you may be safe. But error is dangerous indeed, if you err when you choose a religion for yourself.' Yet Johnson did try to rid himself of the superstitious beliefs that dominated his mother's life, resenting the way they had kidnapped his intellect.

Perhaps Johnson's writings still engage us in a way that those of, say, Hume or Descartes never quite do because he speaks so directly to us as fellow human beings struggling to create sense and order out of a world that makes no sense, in which suffering is randomly apportioned and individuals are constantly reminded of their ephemeral insignificance. Rarely a day passes without something Johnson once wrote or said being quoted in the papers, on the web or on the radio, precisely because he gives us so many piquant illustrations of life's inexplicable troubles and our own inadequate understanding of how to respond to them.

When Johnson set out to pin down meaning in his literary and scholarly works, he was trying to create a defence against the superstitious world that lies so close beneath the surface. His *Dictionary of the English Language* and the *Lives of the Poets* catalogue knowledge in a concrete way, producing works of definition, of containment. In them he was struggling to keep at bay the unruly, uncontainable forces which we cannot know or understand.

Once the ordeal of the touching ceremony was over, Sarah went shopping for souvenirs: a linen frock for her son – cream-coloured, with a 'speckled' pattern – and a silver cup and spoon. She had them engraved with the letters 'SAM J' (rather than just the initials SJ) so that they would never be confused as belonging to her and taken from him if she died. Sarah was perhaps already dreading the terrors of giving birth a second time. Johnson took the cup with him when he left home as a young man and would have kept it all his life had he not been forced to sell it when he was struggling to make a living as a journalist in London, a newly married man with a wife to support. The spoon he still had among his few household possessions when he died.

Somehow, almost miraculously, Samuel did recover, the wounds healing, his body recovering its immunity against infection. He grew up into a sturdy and athletic teenager, an enthusiastic tree-climber and a strong swimmer. Sarah's determination and her tenacity played their part in this. She also encouraged the development of her son's extraordinary intellectual powers. Every Sunday, Sarah made Samuel memorise the collect of the day as written in the *Book of Common Prayer*. By the time he was eight, he could do this so speedily she only had to climb the stairs from the kitchen in the basement to her bedroom on the first floor for Samuel to be able to recite the collect back to her without a mistake.

Sarah schooled her son in the works of some of the best writers in the English language – Thomas Cranmer, Lancelot Andrewes and William Tyndale. These sixteenth-century theologians, who created the devotional books of the new Church of England, were part of that great Elizabethan flowering of verse and prose writing which also included Shakespeare, Ben Jonson and Robert Herrick. The words and cadences of their prayers and translations resound throughout his writings.

Johnson later recalled how one morning when he was very young and lying cosily in bed with his mother, after his father had left the house to visit his scattered out-of-town customers, Sarah began teaching him about Heaven and Hell and the Day of Judgement. As soon as she had finished, she told her toddler son to go downstairs to find the servant 'to whom she knew he would communicate the conversation while it was yet impressed upon his mind'. Sam never forgot the lesson or the method by which his mother had taught him.

As an adult he had a phenomenal memory, with the ability to compose in his head seventy lines of poetry, or an entire essay of 2,000 to 2,500 words, before writing them down. He knew that he owed this in part to the early training his mother had given him. When many years later Hester Thrale asked him for advice on the best way to teach her young children, he told her, 'Little people should be encouraged always to tell whatever they hear particularly striking, to some brother, sister, or servant, immediately before the impression is erased by the intervention of newer occurrences.' He knew that it was his mother who should be given credit for his 'uncommon felicity of remembering distant occurrences, and long past conversations'.

Sarah had perceived, beyond her son's physical difficulties and awkward appearance, his exceptional abilities. She taught him to read from books about St George and the Dragon, and made sure that he did not become bored and disheartened when he was struggling to learn the Latin declensions taught him by the rigid learning-by-rote system of Lichfield Grammar School. The school was famous throughout the Midlands as the alma mater of many lawyers and politicians and several bishops. The actor David Garrick and the botanist, geologist and philosopher Erasmus Darwin, grandfather of Charles, were also pupils there in these years. Standards were high, and teaching methods rigorous, yet also prescriptive. Young Sam hated to do badly and was anxious about his next test. His mother reassured him that fear sometimes is no bad thing; it kick-starts inspiration. 'We often come off best when we are most afraid.' It was a lesson that Johnson followed throughout his life, always testing himself to the limit by setting himself extraordinary goals – containing the language in the *Dictionary*, providing a comprehensive guide to English poetry in the *Lives of the Poets*, and composing useful prefaces to Shakespeare's plays – and then not giving himself enough time to meet the deadlines.

Johnson, though, was a self-opinionated teenager who soon outgrew his mother's lessons and became irritated by her small-town outlook. He despised the way in which Sarah was so concerned about what the neighbours might think. 'You puppy!' she scolded him after he had been particularly self-willed. To which young Sam replied, 'What then do they call a puppy's mother?'

Sarah had the misfortune to give birth to a gifted child whose mental facility was way beyond his parents' experience and understanding. 'I was born in the house of discord,' he wrote in the *Rambler* in February 1751, 'so that from the first exertions of reason I was bred a disputant, trained up in all the arts of domestick sophistry, initiated in a thousand low stratagems, nimble shifts, and sly concealments; versed in all the turns of altercation . . .' If we assume that Johnson was writing from experience, we can only pity Sarah. What chance had she against a child so determined to flex his wits against her?

When Samuel was nine years old, he and his younger brother Nathaniel were sent away to stay with relatives for the Whitsun holiday, first with an aunt and uncle in Sutton Coldfield and then in Birmingham with their mother's widowed brother-in-law. Sarah must have been having trouble keeping her sons from scrapping in the shop while their father was away from home looking after his customers. 'My mother had some opinion that much improvement was to be had by changing the way of life,' wrote Johnson much later in the memoir of his early life.

Birmingham was just sixteen miles from Lichfield, but it was then a world apart. Although Lichfield was a prosperous, characterful town with a distinctive three-spired cathedral and a busy cattle and leather market, Birmingham was a new town, fast expanding as the local centre of the new metal-working industries. Its back streets were filling up with canneries for making pots and pans, button-making factories and armouries, where guns were produced in new industrial quantities. Johnson's uncle, the saddler John Harrison, lived on the High Street, as did his father's brother Andrew, who had once been a prize boxer in London, unchallenged in the ring at Smithfield for 'a full year'.

Johnson later remembered little of the trip except that his aunt was shocked by the amount of meat he greedily ate from a leg of mutton, much more than anyone else. The story of Samuel's voracious appetite, and his lack of table manners, was apparently talked about for years afterwards, acutely embarrassing his mother. Johnson, too, must have felt some sense of guilt, conflating the memory of how much he disliked the way his mother fussed over trifles with his own fear that he lacked self-control. The boys were never sent to Birmingham again.

Samuel had upset his parents still more by writing home to his father, telling him not to come and fetch the brothers on Monday, as had been planned, but to wait until Thursday, 'and then, and not till then' would he and Nathaniel be happy to leave. As an older mother, who had struggled so hard to keep her son alive, Sarah had always encouraged Samuel's precocity, teaching him to act out 'Little Natty's' name for the guests at his younger brother's baptism party. But as an awkward, unattractive child, Samuel resented the way his parents, both of them, delighted in parading him in front of their relations, almost as if he were a prize bull. An old man's offspring, warned Johnson, 'leads much the same life as a child's dog; teased like that with fondness through folly, and exhibited like that to every company, through idle and empty vanity'.

In her *Anecdotes of the Late Samuel Johnson*, Hester Thrale records a strange conversation she once had with Johnson about his father (she never met either of his parents and was intrigued to know something of them):

The trick which most parents play with their children, of showing off their newly-acquired accomplishments, disgusted Mr Johnson beyond expression; he had been treated so himself, he said, till he absolutely loathed his father's caresses, because he knew they were sure to precede some unpleasing display of his early abilities.

In her unpublished diary (later known as the *Thraliana*) Hester tells the story rather differently. Johnson, she says, had once complained to her in confidence that his father had persisted in 'caressing' him long after the age when such caresses were welcome:

> A Child says he is capable of resentment much earlier than is commonly suppos'd, & I never could endure my Fathers Caresses after he had once rendered them displeasing to me by mingling them with Caresses I did not care to comply with.

With our over-sensitive antennae, alert to any suggestions of inappropriate behaviour, Hester appears to be telling us something very strange. What are we to make of these 'caresses' that Johnson 'did not care to comply with'? And why did Hester alter her account for the published *Anecdotes*, as if she knew that what she had written in private was not suitable for publication?

There's nothing in Johnson's papers to suggest that his relations with his father were in any way out of order, other than the fact that as a clever child he soon outdistanced his parents before he was old enough to understand or accept his sense of separation from them. He had difficulty in respecting them, especially once he recognised that his father was not disciplined enough to be a successful businessman. Yet although he accused his parents of failing to realise how much he disliked being made to show off as a child, as an adult he always desired attention, holding court among his friends by withholding his contribution to the conversation until asked a question, and then dominating the debate with his loud, insistent voice.

Memory, as Johnson himself recognised, is not always an accurate reflection of what we have actually experienced, and especially in childhood. 'I know not whether I remember the thing, or the talk of it,' he admitted. Our perceptions of what happen to us in childhood vary throughout our later lives. Incidents that we recall with perfect clarity change shape as we grow older, and are often placed by us in a very different context from that in which they originally occurred. Johnson's brother Nathaniel died in 1737 when he was just twenty-four. Thereafter Johnson knew no one who could verify what he remembered with such vividness.

Nathaniel, less determined and mentally agile than his elder brother, always lost out in comparisons with Samuel. He later wrote bitterly to his mother that his brother would 'scarce ever use me with common civility'. Johnson scarcely mentions Nathaniel in his letters, or even refers to brothers in his *Rambler* or *Idler* essays. It's as if Nathaniel never existed; an aspect of Johnson's life that is also largely unexplored.

Samuel was undoubtedly a difficult child, whose personality never really fitted into the confines of his home, or Lichfield. After the never-to-be-repeated visit to Birmingham, he was sent away again, this time without Nathaniel and to stay with his cousin, Cornelius Ford, a graduate of Cambridge and by then the newly married rector of Pedmore in Worcestershire. Ford later moved to London, where he met Alexander Pope and was part of an intellectual circle that included Philip Stanhope, who became the Earl of Chesterfield, and eventually one of the patrons who funded the *Dictionary* (to whom Johnson wrote his infamously rude letter bemoaning lack of interest in the project). In the early 1730s, Ford was probably the model for the drunken parson in Hogarth's satirical print 'A Modern Midnight Conversation'.

Ford is shown smoking a pipe and holding a punch ladle, surrounded by a group of drunken friends in a chaotic room, chairs overturned, candles burnt down almost to stubs. Soon afterwards he was found dead in a Turkish bath in the West End of London. Not on the surface, then, a very suitable mentor for the bored and wilful elder Johnson boy. But in 1725, when Samuel spent several months with him, he was still a respectable parish priest with an elegant wife and enough money to equip himself with a substantial library. Cornelius took it upon himself to rescue his younger cousin from his teenage misery by encouraging him to spend his time reading through a highly influential collection of works by Ovid, Seneca, Juvenal, Petrarch, Homer and Virgil.

When Samuel did eventually return home, he was not allowed back into lessons at the grammar school because he had been away for so long (from the autumn holiday until the following Whitsun). As a teenager, Johnson was a truculent school absconder, expelled for his truancy. Expulsion, though, was just what he needed. He had picked up the habit of reading from Cornelius and, instead of wasting his time in lessons that taught him nothing he did not already know and understand, he lounged around at home, roaming through the shelves in his father's bookshop.

Many of the 2,900 volumes from the sale of the Earl of Derby's massive library which Michael Johnson had unwisely bought in 1706 in the flush of enthusiasm he experienced on marrying Sarah, were still unsold, too scholarly and expensive for his Lichfield clientele. Some of these books later made their way into the Cathedral Library where they can still be seen, such as a lavish edition of *De L'Art de Regner* by Le Père Le Moyne de la Compagnie de Jésus, which was printed in Paris in 1665 (a vast and esoteric tome on courtly rituals and the exercise of kingship). Now at last they found a reader in Samuel. One morning he was sent by his mother to look for a box of cooking apples she had stored on a top shelf in the shop. Before he found the apples he was waylaid by a rare volume of Petrarch's sonnets and spent the rest of the day lost in the Italian, picking up the meaning of the words he didn't know by browsing through the Italian dictionary that was lying further along the shelf.

This was the best kind of education for Johnson's scavenging mind. He says later that he read so hard in the years before he reached eighteen he knew then 'almost as much as I do now. My judgment, to be sure, was not so good, but I had all the facts.' At Oxford as an undergraduate, he astonished his tutor by quoting from an obscure Roman philosopher, Macrobius, whose works no ordinary student would have had the opportunity, or inclination, to read.

Johnson liked to boast that as a teenager he 'knew more books than any man alive'. Those months with Cornelius Ford in Pedmore, and later in the bookshop, gave him the opportunity while his mind was still flexible and impressionable to read most of what were then considered to be the major books of the literary canon. When later he began work on the *Dictionary*, compiling the quotations to illustrate his definitions, he already had stored in his mind an extraordinary range of suitable examples from Chaucer, Roger Ascham, Francis Bacon and Richard Hooker onwards through the centuries, memorised through the techniques taught him by his mother.

University was the obvious next step for such a bookish boy, but by the 1720s his father's business was doing so badly there was not enough money to send Samuel away. Michael had overstretched himself with the purchase by mortgage of his grand house on the market square, plus all the books in the Earl of Derby's library, as well as the expense of setting up the tannery. He was also in trouble with the Excise for not acquiring the right licences for his business dealings. The accusations were false, and his customers in Lichfield supported him throughout the protracted legal wrangling, but Michael never quite recovered from the unexpected costs he incurred in trying to clear his name, or the slur to his reputation.

Johnson later talked of his childhood as being 'beggarly', with none of the luxuries that the families of his friends at the Grammar School were beginning to acquire. His mother complained that the housekeeping money was never enough to buy tea (a great luxury at one shilling a pot for the best-quality leaves), which prevented her from entertaining as often as she wished. Her tea-set included just two silver teaspoons. But in 1728 she inherited £40 (worth now about £3,400). The money was left to her by an enlightened aunt, with the provision that it was 'for her own separate use', presumably to give Sarah some belated independence from her husband. She chose instead to devote the inheritance to her elder son's further education, sacrificing her desire for a china teapot with matching cups and saucers so that he could go to Oxford. Her son would become known for his love of tea, and his ability to drink up to twenty-two cups in a single day, Boswell remarking in the *Life* 'that his nerves must have been uncommonly strong, not to have been extremely relaxed by such an intemperate use of it'. But Sarah was always conscious of the price of the leaves used to make a single pot.

Samuel was signed in as a Commoner at Pembroke College on the last day of October 1728, quite late in the term. The money from his mother turned out to be nowhere near enough to fund his life at university, even though his father had also supplied him with a bundle of books from the shop. After paying for his gown, Johnson soon ran out of cash to pay his buttery bills (from the college bar and dining hall). He was too proud, though, to admit he had a problem, or to accept help. When a friend, who was noticeably better off, left a pair of shoes outside his college room, after noticing that Johnson's were worn through, Samuel threw them away, outraged that his poverty had been discovered. Thirteen months later, he was forced to give up the pretence that he could manage on no money, and he returned home for the Christmas vacation. 'I was miserably poor,' he later said of his time at Oxford, 'and I thought to fight my way by my literature and my wit; so I disregarded all power and all authority.'

In truth Johnson was always a difficult student, unimpressed by his tutors and bored by the Classics curriculum, which had changed little since the college's foundation in 1624. He left behind most of his books and papers in his room at Pembroke so perhaps he had intended to return after Christmas, but he arrived back in Lichfield to discover that his father was very ill. Johnson never completed his degree, even though his father recovered from that bout of illness to survive another two years. Instead he languished at home, idling away his days. Sarah had the sense not to berate her son, or to insist that he should help in the shop. When Michael eventually died, in December 1731, of 'an inflammatory fever' (probably pneumonia), leaving behind a failing business and unpaid debts, she merely bit her lip and got on with what needed to be done, leaving Samuel to his own devices. She could not even rely on him to help with his father's funeral, which in the end was arranged by her maid, Catherine ('Kitty') Chambers.

While Samuel stayed in bed until noon, Sarah soldiered on in the shop. She had no choice but to rely on her younger son, Nathaniel, to provide the assistance she might have expected from Samuel. He did attempt to find some paid work as a schoolteacher to relieve the household finances, leaving home to teach at a second-rate grammar school in Market Bosworth, about twenty-five miles away in Leicestershire. But after just three months he gave up, complaining of the drudgery of trying to teach dull boys the rudiments of Latin and Greek. (Without a degree Johnson was unemployable in any of the best schools, such as Rugby, Westminster or Harrow.) He did not, though, return to Lichfield. Instead he found a reason to stay away in an invitation from Edmund Hector, a schoolfriend, who was now living in Birmingham. Hector was lodging on the High Street, close to the Swan Tavern, and had a spare room, which he offered to Johnson.

The house was owned by Thomas Warren, who had just launched the weekly *Birmingham Journal*. With Hector's encouragement, Johnson wrote some essays for the newspaper. Hector, son of the midwife who had saved Johnson's life, was himself already practising as a surgeon. He tried to encourage his friend to find work, and suggested that he should set himself up as a translator. Booksellers and printers were looking for writers willing to translate classic works from French, Italian and German, not yet available in English. There were plenty of them and the work was reasonably well paid. Johnson, somewhat half-heartedly, began translating, from the French, the *Voyage to Abyssinia* by Father Jerome Lobo, a Jesuit missionary. Translation, though, is slow work, methodical and sometimes tedious, and was not at all suited to Johnson's temperament. He made little progress, as if disappointment at his failure to gain a degree from Oxford had engendered in him a bitterness that stalled his development. It took him three years to complete the translation (which was eventually published in 1735, Johnson earning five guineas for his work). Sarah bided her time, giving Johnson the freedom to malinger while she struggled to keep the bookshop going as their only source of income.

Many years later Johnson recalled how once, while he was at Oxford, he was turning the key of the door into his room in college when he heard his mother's voice 'distinctly call *Sam*'. He was unnerved by the experience. There was no question in his mind. It was his mother's voice. This was not a trick of his imagination. She was there, with him, in the room.

But Sarah never did call Sam home after he had left Lichfield behind, even when money was tight and she was in poor health. That incident in Oxford was not so much a haunting as a subconscious acknowledgement by Johnson of how much he owed his mother. She could well have insisted that he stayed on at the bookshop to help her after Michael's death. But she was always 'too tender a parent' – as James Boswell concluded in his *Life of Samuel Johnson* – to make demands on her son.

Boswell, alone among biographers, took the trouble to talk in Lichfield with those who had known Johnson's mother. He concluded, 'She had too much sense to be vain, but she knew her son's value.' Sarah could always be relied upon to support Johnson's endeavours – even when in the summer of 1735 he announced that he was about to marry a forty-six-year-old widow with three children. At the time Samuel was jobless, penniless and a callow twenty-five-year-old with no qualifications and no thought of a career other than a vague idea that he might teach. But alone among the family and friends, Sarah did not oppose the match. 'She knew too well the ardour of her son's temper.'

3

Love and Death

That the creator of the *Dictionary*, and the hero of Boswell's *Life*, was once married, and remained so for seventeen years, is a fact not often discussed by his biographers. It's just too difficult to reconcile the thought of Johnson as a husband with our favourite image of him enjoying the convivial atmosphere of a tavern, a giant among men, talking late into the night with the other members of his Literary Club. The fact that he once had a wife is inconvenient, a distraction. It's also not easy to find out anything about Tetty Johnson. Just as we know very little about his mother, so we have no letters from his wife, and only one letter from Johnson to her. With so few documentary sources, we can only speculate what their marriage might have been like, conjuring up an image of the couple at home from what Johnson himself wrote in his essays about the trials of wedlock.

Young Sam and mature Tetty are an odd, provoking couple; their connection as husband and wife difficult to understand. When they married, on 9 July 1735, he was little more than a youth who had yet to make anything of his life. She, at forty-six, was old enough to be his mother. What did they see in each other?

Second marriages, Johnson once commented, are 'the triumph of hope over experience'; perhaps one of his most often-quoted remarks. Was he thinking of Tetty when he said this? Was he suggesting that she had bitterly regretted marrying again after the death of her first husband, Henry Porter? Johnson is also thought to have been thinking of his own marriage when he advised, 'A man of sense and experience should meet a suitable companion in a wife. It was a miserable thing when the conversation could only be such as, whether the mutton should be boiled or roasted, and probably a dispute about that.' Did he see himself as that man of 'sense and experience'? Was Tetty that nagging wife?

We cannot know. Without Tetty's witness, without her thoughts on Johnson, there is not enough evidence to paint an accurate picture of their relationship. If there are connections between what Johnson said about marriage and his own experience of it, we cannot be sure of their significance without knowing Tetty's side of the story. Those clever remarks about marriage so carefully documented by Boswell in his *Life of Samuel Johnson* were often made in response to the provocative questions that Boswell, who never met Tetty, laid as bait for Johnson, hoping to find out something about Johnson's life with his wife. Johnson always fell for it, but not quite in the way Boswell intended. Instead of revealing the intimate details of his fondness for Tetty, Johnson would launch into an exposition of marriage, celibacy, the quest for love and contentment, airing his views on the conundrums that often obsess our internal thoughts but which we rarely have the honesty to admit, even to ourselves. Why did I choose to marry/live with this person rather than another? Could I have been happier with someone else? What, in any case, is happiness?

Johnson was never afraid to look deeply into life's big questions, yet he rarely probed his own most personal relationships. He tells us little of what Tetty herself thought and felt. In a *Rambler* essay on the subject of biography, Johnson argues, 'The most authentick Witnesses of any Man's Character are those who knew him in his own Family.' Marriage, family life, personal relations: these are the aspects of life which determine a person's character, shaping and moulding them. If we wish to know him, he appears to be implying, then we need to understand his wife and his relationship with her. Yet Tetty has been written out of his personal history. 'The most authentick Witness' to Johnson's life has been for the most part forgotten.

Tetty was of immense importance to Johnson and to his slow 'rise to worth', out of poverty to success and esteem as a writer and literary figure, champion of the English language and of its chief poets. She was, after all, the only woman to have known Johnson intimately as a wife. Mrs Desmoulins (whom we shall meet later) shared his bed on occasion, but she did not, as far as we understand, go so far as to have sex with him. Tetty, alone, had that experience. She was closer than anyone to Johnson as he grew out of being the miserable misfit she first knew in Birmingham. The stability, the support, the stimulus she gave him can perhaps be gauged from the fact that while he was married to her he never suffered from the 'black dog', the paralysing depression which afflicted him at intervals throughout his adult life.

Tetty rescued Johnson from his inertia and his inability to overcome the financial and emotional difficulties that beset his teenage years. She lived with him through his most challenging period, as he struggled to make his name as a writer in London. She is a woman whose importance not just to Johnson but also to our understanding of him should be celebrated. Yet we know very little about her. So who was Mrs Elizabeth Johnson? And what can she tell us about Johnson at home, in the main of life, amid the daily tedium of small incidents and petty occurrences?

Elizabeth ('Tetty') Jervis (or Jarvis as it was pronounced and often spelt) was born on 4 February 1689 in the village of Great Peatling in Leicestershire. The Jervis family were gentleman-farmers, owning their land, from which they made enough money to send both of Tetty's brothers to boarding school at Rugby and then to Cambridge University. Tetty stayed at home, a much-loved and precious daughter after the death of her two sisters in childhood. As the only surviving granddaughter, Tetty inherited money and jewellery from her grandmother, which provided her with an unusual degree of inde-pendence. Nonetheless, on 4 February 1715, her twenty-sixth birthday, she married Henry ('Harry') Porter of Birmingham, by special licence issued from Lichfield. Their first child, Lucy, was born nine months later. A son Jervis was born the following year, and Joseph, the youngest, arrived sometime in 1724.

Just as Sarah Johnson had done before her, moving from the rural squire-archy downwards into commerce when she married, Tetty lowered herself socially by marrying Harry Porter. This was not something to be overlooked easily. The Jervis family were proud of their landowning ancestry. The Porters were tradespeople, Harry inheriting his father's drapery shop on the High Street in Birmingham. Tetty, though, was tempted by the prospect of moving away from the settled agricultural community of her childhood into the heart of the expanding town, with its sense of change and opportunity as new businesses kept opening, selling buttons, buckles, toy soldiers and teapots.

The Porters had been in Birmingham for generations; their store, next to the Castle Inn, was a family business with a long pedigree, passed on from father to son. As well as household linens, the Porters sold shirts and undergarments. Harry, like Tetty's brothers, had been given a scholar's education and was far more interested in books and ideas than the price of cotton or the changing fashions in corsetry. Unfortunately, he had no head for business and he failed to notice that his customers were becoming much younger and more style-conscious. They wanted cheaper shirts for everyday work in the factories, and more fashionable stays and corsets. By the summer of 1734, the store was looking outmoded, and the business was in trouble. Harry had been too busy enjoying the company of his friends, who included Thomas Warren, the enterprising bookseller and printer whose newspaper, the *Birmingham Journal*, was published from his home and workshop just along the High Street.

Warren was also the landlord of Johnson's friend Edmund Hector and, through the close networks that developed in these as-yet-small urban communities, Harry was introduced to Hector, just at the time that Johnson arrived in Birmingham to stay with Hector. Warren needed to find writers with a distinctive voice who could attract readers to his weekly newspaper, and Hector hoped that Johnson might be persuaded at last to write something for publication. Maybe this would stir Johnson out of the lethargy that threatened to waste away his talent?

Johnson's first published essay appeared in the *Birmingham Journal* sometime in 1734 (those early issues of the paper have not survived). Hector also introduced Johnson to Warren's friends, the Porters, and their three children, who included Lucy, a shy eighteen-year-old.

The young man whom Tetty and her family first encountered over tea in her High Street drawing room was uncommonly thin, a lanky scrap of skin and bone. As he entered the room, Samuel hesitated, confused for a moment by the company who because of his short sight he could only see as a blur, their faces indistinguishable. His clothes were shabby and not all that clean, his shoes worn down to the heel. He appeared unable to keep still, constantly jerking his neck from side to side and throwing his arms about.

His rough manner and strange appearance frightened Lucy at first. Years later she gave Boswell a vivid description of the man who was to become her stepfather. She recalled how his thinness was so extreme that he was little more than an 'immense structure of bones' with no muscle, nothing fleshy, like a skeleton, 'hideously striking'. The scars on his neck from the scrofula he suffered as a child were 'deeply visible' and quite shocking. His hair was uncut, long and thin but oddly 'straight and stiff, and separated behind', as if he had tried, rather badly, to tidy it up for the occasion. Most disturbing, though, were those 'convulsive starts and gesticulations', which 'tended to excite at once surprize and ridicule'.

Yet these 'external disadvantages' disappeared as soon as Samuel began to talk, in his deep, ponderous voice, thickened by his long-drawn-out Midlands accent. The room fell quiet as everyone turned to listen to the young man: 'Life is made up of little things; and that character is the best which does little but repeated acts of beneficence; as that conversation is the best which consists in elegant and pleasing thoughts expressed in natural and pleasing terms.' The woman behind the teapot turned to her daughter with an engaging, thoughtful smile and whispered, 'This is the most sensible man I ever saw in my life.'

By 'sensible' Tetty was investing Johnson with far more subtlety of character than we would now understand. Johnson gives us eight definitions in his *Dictionary*:

> Having the power of perceiving by the senses; Perceptible by the senses; Perceived by the mind; Perceiving by either mind or senses; having perception by the mind or senses; Having moral perception; having the quality of being affected by moral good or ill; Having quick intellectual feelings; being easily or strongly affected; Convinced; persuaded; In conversation, it has sometimes the sense of reasonable, judicious; wise.

Tetty could see beyond Johnson's outward flaws that his greatest gift was his 'moral perception'. He discerned the true meaning of things, not just through the exercise of his reason but by interpreting his senses, his intuition.

After the success of his first meeting with the Porters, Johnson began to call on them frequently, enjoying the happy ease of their domestic life, a solace to his lonely, confused mind. Then, suddenly, sometime in late July or early August 1734, Harry fell dangerously ill, perhaps brought on by worries about money and his dwindling business. By September he was dead, leaving Tetty with bills to pay and three children to settle in life. The

Lichfield gossips loved to insinuate that 'young Johnson' had attended the sickbed of Harry Porter 'with great assiduity' – as if angling for the widow even before her husband was dead. This was an odd accusation to make against a shy and inexperienced young man who had left Lichfield to avoid the domestic obligations that home, a widowed mother and the bookshop represented. Would Johnson really have been tempted to saddle himself with not just a wife but also her three children and a business selling underclothes?

There must have been something about Tetty that Johnson hoped could rescue him from his deep gloom and his abiding sense of failure. In his *Life*, Boswell gives us a rare portrait of Tetty, taken from the actor David Garrick, one of very few people to have known her. Unfortunately, Garrick's description of Tetty is both memorable and unkind.

Quoting Garrick, Boswell writes:

> She was very fat, with a bosom of more than ordinary protuberance, with swelled cheeks of a florid red, produced by thick painting, and increased by the liberal use of cordials; flaring and fantastick in her dress, and affected both in her speech and her general behaviour.

Boswell warns us that Garrick probably 'considerably aggravated the picture', but his character-sketch is so well written, so filled with telling details, that Tetty has become that fat, little woman, who was too fond of the bottle, shared none of her husband's literary interests and spent most of her time lounging in bed and reading cheap French romances while eating sweets and taking opium.

In her *Anecdotes of the Late Samuel Johnson*, Johnson's friend Hester Thrale (who herself never knew Tetty) also quotes from Garrick when trying to describe Johnson's wife:

> Garrick told Mr Thrale that she was a little painted puppet, of no value at all, and quite disguised with affectation, full of odd airs of rural elegance; and he made out some comical scenes, by mimicking her in a dialogue he pretended to have overheard.

She warns her readers not to take what Garrick says too literally: 'I do not know whether he [Garrick] meant such stuff to be believed or no, it was so comical.' And she gives us a clue as to what might have inspired this caricature. 'Nor did I ever see him represent her ridiculously, though my husband did.' Garrick, according to Hester Thrale, loved to entertain his friends with his genius for mimicry, usually to ribald effect. But he only performed his 'Tetty sketch' when in exclusively male company, as if he knew it was too risqué, too mean, and would never amuse his female friends.

There is nothing in Garrick's account of Tetty to suggest she had anything in common with Johnson. On the contrary, his view of Tetty taps into the simplest, most basic explanation for their unconventional liaison – sex. According to Garrick, Johnson once confessed to him that he could no longer come to see him backstage at Drury Lane because the sight of all the actresses wandering round the corridors wearing nothing more than petticoats and stockings excited his 'amorous propensities' (or, as Boswell writes in his journal, his 'genitals'). Johnson was a man of 'active parts' but moral principle; Tetty was a mature, experienced woman with a sensual figure. Johnson married Tetty to have his way with her, or so Garrick and Boswell would have us believe.

Other biographers, reluctant to think of Johnson as a married man, let alone the husband of a middle-aged widow from Birmingham, have suggested that he fell in love not with Tetty but with her daughter. After all, Lucy was at the time of their meeting a blushing eighteen-year-old while he was just twenty-five. Is it not more likely that he would have fallen in love with her rather than with her middle-aged mother? He only turned to Tetty out of pique when Lucy refused him, put off by his umpromising behaviour and charmless looks. Boswell was given this story by the gossips of Lichfield when he was researching his *Life* several decades later, but he found it difficult to believe. He preferred his own interpretation.

Hester Thrale, who knew Johnson better than most in his later years, writes rather differently about Tetty. She says in the *Anecdotes*, 'Mr Johnson has told me that her hair was eminently beautiful, quite *blonde* like that of a baby; but that she fretted about the colour, and was always desirous to dye it black, which he very judiciously hindered her from doing.' Hester was fascinated by Tetty and by her portrait, which she was shown by Lucy many years after Tetty's death. 'The picture . . . was very pretty,' she tells us, 'and her daughter Mrs Lucy Porter said it was like.'

This portrait, by Marie Verelst, a Dutch painter who worked in London as a society artist, still survives (in the Hyde Collection at the Houghton Library) and shows Tetty as a genteel lady of the Restoration with fine blonde hair, lightly curled, hanging long over one shoulder. It's a straightforward, if old-fashioned, portrayal, not overly dressy or foolishly flirtatious. Tetty's rich silk gown matches the deep blue of her eyes and is draped low across her bust to accentuate her womanly shape, but decorously so. There's no danger of the silk slipping to reveal a pert nipple (as in the courtly portraits of Sir Peter Lely). Tetty is of the fashion, but at the same time she is very much her own person. She has lightly rouged her cheeks to give that attractive pinkish flush, but only just enough to enhance the pure white skin of her bosom. There's a sweetness, a delicacy of feeling in her expression as she looks out at us with no reserve or affectation, her questing eyes hiding nothing.

Hester Thrale once asked Johnson if he had ever disputed with his wife, to which he replied, 'Perpetually,' before explaining, 'My wife had a particular reverence for cleanliness, and desired the praise of neatness in her dress and furniture, as many ladies do, till they become troublesome to their best friends, slaves to their own besoms, and only sigh for the hour of sweeping their husbands out of the house as dirt, and useless lumber.' Tetty, Hester recognised, had wit enough to banter with her husband: 'But, Sir, a clean floor is *so* comfortable!'

Tetty's misfortune was that Johnson so soon grew apart from her. When she married him, he had written nothing of any worth, and for much of the time he could not write, overwhelmed by lowness of spirit and constrained by self-doubt. Who knows what Tetty saw in such a troubled young man? Perhaps she adopted him as a cause. Perhaps she was comforted by him when her life fell apart after Harry's death. The marriages of even our dearest friends are sometimes difficult to fathom.

The wedding day itself was not an auspicious beginning. Elizabeth Porter (née Jervis) and Samuel Johnson married not in Lichfield or Birmingham, but in Derby, in the church of St Werburgh's. They had to hire a horse for the ride, which took all morning. Boswell suggests in the *Life* that even before they were husband and wife the Johnsons fell out with each other and that Tetty cried on her wedding day not from happiness, but disappointment. He tells the story as if he is in conversation with Johnson:

> 'Sir [says Johnson], at first she told me that I rode too fast, and she could not keep up with me; and, when I rode a little slower, she passed me, and complained that I lagged behind. I was not to be made the slave

of caprice; and I resolved to begin as I meant to end. I therefore pushed on briskly, till I was fairly out of her sight. The road lay between two hedges, so I was sure she could not miss it; and I contrived that she should soon come up with me. When she did, I observed her to be in tears.'

According to Boswell, Tetty, even at forty-six, was a foolish, flirty female, schooled in the arts of coquetry.

Hester Thrale also tells the tale in her *Anecdotes*, and also as if Johnson himself is talking directly to us:

'I was riding to church (says Johnson), and she following on another single horse: she hung back however, and I turned about to see whether she could get her steed along, or what was the matter. I had however soon occasion to see it was only coquetry, and *that I despised*, so quickening my pace a little, she mended hers; but I believe there was a tear or two—pretty dear creature!'

But did Johnson really use those words, 'pretty dear creature', of Tetty, a mature mother of three? It's the kind of language he perhaps used about Hester's children, when he was in his seventies and Hester herself was little more than thirty.

Hester had been told the tale when she visited Lichfield with Johnson in 1774. Why was the wedding still being talked about so long after it had taken place? No one travelled with Tetty and Samuel to Derby from Lichfield. No one knew what had passed between them on that day. Apart from the presiding minister, the Revd William Lockett, and the two signatories on the marriage certificate, neither of whom figure in Johnson's later life, no one else was there.

Boswell tells us that Tetty's in-laws from her first marriage virtually cut her off, appalled by her decision to marry a man with so few prospects. What would happen to her children? Even Lucy did not attend the ceremony. Tetty's elder son Jervis (named after Tetty's family) was already in the merchant navy, but the youngest child Joseph was only eleven. He was sent away to stay with his uncle, also called Joseph, a successful merchant, trading with the Hanseatic ports in cloth, timber and furs, who owned a large home in Ironmonger Lane in the City and also a country retreat in Mortlake, on the banks of the Thames to the south-west of the capital.

Lucy, as far as we know, never reproached her mother for what she had done. Johnson's mother, too, was compliant, at least according to Boswell. Sarah, he says, 'was too tender a parent to oppose his inclinations'. But he adds, straight from the acid tongue of his Lichfield witness, Anna Seward, that Johnson could only persuade his mother to accept his decision by telling her:

> Mother . . . I have told her [Mrs Porter] the worst of me; that I am of mean extraction; that I have no money; and that I have had an uncle hanged. She replied, that she valued no one more or less for his descent; that she had no more money than myself; and that, though, she had not had a relation hanged, she had fifty who deserved hanging.

Anna Seward's gossip against Johnson was fuelled by jealousy (she envied his literary success in London) but also by the misfortune of her sister, Sarah, who was once engaged to Tetty's son Joseph. Having made a commitment, Joseph then prevaricated, delaying the arrangements for the wedding. Sarah fell ill while she waited for him to make up his mind, and she died a few months later. Johnson was not of low birth, nor did he have an uncle who was hanged (as far as we know). But there was perhaps a grain of truth in Anna Seward's story. Tetty's sharp retort about her relatives shows again that she was a woman of character and wit.

Most of what we know about the Johnsons' marriage is actually hearsay, gossip or conjecture. All we have from Johnson himself is what he writes in his letters *after* Tetty's death, when grief clouded his vision: 'I have ever since seemed to myself broken off from mankind a kind of solitary wanderer in the wild of life . . . A gloomy gazer on a World to which I have little relation.' He writes prayers filled with remorse at his neglect of her and longing for her company. He did not intend anyone else to read them, but they were discovered among his papers after his death and published soon afterwards in early 1785, along with a selection of his meditations.

'Poor Tetty,' he mused on Easter Day 1778, almost thirty years after her death, 'whatever were our faults and failings, we loved each other—Could'st thou have lived!' On reading this, in the published version, a Mrs Nicholas of Chichester told a friend, 'Every woman must love and reverence the man whose tender affection and grief for his wife was not abated by a separation of thirty years.' In these prayers, Johnson appears as the loving husband, a gentle, caring man attuned to Tetty's personality and deeply mourning his loss.

Johnson never stopped missing Tetty, after her death. But there was something troubling about their relationship. 'Whatever was good in the example of my departed wife, teach me to follow, and whatever was amiss give me grace to shun . . .' he prayed. He could not forget that there had been things 'amiss' in her character. In 1762, he warned his friend, Giuseppe Baretti, the volatile Italian writer, about the perils of love and marriage. Baretti was wondering whether he should marry. Johnson advised him, 'There is indeed nothing that so much seduces reason from her vigilance, as the thought of passing life with an amiable woman.' He goes on to explain:

> Love and marriage are different states. Those who are to suffer the evils together, and to suffer often for the sake of one another, soon lose that tenderness of look and that benevolence of mind which arose from the participation of unmingled pleasure and successive amusement. A woman we are sure will not be always fair; we are not sure she will always be virtuous; and man cannot retain through life that respect and assiduity by which he pleases for a day or for a month.

Is this what he really thought about his own marriage?

Less than a fortnight before their wedding, on 25 June 1735, Johnson wrote to his old Oxford friend Richard Congreve, 'I am now going to furnish a House in the Country and keep a private boarding-school for Young Gentlemen whom I shall endeavour to instruct in a method somewhat more rational than those commonly practised . . .' Johnson was thinking about setting up a school and needed advice on the curriculum. 'Before I draw up my plan of Education, I shall attempt to procure an account of the different ways of teaching in use at the most celebrated Schools, and shall therefore hope You will favour me with the method of the Charterhouse, and procure me that of Westminster.'

Congreve had been a boarder at both Charterhouse and Westminster. Johnson had not, and did not know what parents would expect such a school to provide. His letter is full of optimistic plans for the future, but makes no mention of the wife with whom he intended to run this school – and on whose money the plan depended (he had no money and was reliant on Tetty's 'fortune', her inheritance from her grandmother, which she must have preserved intact during her first marriage).

At the same time he was writing letters to the editor of the newly established *Gentleman's Magazine* in London, Edward Cave, hoping to find work. Signing himself 'S. Smith', Johnson suggested that if he were allowed to contribute to the magazine's pages he would improve them:

> Sir, As you appear no less sensible than your readers of the defects of your poetical articles, you will not be displeased, if, in order to the improvement of it, I communicate to you the sentiments of a person, who will undertake, on reasonable terms, sometimes to fill a column.

Cave, not surprisingly, never replied to such a presumptuous letter but he must have kept it, for it still survives, presumably kept by Cave and returned to Johnson's estate upon his death.

Cave was a self-made man, enterprising and creative. Born a cobbler's son, he was sent to school at Rugby to improve his chances. While there he became interested in printing and publishing, and in 1731 he seized the opportunity of the relaxation of taxes on paper and the freeing up of government censorship to launch his *Gentleman's Magazine*, a digest of news, poetry (often in Latin and Greek), book reviews, theatre bills, stocks and shares, ship movements, geology, geography, fauna and flora. The magazine, which was finely illustrated with maps, architectural plans and line drawings from nature, was such an original idea and so accomplished it was an immediate success and in just a few years established a circulation of 10,000 copies, a huge readership for that time. In the *Dictionary* Johnson credits Cave with having given birth to the term 'magazine' in its modern sense, taking the word 'magazine' meaning 'a storehouse' and applying it to his weekly treasury of news and information. 'Of late this word has signified a miscellaneous pamphlet, from a periodical miscellany named the *Gentleman's Magazine*, by Edward Cave,' reads the entry.

Did Tetty know that Johnson was trying to get work as a writer for a London magazine? Did she encourage him to do so? There is no record. But after marrying Samuel Johnson she at first moved to Lichfield, above the bookshop, where she lived with her mother-in-law and the occasional presence of her husband's younger brother Nathaniel. The couple do not appear to have made careful plans for the future. On the contrary, they rushed into marriage without really contemplating its consequences.

Almost a year later, in the June edition of the *Gentleman's Magazine*, an advertisement declared:

> At Edial, near Litchfield in Staffordshire, Young Gentlemen are Boarded and Taught the Latin and Greek Languages, by SAMUEL JOHNSON.

Why Samuel and Tetty thought that printing his name in capital letters would sell the school to parents is a puzzle. No one beyond Lichfield, and a few friends in Birmingham and Oxford, would have known of Samuel Johnson. He had not published anything beyond those few pieces in the *Birmingham Journal* and, more pertinently, he had no academic (or any other) qualifications. No Oxford degree, let alone a doctorate. How did he and Tetty expect to attract pupils? But they went ahead anyway, opening the school in a large house at Edial, which they must have rented with Tetty's money.

The advertisement was a waste of that money, yielding few, if any pupils. At most the Johnsons only ever attracted eight boarders, and these were mostly the children of friends and acquaintances from Lichfield. David Garrick, the future actor, was among them, just a few years younger than Johnson himself, and ungovernable. Johnson was not equipped to teach; feeling awkward and ungainly himself, he was unable to impose his authority on teenage boys. He was also not interested in the rigid Classics curriculum then expected by parents and the universities. Neither he nor Tetty enjoyed sharing their home with a group of hyperactive teenagers. In less than a year they sent away their pupils and gave up the house. Either they had run through all of Tetty's inheritance, or she was unwilling to lose all her money in a venture which she knew could never guarantee them sufficient income.

The failure of their Edial experiment did more than dent their finances and their confidence. Garrick and his fellow pupils had once spied on the Johnsons through the keyhole of their bedroom door. As a bumptious eighteen-year-old, Garrick had watched the awkward couple tossing and tumbling between the sheets. He never forgot the scene, nor could resist re-enacting in graphic detail what he had witnessed. Tetty was unfortunate enough to have been caught in flagrante delicto by a boy who would grow up to be the greatest mimic of his age, of whom Johnson once said his face had aged because 'no man's face has had more wear and tear' as he acted out his roles. Her character and her reputation have never recovered.

*

Not long after leaving Edial, on 2 March 1737, Johnson set off for London, but without Tetty. He was inspired to take action and attempt to achieve his ambition by Garrick, who was determined to try his luck in the capital as an actor. Johnson hoped to find work as a writer. Garrick had connections in the city, through his brother Peter, who was setting himself up as a wine merchant. Peter had already met and befriended Charles Fleetwood, manager of the successful small theatre at Goodman's Fields in Whitechapel. David Garrick hoped to impress Fleetwood with his talent as an actor. Johnson took with him the manuscript of a half-finished play. Both were so short of money, they shared a horse, riding or walking in turn.

Maybe Johnson left without cash because he did not want to spend what he had not earned himself? Maybe Tetty agreed to stay behind in Lichfield to help Sarah Johnson make more of a success of the bookshop? We do know she encouraged him to leave, hoping that he would be able to sell his play to Fleetwood. She believed in her husband's exceptional talent and in the possibility of success. Johnson later said of Tetty, with regret, that she could recite comedy better than anyone he knew (even Garrick?), but that in tragedy 'she mouthed too much'.

His manuscript was a half-formed tragedy, *Irene*, with not one, but two heroines, Irene and Aspasia, both of whom are supposed to have been modelled on Tetty. It's an exotic fable, set in Constantinople in 1453 as the Byzantine capital is being ransacked by the Ottoman Turks. Irene is trapped in the city, a Greek Christian who is forced to become the mistress of the Sultan Mahomet II. But the Sultan soon begins to resent being in thrall to a woman and he orders Irene's death to prove that he is in command of his passions. A woman's life is sacrificed on the altar of a man's reason in a scenario that has contemporary resonances.

The Eastern theme and setting were very popular in the first half of the eighteenth century, as travellers began wandering across the Mediterranean as far as Beirut, Jerusalem and Constantinople. Playwrights could make huge amounts of money, both from the theatre performances and the publication of the text. Having experienced failure at Edial, Tetty and her husband took a huge risk when they staked their future on the success of a grandiose play set in the East and inspired by the clash of civilisations between Christianity and Islam. Or did they? Tetty had no doubt that her husband was unusually gifted; Johnson had read more plays than most people, and he knew what made them work – at least on the page. He was crippled by insecurities, partly derived from his very real disabilities: he was deaf in one ear, partially sighted and afflicted with nervous tics. But he had a compulsion to write and a talent for putting words together.

As the play begins, the golden city of Eastern Christendom is being ripped apart by the heathen Turkish conquerors.

> From ev'ry palace burst a mingled clamour,
> The dreadful dissonance of barb'rous triumph,
> Shrieks of affright, and wailings of distress . . .

Irene's virtue and that of her companion Aspasia is gravely threatened by the barbarian hordes:

> Behold the monsters gaze with savage rapture,
> Behold how Lust and Rapine struggle round her.

Aspasia laments the weakness of her sex:

> The weakness we lament, our selves create,
> Instructed from our infant years to court
> With counterfeited fears the aid of man;
> We learn to shudder at the rustling breeze,
> Start at the light, and tremble in the dark;

But Irene will have none of it, rallying her friend by declaring boldly:

> Then let me once, in honour of our sex,
> Assume the boastful arrogance of man . . .

> Do not we share the comprehensive thought,
> Th' enlivening wit, the penetrating reason?

It's stirring stuff. Fifty years before Mary Wollstonecraft asserted in her *Vindication of the Rights of Woman* that men and women should be equal, Johnson's dual heroines, Irene and Aspasia, demand that their voices be heard. But *Irene*, in spite of its exotic setting and some powerful speeches, was too serious, too moral, too philosophical a drama for a West End audience, with not enough plot.

Once again, Tetty and Johnson had misjudged the market, and it was years before Johnson could persuade anyone to stage *Irene*. When, in February 1749, it was at last put on at Drury Lane (where David Garrick was by then the manager), Tetty was too ill to attend the performance. Garrick ensured that it ran for a respectable nine nights and yielded £200 profit for the Johnsons (worth about £17,000 now), but the reviews were lukewarm and *Irene* was never revived.

Johnson, though, was not deterred by his inability to sell his play, or find enough paid work. He was enthralled by life in the capital. As he walked down the Strand towards Fleet Street, brushing shoulders with the whole gallery of humankind, from beggars and prostitutes in rags to ladies in fine silks, or a footman in breeches, a judge in his wig, actors rushing home from the theatre still in their greasepaint, a milkmaid leading a cow, a blind fiddler and his dog, he began to feel that anything was possible. He was at last among people like himself. Even if he only had less than £30 a year to live on, he knew that he could survive and live reasonably well.

After allowing £10 a year for his clothes and linen (presumably including the cost of laundry), he calculated that 'a man might live in a garret at eighteen-pence a week . . . By spending three-pence in a coffee-house, he might be for some hours every day in very good company; he might dine for six-pence, breakfast on bread and milk for a penny, and do without supper. On clean-shirt-day he went abroad, and paid visits.'

But his income-and-expense balance-sheet failed to take account of his wife's expenses, and her desire for more comforts than the stark boards of a garret and only bread and milk for breakfast. Had he abandoned her for ever to Lichfield and his mother?

In the autumn of 1737, he went back to the Midlands to collect Tetty, agreeing to move into better lodgings in the West End, just off the newly built Hanover Square, as an enticement. He wrote again to Edward Cave, suggesting that a translation of a history of the Council of Trent should be published in the *Gentleman's Magazine* and that he should be the translator. Cave did not reply, at first, but at last in March 1738, after several more attempts to interest Cave in his work, his persistence paid off and his first published poem appeared in the magazine – verses in Latin in praise of Sylvanus Urban, Cave's pen name. A few months later Johnson saw in print for the first time his verses in English.

'To Eliza Plucking Laurel in Mr Pope's Gardens' celebrates Johnson's introduction to literary London. His 'Eliza' was a new friend, Elizabeth Carter, whom he met at Cave's office in St John's Gate, a scholar and linguist who also arrived in London hoping to make her name as a writer. Such was the prestige of the *Gentleman's Magazine* that she and Johnson, together with their colleague on the magazine, Thomas Birch, were invited by the scholar and translator Alexander Pope to visit his river garden and grotto at Twickenham. Pope's reputation was based on his hugely successful versions of the *Iliad* and the *Odyssey*. Tetty was not included in the trip.

In London, Johnson had discovered a place so endlessly absorbing and inspiring that his discomforts of mind and body were forgotten. At the offices of the *Gentleman's Magazine*, he met men and women of like mind who, by assisting Cave and providing him with copy each month, were earning enough to survive, just, in the endlessly absorbing city. Their arrival in the capital had coincided with the start of a new kind of publishing, which was cheap, immediate and with a broad circulation, taking in the interests of not just a select band of academics and wealthy indolents but a new breed of readers, often self-educated, required to earn their own living but with sufficient leisure to read magazines and books. Even though Tetty was now in London, Johnson did not stay at home with her, eating meals at regular hours and spending the evenings in her company. He preferred to wander the city through the night, from Tyburn to Limehouse, dropping in to a tavern, then walking some more, until hungry at dawn he found a pudding shop still open, busy with other rootless young men who were bursting with ideas and dreams of how to fulfil them. Not to have money was no hardship when there was always company to provide distraction.

Tetty did not agree. She did not find the city a source of never-ending interest and stimulation. She felt dowdy, slow-witted, unable to make herself understood or to decipher the flat vowels and London slang of the shopkeepers. Life, even in the more salubrious West End, was exhausting, dangerous – and far too expensive. Johnson in no way made enough money from what he wrote, and without regular income the capital was a dreary, uncomfortable, frightening place. Tetty had swapped a settled life in a companionable market town for the peripatetic existence of a writer's companion, moving lodgings every few months to find somewhere cheaper. While her husband spent his day – and much of the night – in and around Fleet Street among the print-shops and publishers, dining with his new friends Elizabeth Carter and Thomas Birch and wandering the streets with the poet Richard Savage, she had nothing to do except endlessly struggle to keep clean a home that would never be free of soot, mud and vermin.

At least she still had some money of her own, and while Johnson moved closer to Cave's office in Clerkenwell, Tetty retreated to lodgings beyond London Bridge away from the foetid fumes of the crowded inner city. Johnson was preoccupied and determined to find success as a writer. Tetty was bored and abandoned. How different her life had become, with no family, no friends and no settled home.

Johnson, though, was at last becoming productive. In May 1738 his first major work was published, a poem celebrating London, written in imitation of the Latin poet Juvenal. On the surface, *London: A poem* satirises the perils of city life, but it can also be read as Johnson's paean to metropolitan life, his anthem to its fascinating chaos, its endless possibilities:

> Here Malice, Rapine, Accident, conspire,
> And now a Rabble rages, now a Fire;
> Their Ambush here relentless Ruffians lay,
> And here the fell Attorney prowls for Prey;
> Here falling Houses thunder on your Head,
> And here a female Atheist talks you dead.

He kept his authorship secret, at first, but *London* was so successful it was reprinted several times within a year, and attributed to this new young writer, Samuel Johnson. He was beginning to establish a name for himself, although he still had no financial security. By August 1739, he and Tetty were so desperately short of money they were forced to sell the silver cup that Johnson's mother had bought for him on that long-ago visit to London.

Johnson made one last, rather half-hearted attempt to find paid work as a schoolteacher, leaving London (without Tetty) to apply for a vacancy at Appleby Grammar School, not far from Lichfield. He failed to get the job, which was no surprise given his unprepossessing appearance and his ineptitude as a teacher. Strangely, though, he did not return immediately to London but instead lingered in the Midlands visiting friends from Oxford and staying on in Lichfield at the bookshop (where his stepdaughter Lucy was now helping Mrs Johnson senior) not just for weeks but for several months, even though he knew Tetty was miserable and alone in London.

*

On 31 January 1740, six months after abandoning Tetty, Johnson wrote to her from Lichfield. It is the only letter to her which has survived, and thereby holds a significance far beyond any that Johnson might have intended when he wrote it. Tetty had moved again and was now staying at a Mrs Crow's in Castle Street, close to Cavendish Square in the West End. She was worried about money while Johnson had enjoyed several months of freedom from his financial and household responsibilities.

'Dearest Tetty,' the letter begins, in tight-fisted, contorted handwriting, as if Johnson was holding back a great deal of emotion:

> I shall be very uneasy till I know that you have recovered, and beg that you will omit nothing that can contribute to it, nor deny yourself any thing that may make confinement less melancholy.

Tetty had injured her leg, perhaps having slipped on the ice. It had been one of the coldest and most dangerous winters on record. The Thames had frozen over, people had died in the street, and the snow and ice stayed on the ground until March:

> You have already suffered more than I can bear to reflect upon, and I hope more than either of us shall suffer again. One part at least I have flattered myself we shall avoid for the future, our troubles will surely never separate us more.

But Johnson does not suggest that he should rush back to London to help Tetty:

> I still promise myself many happy years from your tenderness and affection, which I sometimes hope our misfortunes have not yet deprived me of.

To assuage his guilt he instructs Tetty to spare no expense and to consult the best physicians in London, either John Ranby or John Shipton, both of whom were doctors at Court. (Ranby was an expert surgeon who in 1744 published a pamphlet, *The Method of Treating Gun-shot Wounds.*) Johnson is worried, and wants Tetty to have expert treatment, at a time when a neglected wound, even though not originally very serious, could prove fatal. But his remorse pulled them further apart:

> My dear Girl—I have seen nobody in these rambles upon which I have been forced, that has not contributed to confirm my esteem and affection

for thee, though that esteem and affection only contributed to encrease my unhappiness when I reflected that the most amiable woman in the world was exposed by my means to miseries which I could not endure.

I am, My Charming Love,

Yours

Sam. Johnson

Tetty has by now become Johnson's 'dear Girl', almost his daughter. Her life with him had begun with her instilling in him the confidence to apply himself and become the successful writer she knew he could be. Now, not five years later, it is Samuel who has to chivvy Tetty out of her misery.

He adds a postscript:

Lucy always sends her Duty and my Mother her Service.

He is with family. Tetty, in contrast, is alone in an unfriendly city, with no one to visit and comfort her. Johnson's few lines of consolation will have done little to help, and he knows this. The letter is full of uncharacteristic crossings-out, changing 'We' to 'I' when he writes 'I have often flattered myself', and turning 'diffi . . .' into 'hazards'. Johnson is lost for words.

What Tetty thought of the letter we do not know. If she sent a reply, it has not survived. But she was left alone for another three months before at last Johnson came back to London. His return made little difference to Tetty. Johnson at first lived with her in Castle Street, but he was rarely at home, getting up late, staying out until the early hours, and preferring the company he could find at St John's Gate or in the coffee-houses of Fleet Street. Johnson was not happy in the West End, which was too far away from the printers and publishers of Grub Street and St Paul's Churchyard. He insisted that they move further east, first taking rooms in Durham Yard, off the Strand, then moving on to Fetter Lane and Holborn.

They were still short of money, with only the meagre income Johnson earned from Cave for his editorial help and the occasional essay, and Tetty had to scrimp and save, until Johnson complained, 'huffing' his wife about the toughness of the meat. One day when he was about to say grace before dinner she stopped him with the words, 'Do not make a farce of thanking

God for a dinner which you will presently protest not eatable.' Tetty's spirit was crushed by metropolitan life, their lack of money, and her succession of misfortunes, but she still tried to hold her own against her infuriating husband.

Cave then asked Johnson to provide weekly reports on the debates in the House of Commons. Journalists were not allowed into the House, and so Johnson came up with the idea of inventing the proceedings, in the style of Swift's satirical *Gulliver's Travels*. His column proved a huge success, giving birth to the satirical parliamentary sketch, still a staple of newspapers. Johnson also began writing short 'lives' for the magazine, creating in the *Life of Richard Savage* the first 'biography' to explore the inner workings of character. Savage, a brilliant poet and colleague on the magazine, had been his friend but Johnson did not flinch from analysing his unruly and contradictory personality, remarking, 'It cannot be said, that he made Use of his Abilities for the Direction of his own Conduct; an irregular and dissipated Manner of Life had made him the Slave of every Passion that happened to be excited by the Presence of its Object, and that Slavery to his Passions reciprocally produced a Life irregular and dissipated.'

Savage was tried for murder and convicted but given a royal pardon, after which he did not reform but fell heavily into debt, dying young in a debtors' jail in Bristol in August 1743. Out of his grief, Johnson created a powerful portrait of a flawed genius, attractive, talented, but out of control. His 'life' was as original as his accounts of the sessions in Parliament. He was beginning to show that he could write with equal ease as a poet and satirist, historian, biographer and bookish scholar. Tetty's faith in him was at last beginning to bear fruit.

In early 1746, Johnson signed an agreement with a consortium of booksellers to prepare a dictionary of the English language. Johnson promised to complete the project in just three years, and was given a very generous advance of £1,575. This figure of about £135,000 in today's money would have been lavish if Johnson had managed to complete the project in the time allotted. But at least he and Tetty now had a proper income, and guaranteed economic stability for the next three years, if not beyond. They moved into No. 17 Gough Square, an imposing five-storey house in a quiet square behind Fleet Street.

They chose this new home wisely. No. 17 had, and still has, a huge garret that stretches across the whole breadth of the house, with plenty of windows to provide maximum daylight for Johnson and his copyists to work in while also having plenty of rooms below for entertaining. Tetty, though, was still not happy. Gough Square was convenient for Johnson, close to Cave's office and his printers in St Paul's Churchyard, but it was in the heart of the commercial City, far too close to the pungent, disease-ridden Fleet ditch, and a long way from the gracious squares of the West End. Johnson, too, was even more preoccupied than before, struggling to work out how to compile the dictionary and develop a filing system for the illustrative quotations which he could easily refer back to when writing up the definitions. Looking back on these years in Johnson's life there are no references to Tetty, and yet when she died, on 18 March 1752, after a long, debilitating illness, Johnson was bereft, as if he had lost a bosom companion.

Tetty's ill health can be dated back to that winter of 1739–40 when she struggled on alone in London as Johnson gallivanted in the Midlands. She never recovered properly from the injury to her leg and by 1743 was more or less housebound. On Sunday 2 January 1743, Johnson wrote to an old schoolfriend John Taylor, who was now rector of Ashbourne in Derbyshire and with whom he had stayed on that long trip away from home: 'Soon after I received your last Letter, Mrs Johnson was seized with such an illness, having not been well for some time before as will easily make You excuse my neglect at answering You, I believe it is now the twelfth Week since she was taken with it . . .'

Very few of Johnson's friends had met Tetty, and they decided she must be a difficult hypochondriac, a lazy woman, who indulged herself by absconding to more expensive lodgings while Johnson slaved away over his *Dictionary* 'in the smoke of London'. Gough Square was a fine house but Tetty craved green space and cleaner air. She had never adjusted to life in the capital, or the loss of her children. Jervis was still away at sea, Joseph was now living in Leghorn to develop his uncle's trading connections with the Mediterranean sea ports, while Lucy stayed on in Lichfield. Lonely and isolated, she then began to show the symptoms of some kind of wasting illness, probably cancer.

By the spring of 1751 Johnson was sending regular letters to a bookseller named John Newbery, in St Paul's Churchyard, for loans of sometimes a guinea, sometimes £2. He did not say for what 'sudden needs' these loans were required, but they were probably to pay the physicians whom he consulted to help Tetty. She took rooms in Hampstead, just beside the heath, where she could see trees in the distance and breathe cleaner air. But by the first weeks of 1752 she had become so ill she returned to Gough Square to be cared for by Johnson and to be closer to the physicians who were treating her.

On 12 March, Charlotte Lennox, a young novelist and protégée of Johnson, received a letter from him thanking her for the 'present' (her latest novel, *The Female Quixote*, was published on 15 March). The letter ends, 'Poor Tetty Johnson's illness will not suffer me to think of going any whither, out of her call. She is very ill, and I am very much dejected.'

Tetty died in the early hours of Tuesday 18 March, in her bedroom at Gough Square, leaving Johnson so distraught that he wrote immediately in desperation to John Taylor, who was an absentee prebendary of Westminster but happened to be in town fulfilling his clerical duties. The letter, which Johnson wrote at three in the morning just as Tetty died, is an outpouring of his grief. Taylor was not impressed, suspecting, not without cause, that Johnson was consumed by guilt.

In the sermon that he wrote to be delivered at Tetty's funeral Johnson declared that 'kindness' had been 'snatched from his arms, and fidelity torn from his bosom'. He had lost his companion, his support, but also the person with whom he shared his work, reading aloud together not only his poems but also works that they both appreciated:

> Yet, let it be remembered that her wit was never employed to scoff at goodness, nor her reason to dispute against truth. In this age of wild opinions, she was as free from scepticism as the cloistered virgin. She never wished to signalise herself by the singularity of paradox. She had a just diffidence of her own reason, and desired to practise rather than to dispute . . .

But the sermon was never delivered. Johnson was too upset even to attend Tetty's funeral, let alone give the oration, and John Taylor, who was supposed to do it for him, refused to use what Johnson had written, shocked by what he believed to be its insincerity. Taylor disliked Tetty and thought of her as having been a hindrance to Johnson as he struggled to achieve his potential. He had himself acrimoniously divorced his first wife, and he spread abroad the story that Tetty 'was the plague of Johnson's life'. I suspect, though, that he refused to use Johnson's sermon not so much because of what Johnson says about Tetty but because of the way Johnson harps on about death.

'It is impossible to think, and not sometimes to think on death,' Johnson wrote. 'Let everyone whose eye glances on this bier, examine what would have been his conditions, if the same hour had called him to judgement . . .' And so it goes on, and on, for the next six paragraphs. Johnson wanted to remind the mourners, who would all have been standing in front of Tetty's coffin, 'Hope, indeed, has many powers of delusion; whatever is possible, however unlikely, it will teach us to promise ourselves; but death no man has escaped, and therefore no man can hope to escape it.' Taylor must have been concerned that Johnson's relentless focus on our too brief mortality was too harsh for the occasion.

William Shaw, who was one of the first to publish a biography of Johnson and who knew both Taylor and Johnson's friends in Lichfield, said of Tetty, 'Johnson often said he never knew how dear she was to him, till he lost her.' Shaw did not know Tetty but he did talk to Mrs Desmoulins (pronounced Des Mullins), the daughter of Johnson's godfather Dr Swynfen. Mrs Desmoulins had befriended Tetty and kept company with her in Hampstead while Johnson was living in Gough Square slaving away over the *Dictionary*. Shaw retails the gossip that Tetty took to drink 'and, some say, opium'. He admits, too, that she and Johnson grew apart, although he is careful not to lay the blame on Tetty by adding, 'probably he grew peevish by study and disease'.

Shaw adds to the mystery of the marriage by asserting, 'A suspicion of his conjugal infelicity on this account certainly went abroad, and procured him much commiseration from his friends.' Mrs Desmoulins had told him that when Johnson visited Tetty in Hampstead she would refuse to let him sleep with her. Johnson would then retreat to Mrs Desmoulins's room and ask for comfort, which extended to physical caresses but, she insisted, no more. Shaw did not want his readers to gain the wrong impression, and he makes clear that Tetty and Johnson always 'regarded each other with true cordiality and affection'. Tetty, according to Shaw, shared Johnson's interest in books and reading. But what was the true character of Johnson's relations with Mrs Desmoulins? Or indeed with Tetty herself? What kind of marriage did they have?

*

Here then are the facts about Tetty's life with Johnson of which we can be sure. While Tetty was married to Johnson he did not suffer from the terrible depressive periods which troubled him throughout his life. By the time she died not only had his tragedy *Irene* finally been staged but he had also acquired the literary reputation he had desired for so long. Tetty, too, gave Johnson a firm foundation in friendship. She never lost faith in her husband's unusual degree of sensibility.

After her death Johnson always took his breakfast on a plate that he thought of as 'Tetty's plate', so that she would be with him every day. He always kept in a wooden box her wedding ring, which was inscribed with the date of their marriage (wrongly etched as 1736, not 1735) and the date of her death. He missed her quick wit, her habit of answering back after one too many complaints. Above all, he missed the companionship of someone at home with whom he could chew over the petty thoughts and complaints of the day.

Tetty, in contrast, lost everything when she married Johnson. Her sons no longer communicated with her, refusing to acknowledge their stepfather. Jervis, the sailor, did once try to visit his mother in Gough Square. They had not seen each other for fifteen years but he was home from abroad and had heard that his mother was not well. He called on her without warning. Johnson was out; Tetty was lying in bed upstairs, weak and unwilling to see visitors. By the time she realised her son was downstairs, her Porter son from Lichfield, and had washed and dressed herself for the occasion, her hair powdered, her dress freshly pressed, Jervis had fled, regretting his impulse to call on her. He never returned.

Tetty's younger son Joseph was in London for most of the time that Tetty was also living in the city but he never took the trouble to make contact with her. She also never saw her daughter Lucy after moving to London. Lucy has become part of the Johnsonian tableau, a 'hoary virgin' as her stepfather called her, with what he thought of as affection. She always remained on good terms with Johnson, writing letters and exchanging gifts. He sent her a diamond ring (once he had money and a pension), a sewing bag, and from his visit to Paris in the autumn of 1775 a decorative snuffbox. 'Dear Miss,' writes Johnson to Lucy after both his mother and his wife have died, 'every heart must lean to somebody, and I have nobody but you . . .' Yet of her relationship with Tetty, her mother, we know nothing.

Tetty was buried far from home and family in the nave of the parish church at Bromley in Kent, simply because Johnson was too upset to arrange his wife's funeral. His friend, John Hawkesworth, who lived in the small market town, offered to organise the funeral for him, which took place on 26 March 1752. Tetty had stayed with the Hawkesworths in Bromley on several occasions before she became ill, delighting in the country-town whirl of gardening, tea parties and parish life. But if Tetty had been buried in Tothill Fields in Westminster (which Johnson's friend John Taylor could have arranged), Johnson would have been able to visit his wife's grave. Instead Tetty's body was carried ten and three quarter miles by horse and carriage to a church far from the city, where she was laid to rest among strangers and without any of her family present.

Johnson's funeral took place with great pomp in Westminster Abbey, but his wife had few mourners and her grave was left unmarked for thirty years. Not until he became acutely aware of his own approaching death did Johnson arrange for a simple black marble stone to be laid over Tetty's place of burial at Bromley. Her epitaph was etched in Latin, a language which she did not know.

In translation, the memorial reads:

Here are interred the remains of
ELIZABETH
Descended from the ancient family of JARVIS
Of Peatling, in the county of Leicester;
Beautiful, polite, ingenious, pious;
Wife, by her first marriage, of Henry Porter,
By her second, of SAMUEL JOHNSON,
Who over her much loved and long lamented Remains
Placed this Stone.
She died in London, in the Month of March
AD MDCCLIII

Johnson was too close to death in 1784 to travel to Bromley to see the newly inscribed stone and to notice that the stonemason had made a mistake. Tetty died in March 1752, not 1753.

The church of St Peter and St Paul in Bromley where Tetty lies buried was destroyed by a Nazi bomb in 1941, but her stone was remade and placed on a cloister wall in the rebuilt church. In the 1960s, when the town centre was remodelled, a new road was built alongside the church and named 'Tetty Way'. The proceedings of the council indicate that its intention was 'to perpetuate the name of Dr Samuel Johnson's wife'. Tetty is now immortalised in a back road servicing the newly built shopping centre of Bromley.

Four days before she died, Johnson had presented Tetty with a finely bound collected edition of his *Rambler* essays, which he began on 20 March 1750. These twice-weekly essays on moral questions, social injustice and the dangers of envy were an immediate success, even as far afield as Boston, Massachusetts. Tetty told Johnson, 'I thought very well of you before; but I did not imagine you could have written any thing equal to this.' He stopped writing them in the week of her death, and for months afterwards did no work, lost in grief and probably remorse.

Tetty was dearer to Johnson than a friend; she was the woman through whom he became the Johnson of the *Dictionary*, *Rasselas* and the *Prayers and Meditations*, who would write in the *Rambler*:

> The Main of Life is, indeed, composed of small Incidents, and petty Occurrences; of Wishes for Objects not remote, and grief for Disappointments of no fatal Consequence; of insect Vexations which sting us and fly away, Impertinences which buzz a while about us, and are heard no more; of meteorous Pleasures which dance before us and are dissipated, of Compliments which glide off the Soul like other Musick, and are forgotten by him that gave and him that received them . . . It is, indeed, at home that every Man must be known.

Through Tetty we can come to understand Johnson better. Not because their marriage was a brilliant success, but precisely the opposite. Their difficulties helped him to understand himself better, and to touch upon the problems that most of us face, muddling along in the main of life. At home with Tetty, Johnson experienced the 'meteorous Pleasures', the 'insect Vexations', the 'small Incidents' and 'petty Occurrences' which shape our lives from day to day. His marriage to Tetty, her relationship with him, helped him to become the writer so often quoted today because of his keen understanding of how to temper the cruel disappointments of life with its sheer delights.

In December 1740 Johnson gave Tetty a fine leather-bound edition of the

Book of Common Prayer. A present at Christmas in recognition that she had suffered a terrible year of ill health, and an attempt, perhaps, to make amends for their increasing separation. Johnson wrote on the front page her name and the date, as a sign of his dedication to her. The book itself was an expensive gift, not just in financial terms. Johnson thought of it as a manual for living, a document of faith. That he chose to give it to Tetty in that year was an acknowledgement of what she meant to him.

4

An Equal Mind

After Tetty's death in March 1752, one of the few people to visit Johnson in his 'great affliction' was Elizabeth Carter. They had known each other since Johnson's arrival in London, and had much in common. She, too, had left her home in a small town beyond the capital to find work as a writer, arriving just seven months after Johnson. But, unlike him, she had already been published in the *Gentleman's Magazine*. Her first poem, a riddle whose intricate solution was 'FIRE', had appeared anonymously in November 1734 when she was just sixteen. Encouraged by her success, Elizabeth sent off a stream of verses translated from both Latin and Greek. One of them, from the Roman satirist Horace, includes the lines:

> Whene'er ill fortune's to your lot assign'd,
> With courage bear it, and an equal mind;
> The same right temper; steady and sedate
> Which calm'd your soul amidst the storms of fate
> Will, when you're driven by too propitious gales,
> With prudent care contract the swelling sails.

By 'equal mind' Elizabeth meant 'equilibrium', 'peace of mind', but it's a phrase which neatly fits her character. She was the equal of all those she encountered at the magazine's office in St John's Gate. Already fluent in Latin and Greek, she applied herself to learn Hebrew so that she could read the Bible in the original language of the Old Testament. She could also read French, German and Italian, and more unusually Portuguese and Arabic, which she taught herself because she wanted to read the Koran (of which there were as yet no translations) and the works of the Islamic philosophers.

Johnson once accused her of being too modest, too retiring. He was frustrated by her unwillingness to offer her opinion when in company upon subjects which she was 'so eminently able to converse upon . . . for fear of giving offence'. He was keenly aware that her translation of the works of Epictetus was a best-seller, and that she had made available to those not fortunate enough to be educated in the Classics the self-help insights of the Greek philosopher.

'Have not you received Faculties by which you may support every Event? Have not you received Greatness of Soul? Have not you received a manly Spirit? Have not you received Patience?' Epictetus reminds us, in Carter's free and gutsy translation. 'What signifies to me any thing that happens, while I have a Greatness of Soul? What shall discomfort or trouble me or appear grievous to me? Shall I not make Use of my Faculties, to that Purpose for which they were granted me; but lament and groan at what happens?'

Johnson was a little in awe of Elizabeth, reluctantly recognising that her linguistic abilities surpassed his own. She had a deeper vocabulary of Latin and Greek and more languages at her disposal. He also perceived that she had something he knew he could never attain – an unwavering, but not unquestioning, grasp of what truly mattered. 'My old friend, Mrs Carter, could make a pudding, as well as translate Epictetus from the Greek,' he is reputed to have once said, 'and work a handkerchief as well as compose a poem.' Was Johnson trying to put Elizabeth down by linking her with some of the housewifely characters in his *Rambler* and *Idler* essays, such as Lady Bustle? Or was this intended as a compliment – Elizabeth was both scholar and home-maker?

Elizabeth Carter was born on 16 December 1717 in Deal, a busy fishing port on the Kent coast famous for its smugglers. She disapproved of their law-breaking activities, hiding lace, brandy and jewels from the Excise in their small boats as they crossed the Channel to and from the ports of Normandy and Flanders. But she held an equally dim view of the fashionable gentlemen and ladies who were only too eager to buy lace at a knock-down price. 'I am certainly very far from wishing to defend the practice of smuggling,' she wrote to her friend, the elegant and very wealthy Elizabeth Montagu, whose portraits show her dressed in gowns festooned with lace ruffs and collars. 'Yet I cannot help pitying those poor ignorant people, brought up from their infancy to this wretched trade, and taught by the example of their superiors to think there can be no great harm in it, when they every day see the families of both hereditary and delegated legislators loading their coaches with contraband goods.' Carter added, 'The stealing a loaf by a half-starved beggar is a pitiable breach of honesty. The stealing a jewel by one possessed of all the necessaries and comforts of life is execrable, and without excuse.' She was never afraid to speak her mind.

Elizabeth talked of Deal as being 'a sad, smuggling town', distressed by the destitution she witnessed day by day of those families whose husbands, sons and brothers were caught in the act and imprisoned by the Excise men. She also described it as 'a place where nothing remarkable ever happened since the landing of Julius Caesar' (the Romans arrived on the coast at Deal from across the Channel in AD 55, and were terrified when they saw the alien blue faces of the warrier Britons, painted with woad). But, unlike Johnson, she left her home town only to return a few years later, drawn back by its community and her love of its timeless views across the sea or in the other direction to rolling hills across fields of wheat, rye and barley.

Her father, Nicholas Carter, the Anglican priest in charge of the new St George's Chapel, took great pride in his eldest child, Elizabeth, and encouraged her intellectual endeavours. 'Dear Bett,' he wrote to her in 1729 when she was eleven, 'I must do you the Justice to say that your manner of writing is praise-worthy. I could not forbear showing your letter to Sir George, who commended it extremely. He could hardly believe that one of your Age could spell so exactly, & choose such proper Expressions.' (Sir George Oxenden was an old friend from his college days.)

When she was ten her mother died, after falling ill with the shock of losing the family money in the South Sea Bubble of 1720. The value of shares in the South Seas company, which traded with South America, mostly in slaves, plummeted overnight after too many shares had been sold off in a speculative exercise designed to reduce the national debt. The slump brought down the stock market. Many small investors were ruined in one of the worst financial crashes ever. Those who had the confidence and the wherewithal to leave their money where it was for several years did not lose their savings, unlike those who pulled out of the scheme as soon as the slump began. The Carters withdrew, shouldering huge losses.

Nicholas was left with five young children to care for and relied on Elizabeth, the eldest daughter, to take charge. But he was always careful never to take his daughter's help for granted, and Elizabeth received from her father as good an education as if she were being prepared, like her brothers, for university. Nicholas taught her not just the Classics and Hebrew, but also astronomy, geography, mathematics and the natural sciences. He regarded Elizabeth, rather than her brothers, as his true companion of mind. While the rest of the family were soon wearied by their philosophical debates, he and Elizabeth would sit up talking until well beyond midnight, draining the tea-kettle and arguing for and against the merits of Aristotle and Plato.

When she was fifteen Elizabeth was sent by her father to stay with a Huguenot family who had settled in nearby Canterbury after fleeing the anti-Protestant riots in their native France. Nicholas wanted his daughter not just to read French but also to speak the language fluently and with the correct accent. Or at least this was the reason he gave for sending his daughter away from home for several months. There was another cause. Nicholas was about to marry again, and with characteristic good sense he wanted to give his daughter time away from the family to become accustomed to the idea of having a stepmother.

He also took the unusual and enlightened step of encouraging his daughter to enter the poetry competitions that Edward Cave launched in his *Gentleman's Magazine*. Cave was an extremely shrewd commercial operator and was willing to try anything to build up the readership of his magazine as quickly as possible. The 1735 competition generously offered a prize worth £50, enough to support the winner in the capital for a year (£20 more than Johnson thought he could live on). Elizabeth had already had a poem published, her riddle on 'FIRE'. In June 1735 a correspondent named 'Sylvius' sent in his response, addressed to 'Miss CART—R, Author of the Riddle in Nov. 1734'. Elizabeth's poetic talent was recognised immediately.

Sylvius praised Miss Carter's 'pleasing lays' in rhyming verse, pleading with her 'To wake our raptures with thy pow'rful *muse*' and to publish more poems for her fans among the readers of the *Gentleman's Magazine*. Elizabeth replied by submitting a poem addressed 'To Sylvius', which she signed 'E. C—R.', discreetly dropping the feminine title of 'Miss' as a disguise. In the poem she claimed she was too inexperienced, too 'unform'd', too 'unskill'd' in 'poetic flight' to accept Sylvius's challenge. Elizabeth was keenly aware of the difficulties she would encounter if her authorship became public knowledge.

'Our house is frequented by Men of Sense, and I ask Questions when I fall into such Conversation; but I am cut short with something or other about my bright Eyes,' she declared in a letter written in early 1737, just before she left for London. There is, she says, 'a language particular for talking to women in'. This did not please her. She wanted to talk about the same questions as the 'Men of Sense', and to have her opinions treated with equal respect. Conversation, not money, she once said, 'is the noblest commerce of mankind', and 'the MIND' is our 'most precious merchandise'. Why, then, should it be denied her?

Her father, recognising that Elizabeth was becoming restless in the small-town atmosphere of Deal, arranged for her to visit her uncle in London. A silk merchant, he lived in Devonshire Street, just off Bishopsgate, close to the Spitalfields weavers. Nicholas suggested to Elizabeth that she should take the opportunity to visit the offices of the *Gentleman's Magazine* and show the editor some of her work. He had another, self-interested motive, hoping that Elizabeth would persuade Cave to publish his sermons, which Cave eventually did, Elizabeth acting on her father's behalf as a go-between with his publisher.

From Devonshire Street, the half-hour walk across town to Cave's print-works in Clerkenwell took Elizabeth through the working heart of the city, across the grassy stretch of Moorfields and on to Grub Street, defined by Johnson in his *Dictionary* as 'a street near Moorfields, much inhabited by writers of small histories, dictionaries and temporary poems'. She then strode along the Barbican and across Charter House Square to avoid the heaving throng of animals and butchers crowding into the meat market at Smithfield.

The magazine was edited and printed in rooms rented by Cave in St John's Gate, a fortress-like building that once belonged to the Knights Templar. The ground floor was occupied by a coffee-house, which Carter had to walk through, past the men in frock coats sitting round long tables, smoking clay pipes and reading newspapers on poles as they consumed copious cups of thick black coffee sweetened with sugar. She then took a winding stone staircase over the turreted gateway and into a large wood-panelled room, full of tables covered with piles of books and half-set pages of copy.

The pages of the *Gentleman's Magazine* contained not just poetry and book reviews but also articles entitled 'Advice to the Flax Farmers' or the 'Use of Accents in Hebrew poetry'. Nothing like this variety of information in a single publication had been available so cheaply to readers before. In November 1737, just a few weeks after Carter's arrival in London, the magazine announced, 'At 11 o'clock this night, died of a mortification of the Bowels, her Majesty Queen Wilhelmina Dorothea Carolina, Queen Consort of Great Britain, aged 54 years, 8 months and 20 Days.' In the same issue Carter would also have discovered the state of the national accounts (the National Debt stood at £47,866,598.3s.3¼d) or the cure from a French physician for the bite of a mad dog, 'Take the Shells of Male Oysters . . . calcine them in an oven or crucible before grinding them in a mortar and adding them to a pint of white wine . . . Let the patient drink it . . . and by all means not to touch Butter or anything oily during the time of the Cure.'

Each month a list of deaths cryptically suggested the criminality of the time, such as in March 1738, when it was announced that a Mr Johnson of Chelsea (no relation) had died. He had been 'marry'd that morning of Mrs Matthews; as soon as his Wedding Dinner was over, going to salute his wife etc. fell down and dy'd immediately. About 6 Weeks before the said Gentlewoman was marry'd to Mr Matthews, who dy'd in his bed the first night after the marriage.'

Elizabeth's chief attraction for Cave was her ability and determination to supply him with a steady stream of translations. She could read Aristotle, Plato, Erasmus, Cervantes and Madame de Sévigné in the languages in which they were written, and she wanted to make these texts available to those readers, especially women, who had not been given the kind of education she had been fortunate to have from her father. In February 1739 Cave published her translation of a French critique of Pope's *Essay on Man*; three months later she had completed an English version of an essay in Italian that explained Newton's physics for those 'ladies' not trained in science.

At St John's Gate, she met with the group of youngish men who were all working with Cave as his semi-employed assistants on the monthly magazine. Thomas Birch, a dusty scholar who when not at the *Gentleman's Magazine* was busy compiling his own encyclopaedia, the *General Dictionary; Historical and Critical*, was so impressed by Elizabeth's learning and intelligence that he began writing letters to her in Latin. 'I am perhaps unwise to expose my inelegant Latin to your most refined judgment,' he told her on 19 August

1738. What was unwise was his attempt to flatter the clever, commonsensical Miss Elizabeth Carter.

Meanwhile, she encountered the unprepossessing young married man, Johnson, as he hung around Cave's office in the hope of being given some writing and translating commissions. Johnson went much further than Birch in his praise of Carter, declaring in the magazine that the writer codenamed 'ELIZA' 'ought to be celebrated in as many different languages as Lewis le Grand'. Her Latin and Greek poems are so good, he suggested, she should be given the laurel wreath once bestowed on Alexander Pope for his translations from Virgil and Homer.

In 'To Eliza plucking Laurel in Mr Pope's Gardens', originally published in Latin, Johnson teasingly pays homage to 'Miss Carter' as the true inheritor of Pope, whose riverside house and garden in Twickenham he had just visited with her and Thomas Birch. 'Desirous of the laurel bough,' writes Johnson, 'She crops it to adorn her brow.' But he also warns her not to become too presumptuous:

> Yet do not steal it, lovely maid,
> The wreath you wish shall grace your head;
> If *Pope* refuse it as your due,
> *Phoebus* himself shall give it you.

There were dangers for women who became too well known, talked about in the public prints and lauded in verses of lamentable quality. Elizabeth's father received a letter from his friend Sir George (the same Sir George who had once praised her spelling) who was concerned that Elizabeth's success might antagonise her male colleagues and rivals. 'There is hardly an instance of a woman of letters entering into an intimacy of acquaintance with men of wit and parts, particularly poets, who were not thoroughly abused and maltreated by them, in print, after some time, and Mr Pope has done it more than once,' he warned Nicholas. (Pope notoriously vilified his contemporary Lady Mary Wortley Montagu for daring to criticise his work.)

Elizabeth was herself keenly aware that she would be obliged to 'wear off the scandal of my Greek'. The following month she published in the *Gentleman's Magazine* an elegant riposte to Johnson, hastily refusing the honour he had tried to bestow on her:

> In vain, Eliza's daring hand
> Usurp'd the laurel bough;
> Remov'd from Pope's, the wreath must fade
> On ev'ry meaner brow.

She understood the dangers of setting herself up as a female rival to the male galaxy of writers. At the same time, though, she began to interpret the Classics in her own way. She did not waste the opportunities that Cave offered her, working incredibly hard to outdo both Birch and Johnson in the speed and accomplishment with which she produced translations worthy of publication.

Throughout 1738, she contributed to most of the issues of the *Gentleman's Magazine*, signing herself semi-anonymously either as 'E. C———.' or 'ELIZA'. Her poems praise the wonders of the universe, decry the fickleness of fortune and the illusory quality of dreams, while drawing attention to the Nine Muses – all female – by whom art and ideas are diffused from the heavens to its earth-bound creators.

There's a powerful presence behind all these poems, a true 'voice', fully formed and confident. Her 'Poem Upon the Stars' begins:

> Whether clear the night, and ev'ry thought serene,
> Let fancy wander o'er the solemn scene;
> And wing'd by active contemplation, rise
> Amidst the radiant borders of the skies.

And continues:

> Let stupid Atheists boast th'atomic Dance
> And call these beauteous Worlds the Work of Chance:
> But nobler Minds, from Guilt and Passion free,
> Where Truth unclouded darts her heav'nly Ray,
> Or on the Earth, or in th'aethereal Road,
> Survey the Footsteps of a ruling GOD . . .

Carter's religious ardour is of its time, but beyond it there is something inspiring about her enthusiasm, her broad vision of life, her deep understanding. To read her poems and her many letters is to enter into the inner world of a woman whose intelligence veers from musing on the pleasures of dancing at the local country ball to watching the arrival of the British fleet gathering at anchor in the Downs during the Seven Years War, via an erudite reference to a book called *Matho, or Cosmotheoria Puerilis* – 'I have lately read it over for the second time, by which means I am come to understand about one third of it, but that little fills me with ideas that I would not exchange for any others.' Elizabeth Carter was always certain of her own opinions, yet open to those that were new to her, or very different.

Her first collection of poetry, *Poems upon Particular Occasions*, was published in August 1738 by Cave, who thought of Carter as his star writer. It was no more than a pamphlet of eight poems laid out over twenty-four quarto-sized pages, but its production was of a superior quality. For the frontispiece, Cave commissioned illustrations of St John's Gate, clearly captioned, and Pope's grotto in Twickenham. Carter was given the stamp of approval from the newest and most successful publisher in London and the most prestigious poet-scholar. Her name does not appear on the title page: Miss Elizabeth Carter was not yet ready to make her name known. Nevertheless the sophistication of her writing, of a different class from the usual 'anonymous' fare, caused such a stir that rumours soon began circulating as to the identity of their secret author. 'ELIZA' of the *Gentleman's Magazine* was the chief suspect.

By the following March she was confident enough of her success to allow her full name 'ELIZABETH CARTER' to appear at the bottom of a tribute to the much-praised and always decorous poet, Elizabeth Rowe. Two years earlier Carter had written an anonymous poem 'On the Death of Mrs Rowe', but now she was ready to publish a revised version which was no longer simply a celebration of Mrs Rowe's achievement as a writer. Instead Elizabeth delivered a call to arms to women writers.

Women, declared Carter, should dare to publish (as Elizabeth Rowe had done before her), but they should be writing serious works of philosophy, not foolish romances and light-hearted follies designed to entertain young girls. In her revised version of 'On the Death of Mrs Elizabeth Rowe' she argues:

> Oft did Intrigue in guilty arts unite,
> To blacken the records of female wit;
> The tuneful song lost ev'ry modest grace,
> And lawless freedoms triumph'd in their place.
> The Muse, for vices not her own accus'd,

With blushes view'd her sacred gifts abus'd;
Those gifts for nobler purposes design'd,
To raise the thoughts, and moralise the mind.

'Female wit' has not always been used for the most edifying purposes, but has lost 'ev'ry modest grace' and indulged in 'lawless freedoms'. Too many women, she argues, have frittered away their talent in romantic poetry or frivolous fictions rather than attempting to join with the ranks of male poets and essayists in tackling philosophy, history and science, and to 'raise the thoughts and moralise the mind'.

At first Elizabeth was warmly welcomed by her fellow contributors on the *Gentleman's Magazine*. Thomas Birch became particularly familiar, writing to Elizabeth almost daily (in spite of the fact that they met each other frequently at St John's Gate). In his letter to her of 19 August 1738, he added, in Latin, now translated: 'For when I consider you and your writing—as I do daily, and almost hourly—I am indeed shamed and annoyed to have accomplished so little during so many years in assiduously cultivating humane letters. But it would be wrong to envy you—you to whom by divine grace it has been given to surpass your own sex and ours.'

Six days later, on 25 August, Elizabeth dined with Birch and Johnson *à trois*. Four days elapsed before another entry in Birch's diary suggests that Elizabeth had dined with him alone. She was not yet twenty-one; he was thirty-three and a childless widower who might well have been on the lookout for a replacement wife. There were several more occasions on which Elizabeth and Birch dined together without a third party as chaperone. Then, on 14 May 1739, they left London together, travelling to Oxford in a public coach to visit Birch's friend Walter Harte, a scholar and writer. They took an unusually long time over the journey, staying overnight on three occasions at Windsor, Reading and Woodstock when only one night was necessary to complete the seventy-mile journey.

It was not common for a young woman to travel alone with a man without a maid or chaperone. Perhaps Elizabeth believed the journey was purely a scholarly endeavour, to visit the libraries in Oxford and meet with Birch's academic friends. Perhaps she saw Birch as a friend and companion of the mind, just like her father. Something, though, must have happened on the trip, for six days later Elizabeth was back in London, several days earlier than expected. She remained in town just long enough to tidy up her affairs before leaving again for Deal where she stayed for two years, refusing to venture anywhere near the capital. On 4 June, she wrote a short note to Birch from Dover (just a few miles from Deal) but he sent her no reply, or at least none that has survived.

Elizabeth would never again attempt to live in London as an unmarried woman. Just as she was beginning to establish her reputation as a writer of unusual talent, provoking scholars from the Continent to write to Cave with verses addressed to '*La Nymphe Eliza*', she retreated from metropolitan life. Why? What made her turn her back on success and a life in the capital?

In November 1739 she sent Cave 'An Ode to Melancholy' for publication, but only 'upon this express condition' that he promised to publish the verses anonymously '& will never tell any person whatsoever that they are mine . . .' She added, 'Neither my papa or my friends in London know anything of the matter,' as if her exile was not entirely of her own choosing.

This poem includes the lines:

> I from the busy Croud retire,
> To court the Objects that inspire
> Thy philosophic Dream . . .
>
> . . . O tell how trifling now appears
> The Train of idle Hopes and Fears
> That varying Life attend.

Was she thinking of her own life? Her own realisation that her 'Hopes and Fears' were after all nothing but an idle fancy?

No diaries or personal memoir have survived to explain why she gave up so much (her worthy but irritating nephew destroyed them all after publishing a two-volume biography of his aunt). None of her surviving correspondence refers to this mysterious episode with Birch. Much later, however, Elizabeth remembered how she had once been to Oxford with 'a set of very well meaning folks, but some of them were dull, some were peevish, and some were in love'. Was this the trip she made with Birch? Or another excursion to the university? Had Birch been in love with her? Was he dull and peevish?

In the same letter she explains that most of these 'well meaning folks' would have 'considered a consular statue of Cicero and a waxen image of Queen Anne, in pretty much the same light, and merely something to look at. In short,' she complains, 'as I had neither the aid of society, nor the freedom of my solitary thoughts, I scarcely recollect anything of the expedition, but it made me heartily weary.' Elizabeth was far too clever for most of the men of her acquaintance. She would have known the history behind that statue of Cicero, as well as having the taste and the confidence to assess its artistic quality.

Whatever happened on that trip to Oxford with Birch, the experience changed Elizabeth's perception of her position in London. Did Birch propose marriage, or something much more dangerous for Elizabeth's reputation? It seems likely since, in the months afterwards, Elizabeth (or perhaps it was primarily her father) became uncomfortably aware that she could not carry on without a chaperone – or a husband. It was not possible for her to publish under her own name and to live in the much freer social whirl of London without being married. Some circumspection was required.

A poem had already appeared in the *Gentleman's Magazine*, signed 'From PHILANDER'. It was addressed to Miss E— C—' whom the poet called 'dear Maid'.

> Then thou, dear Maid, shall bless my sight,
> Again with mutual love delight,
> Thee when the grateful winter brings,
> The little loves, shall clap their purple wings,
> And joy shall sound on thy Philander's strings.

Elizabeth's growing unease was probably intensified by the association of her name with such excruciatingly bad verse. Her father, meanwhile, wrote her a warning letter: 'If you intend never to marry, as I think you plainly intimate in one of your letters, then you certainly ought to have retired, and not appear in the world with an Expence which is reasonable upon the expectation of getting an Husband, but not otherwise.' He was quite happy for her not to enter the marriage market but, if she wished to remain single and to continue to publish, then to live in the capital was not feasible. She would have to stay at home in Deal, where her family could protect her reputation.

Elizabeth replied, 'To give up one's ease and liberty for the sake of wearing a finer gown, eating a greater variety of dishes or seeing more company and fewer friends, appears to me a very strange scheme.' Several men had wanted to marry her, but she refused them all, preferring to remain single than be 'needlessly thwarted and contradicted in every innocent enjoyment of life; involved in all [a husband's] schemes right or wrong, and perhaps not allowed the liberty of even silently seeming to disapprove them!'

To live as she wished, free of society's expectations of marriage and dependancy, she would, she now realised, have to accept some limitations, living discreetly and ensuring that what she published was not controversial. Yet she never allowed this containment of her possibilities to limit her imagination. 'But is there no such Faculty in our Composition as Imagination?' she asked a friend. 'Yes, certainly; & a most delightful play fellow it is, graciously allotted to enliven & relax us amidst the Duties of our serious Task of Life.'

She once refused the gift of a linnet in a birdcage because she could not bear the thought that the songbird had lost its freedom to give her pleasure. On the bookplate which she designed for her personal library she drew an owl, the symbol of wisdom to the Romans. Underneath she added a text from the New Testament, 'Ask it of God', from the Letter of James: 'If any lack wisdom, let him ask it of God.' The search for knowledge was always the guiding principle of Elizabeth Carter's life, and on that there could be no limit. 'It is by our own fault if human improvement ever stands still,' she wrote in a letter which reveals that she was at the time reading books by both Hume and Rousseau.

Birds, and their freedom to fly, are a leitmotif in Carter's life. 'I am extremely delighted with a buzzard,' she confided to her friend Catherine Talbot, 'whom I have watched all this winter, and who seems to be of the same taste with myself. Whenever it looks clear and shining the creature sits mighty snug and stupid upon his perch, but the moment the sky begins to lour, he descends, claps his wings, and wanders about the garden with a most complete enjoyment of the tempest.'

Elizabeth loved wild weather, the wind and the rain, and would have relished the opportunity to enjoy the full force of the storm with the same abandonment:

> I should certainly have pursued the method of this my fellow-creature
> in rambling up and down the face of the earth in the last blowing

snowy weather, but on my talking one evening something about walking out, there was as much astonishment and outcry in the family as if I had seriously told them I was going to hang myself; and so to avoid the scandal of having absolutely lost my senses I was obliged to content myself with quietly setting by the fire-side, and listening to the storm at a distance.

Some kinds of freedom, Carter was beginning to accept, were not available to women. She refused to be deterred by this, relishing instead the liberty she had to roam within the broad expanses of her mind. As long as she could read, study, communicate with her friends, Carter was content. She had, too, something not available to most men: her gift for languages, which meant she could wander through the literature of many different cultures.

She did attempt to return to London life in the winter of 1740–41, and thereafter she visited regularly, staying with friends or renting rooms in Mayfair. But she no longer frequented the offices of the *Gentleman's Magazine* or the print shops of Grub Street. Instead she contented herself with the intellectual society of the English *salonnières*, becoming one of the first bluestockings. This group of enthusiasts for knowledge was attempting to 'reform' polite society by meeting together not to play cards and drink claret but to talk good thoughts, congregating after supper, teapots at the ready, for an evening of enlightened conversation.

At first the gatherings included both men and women and were informal. In time, though, these social evenings became the preserve of women with wealth and intelligence such as Elizabeth Montagu, Frances Boscawen and Elizabeth Vesey. Elizabeth Carter was a key figure at these evenings, and through her circle of correspondence, which included Montagu, Vesey and Catherine Talbot, she created a tight network of shared ideas, crossed thoughts and friendship.

In 1746 Edward Cave wrote to Nicholas Carter complaining that he had lost one of his star writers: 'I cannot persuade Miss to undertake any thing, and the world wants to know what she is about.' He hoped Nicholas would encourage his daughter to begin writing for the magazine again. But Elizabeth was not to be persuaded.

Her withdrawal coincided with the publication of an indiscreet poem in the *Gentleman's Magazine* in May 1741. The poem, by Samuel Boyse, celebrates an unusual portrait of Carter by a not very proficient artist called John Fayram. She is sitting at a desk with a classical landscape in the distance. Carter looks directly at us, her warm, friendly face and deep-blue eyes suggesting her approachable nature, open to friendship. But she's not, as you might expect, dressed in the silk gown and pearls of the drawing room. Instead she looks as if she's been playing with the dressing-up box and has discovered the costume of a Roman centurion.

Over a white chiffon blouse, she wears a black overdress in scalloped layers to look as if it's a metal breastplate. A heavy bronze medallion encircles her neck depicting the ghastly image of Minerva, the goddess of wisdom (looking more like a harridan than a bookworm). In her left hand Carter holds the shield of knowledge; in her right a leather-bound volume of Plato. On top of her head she has an iron helmet decorated with an enormous fluffy white ostrich feather.

Carter appears as a warrior for truth, a general in the army of knowledge. She looks at ease in this role, perfectly natural, and yet at the very time that Fayram is working on the portrait she was beginning to think she must retreat from London. Who commissioned such a provocative portrait, posing Carter as the general of a female army? Could Cave have been intending to use it as a frontispiece for his magazine? Was it another marketing ruse designed to appeal to women readers, showing them that the *Gentleman's Magazine* was not afraid to acknowledge their talents as readers and scholars?

The poem, 'On Miss CARTER's being drawn in the Habit of Minerva, with Plato in her Hand', as it appeared in the magazine, celebrates the portrait. A closer read, though, reveals more sinister undercurrents:

> What *British* charmer shines with *Attick* grace . . .
> Have we a nymph, who midst the bloom of youth,
> Can think with *Plato*?—and can relish truth?
> One who can leave her sex's joys behind,
> To taste the nobler pleasure of the mind?

Miss Carter, the poem seems to be saying, has devoted herself to Plato and the Greeks and has thereby relinquished her femininity. She has been neutered, desexualised.

Men were not yet ready to accept women working alongside them as colleagues in a close-knit professional capacity. Carter could have continued living in London and working on the magazine, but at the cost of her reputation. She chose instead to retreat, but did so with a clear sense of purpose. Withdrawal, for her, did not entail failure.

When Johnson remarked that his old friend from the *Gentleman's Magazine* could bake a pudding as well as translate Epictetus, he may have been adopting a patronising attitude but he was also being faithful to the woman he came to know as Mrs Carter ('Mrs' being a title of honour to women of a certain age who had not married). He knew that she was responsible for preparing her younger half-brother for his entrance exams to the University of Cambridge. He knew, too, that she neatly and laboriously stitched the dozen shirts this same half-brother needed to take with him when he left home.

Her skills as a pudding-maker were also renowned, and hard won. As a teenager in charge of running the household after the death of her mother, Elizabeth attempted to make a Christmas pudding from a receipt of her own invention. The result was so highly spiced and full of brandy, 'It put the whole family in a flame.' The pudding no one could eat became part of family legend, the details forgotten, the story so familiar it was told in a shorthand incomprehensible to others. 'The children all set up their little throats against Greek and Latin,' Elizabeth recalled, blaming her poor cooking skills on the hours she spent studying, 'and I found this unlucky event was like to prove my everlasting disgrace.' Undaunted, she resolved to make a pudding so delicious that her previous mishap would be forgotten. 'And though I say it, that should not say it, several grave notable gentle-women of unquestionable good housewifery have applied to me for the receipt.'

Carter, having discovered that society was not yet ready for her 'equal mind', determined to excel at what she knew would be appreciated: domestic management. Did she regard this as a loss of opportunity, a deprivation? Like Johnson, Elizabeth Carter experienced a lifetime of severe physical discomfort, suffering for much of her adult life from 'vile head-aches' which incapacitated her for days at a time; headaches which became worse, more intense and debilitating, at about the time she retreated to Deal from London.

'I have had vile head-aches which have confined me most days for some hours to such a lifeless state of *fainéantise* as might have appeared sufficiently mortifying to me, if I had not felt a more sensible pain from the sad apprehensions of losing one of my best friends by the small-pox,' she wrote to Catherine Talbot in October 1744. 'Indeed I cannot tell when I shall be able to get into my former track again, for this long confinement has rendered me so extremely plodding and stupid, that I begin to fear all my gay whimsical ideas, now I am tolerably at ease, will dwindle into a sober relish for comfortable life . . .' She continued:

> It is not to be described how perfectly muzzy I look, nor what a strange fondness I have lately acquired for dumplings . . . Nay, I am so far gone, that I much question whether instead of keeping my senses awake with an enlivening supper of green tea, I could not with very solemn satisfaction regale myself upon lambs wool, or wigs and ale, and get very quietly to sleep by eight o'clock without the interruption of a single dream. In short, my dear, castle building seems to be utterly at an end, and instead of soaring in the air as volatile as a sky lark, I shall soon be reduced to waddle upon earth like a fat goose . . .

Carter was only twenty-seven when she wrote this letter, yet she was already beginning to sound like a much older woman, limiting her ambitions, curtailing her dreams, putting an end to castle building. She has headaches, develops a fondness for puddings, waddles around 'like a fat goose'.

Perhaps the headaches were a symptom of suppressed emotions, of Carter's frustration at having her talents put back into the box, of being contained at home rather than living, like Johnson, in the full flow of life in London. Yet to read through her correspondence is to discover a woman who does not appear to have been denied what she most enjoyed: ideas. It is possible that her zealous nephew was so keen to create a respectable and contented image of his aunt that he destroyed any letters in which she confessed any bitterness or rebellious thoughts. But assuming the letters that have survived are an accurate portrayal of her character, then Carter lived a fulfilled life.

'I am in no sort of danger of falling in love with heroes or conquerors,' she once told Catherine Talbot. They 'are characters I look upon with so little reverence, that I think many an honest old woman who cries hot dumplings, a much greater ornament to human nature than a Caesar or an Alexander'. Women, argued Carter, should not be complicit in the hierarchies which society falsely establishes by idolising leaders. Caesar and Alexander, she seems to be telling us, should not be of more importance to the ordinary citizen than those who make our puddings and dumplings.

After leaving London, but before she stopped publishing her poetry, Carter composed a witty poem in which she sets Body against Mind:

> Says *Body* to *Mind*, 'Tis amazing to see,
> We're so nearly related yet never agree,
> But lead a most wrangling strange Sort of a Life,
> As great Plagues to each other as Husband and Wife.

Body says that it's all the fault of Mind, who has seized control of the 'best Room in my House' and 'turn'd the whole Tenement quite upside down':

> While you [Mind] hourly call in a disorderly Crew
> Of vagabond Rogues, who have nothing to do
> But to run in and out, hurry scurry, and keep
> Such a horrible Uproar, I can't get to sleep.

Mind retaliates:

> 'Tis I, that, methinks, have most Cause to complain,
> Who am crampt and confin'd like a Slave in a Chain,
> I did but step out, on some weighty Affairs,
> To visit, last Night, my good Friends in the Stars,
> When, before I was got half as high as the Moon,
> You dispatch'd *Pain* and *Languor* to hurry me down.

And ultimately Mind triumphs, flying free when Body succumbs to corporeal frailty:

> I've a Friend, answers *Mind*, who, tho' slow, is yet sure,
> And will rid me, at last of your insolent Pow'r,
> Will knock down your mud Walls, the whole Fabric demolish,
> And at once your strong Holds and my Slav'ry abolish:

And while in the Dust your dull Ruins decay,
I shall snap off my Chains and fly freely away.

The Body–Mind dialogue was a popular device for contrasting the physical aspects of being alive and the spiritual awakening of the soul. But Carter subverts the genre by suggesting that Body is male and Mind female, rather than the other way around. She also dreams of a time when Mind could 'fly freely away', free of the constraints put upon it by the 'Husband', the Body.

The poem appeared in the *Gentleman's Magazine* in January 1741 when Carter was safely ensconced in Deal, far from the crowd of 'snarling Criticks', as she called them. No snarling occurred; on the contrary the poem re-affirmed her reputation as one of Cave's most original contributors.

A few years later, in 1748, one of her poems was included by Samuel Richardson in his mammoth five-volume psycho-drama, *Clarissa*, as if written by the eponymous heroine. Clarissa has been imprisoned in her room by her family for refusing to marry the man her father has chosen for her. She consoles herself by setting to music three stanzas of a poem in which the writer seeks the protection of the owl, 'the solitary bird of night' and messenger of Minerva, the goddess of wisdom. With such a shield against the cruelties of her family, she will, she writes, take no notice of:

> The coxcomb's sneer, the stupid lie
> Of ignorance and spite:
> Alike condemn the leaden fool,
> And all the pointed ridicule
> Of undiscerning wit.
>
> From envy, hurry, noise and strife,
> The dull impertinence of life,
> In thy retreat I rest;

She decides instead:

> Thine are Retirement's silent joys
> And all the sweet endearing ties
> Of still, domestic life.

The appearance of Carter's 'Ode to Wisdom' in such a successful novel should have been a huge compliment – but for the fact that Richardson had never asked her for permission to print it. He used it as if it were his own invention. Carter's friends alerted her to Richardson's plagiarism, and she fired off what she called a 'twinkation', complaining about his behaviour. His reply was so generous in its apology that she 'knew not how to be angry with him'. Richardson got away with it.

Carter had circulated copies of the 'Ode to Wisdom' among her friends, but had never intended it for publication. The poem, though, was so accomplished and so admired that further copies were made by others, full of mistakes, and these began doing the rounds of literary London, no one knowing to whom it should be attributed. Richardson was shown it, appreciated its worth, had no clue as to its author, and thought he could use it without finding out. Such was the fate of poems written by women who refrained from publishing, their rights to authorship lost or denied.

After the poem had appeared in *Clarissa*, Carter authorised Cave to publish a correct version in the *Gentleman's Magazine* with a note attached: 'We have had the following beautiful Ode above a year, under an injunction, which was general on all the copies given out, not to print it; but as it has appeared in *Clarissa* with several faults, we think ourselves at liberty to give our readers so agreeable an entertainment from a correcter copy.' Carter asserted her rights as author, but only after she had been forced to do so by Richardson's actions; she rarely did so again.

The contrast with Johnson's burgeoning career is significant. While Carter retreated further and further from Grub Street, Johnson was at last beginning to experience some success. In 1744 his *Life of Richard Savage* created a new kind of biography, short but full of telling details, revealing not just the externals of a life but also the inner workings of Savage's contradictory personality. Then on Tuesday 20 March 1750 Johnson published the first of his twice-weekly *Rambler* essays, printed by Cave on Tuesdays and Saturdays and sold at twopence each. Only 500 copies were at first circulated, but they were read aloud between friends, passed on from family to family, their highly original blend of moral insight, classical learning and domestic incident fascinating readers across London and into the provinces. That very first *Rambler* segues without a pause from Plutarch to the business of love and the dangers of too soon professing yourself a lover; the second quotes from Cervantes and Epictetus on the dangers of living for imagined happiness, for future success, rather than in the present moment.

Carter was impressed by the *Rambler* but also irritated by its metropolitan bias and lofty tone. She wrote to Johnson suggesting ways in which the essays could be improved and enclosing a sample. A few days later she was surprised to discover on opening the latest issue that what she was reading was the essay she had just posted to Johnson. No permission asked for, or granted. Johnson must have decided to save himself the effort of producing 2,500 words at short notice and sent off Carter's essay to the printer, just as it was.

Rambler No. 44, which appeared on Saturday 18 August 1750, tells of 'a very remarkable dream' in which the writer meets 'one of the most shocking figures imagination can frame': Superstition. This baleful figure tries to tempt her away from life into the desolate forest of despair and discontent, but she is saved by the arrival of Religion. 'I do really now wish *you* would write a cheerful paper to the *Rambler*,' teased Catherine Talbot, who wished Johnson's moral teachings could be made more relevant to the lives of those without scholarly learning. 'Whether on Christmas merriment as laudable . . . or on the hoops of these days, compared with those of the Tatlers, &c, and so on all sorts of caps, bonnets, aigrettes, coloured capuchins, &c &c &c on drums . . . or on anything or nothing.'

Carter did write another essay for Johnson, which he also published but this time only after consulting her. But on this occasion he made slight alterations to her text without telling her what changes he was going to make. Both Johnson and Richardson respected and valued Carter's work, but they were less than scrupulous with her professional reputation.

In *Rambler* No. 100 (published on Saturday 2 March 1751), Carter took Catherine Talbot's advice and created a light-hearted essay. Her narrator, Chariessa, berates the Rambler for his failure to address the interests of those who are unfortunate enough to be buried in the country, 'where they labour under the most deplorable ignorance of what is transacting among the polite part of mankind'. Mr Rambler, she suggests, should be writing about the benefits of playing whist or bragg, and giving his readers:

> a compleat history of forms, fashions, frolicks, of routs, drums, hurricanes, balls, assemblies, ridottos, masquerades, auctions, plays, operas, puppet-shows, and bear-gardens; of all those delights which profitably engage the attention of the most sublime characters, and by which they have brought to such amazing perfection, the whole art and mystery of passing day after day, week after week, and year after year, without

the heavy assistance of any one thing that formal creatures are pleased to call useful and necessary.

Carter was annoyed by Johnson's amendments, she told Talbot, because, 'in my opinion, [they seem] to have taken off both from the meaning and what spirit there was in it'. Carter had not meant her essay to be taken very seriously; she intended it as entertainment. Women writers were caught in a conundrum. To live and work as professional writers endangered their social reputation; but not to be able to take control of their published (and even their unpublished) work laid them open to disrespect.

Very few letters have survived between Carter and Johnson. They met from time to time through their mutual connections in the bluestocking circle, but such meetings were rare, as if Johnson was in some way wary of his old friend and colleague. In January 1756 he asked her for help in raising subscriptions for a book of poems written by Anna Williams, the blind woman who lived with him in Gough Square after the death of her father, an eccentric scientist who tried and failed to discover a means of calculating longitude. Mrs Williams had no money to publish herself but Johnson hoped to sign up enough subscribers to pay for the print run in advance. 'From the liberty of writing to you,' he begins his begging letter, 'if I have been hitherto deterred by the fear of your understanding, I am now encouraged to it by the confidence of your goodness.'

The 'fear of your understanding' is a strange choice of words and suggests that although Johnson enjoyed the company of women he preferred them to be young and admiring. With Carter he was always a little intimidated.

Carter never stopped writing, even when living in retreat with her family in Deal, but what could she publish that would enhance her moral reputation but also be a worthy project? Her friend Catherine Talbot suggested perhaps she might like to work on a translation from the Greek of Epictetus, the Stoic philosopher, whose discourses could provide such solace for those suffering from life's griefs and tribulations. This was to become Carter's major contribution to scholarship, making available to the general reader and not just to Greek scholars the robust but also reflective teachings of this former slave.

Epictetus's approach to life's travails was to ask the question, 'How, then, shall one preserve Intrepidity and Tranquillity; and at the same time be careful, and neither rash, nor indolent?'

> How do we act in a Voyage? What is in my Power? To chuse the Pilot, the Sailors, the Day, the Time of Day. Afterwards comes a Storm. What have I to care for? My Part is performed. The Subject belongs to another, to the Pilot. But the Ship is sinking: What then have I to do? That which alone I can do; I am drowned, without Fear, without Clamour, or accusing God; but as one who knows, that what is born, must like-wise die. For I am not Eternity, but a Man; a Part of the Whole, as an Hour is of the Day. I must come like an Hour, and like an Hour must pass away. What signifies it whether by Drowning, or by a Fever? For, in some Way or other, pass I must.

As revealed to us by Carter, Epictetus takes us straight to the heart of our most pressing concerns.

The task of translating his discourses was a huge project and *All the Works of Epictetus* was not ready for publication until the summer of 1758, taking Carter almost as long as it took Johnson to prepare his *Dictionary*. Samuel Richardson, the novelist who also owned his own printworks, compensated Carter for having stolen her 'Ode to Wisdom' (for that is what he did) by helping to organise the publication. To cover his costs in advance, he enlisted 1,013 subscribers, who each paid one guinea and were rewarded by having their names included in the 'List of Subscribers' at the front of the first edition. This was a beautifully produced 539-page quarto volume printed on thick creamy parchment paper. The list is led by HRH the Prince of Wales (later to become George III) and a scattering of dukes, bishops and prebendaries. A fair number of Misses were included, as well as Samuel Johnson and the Revd Dr Birch (by then an ordained minister, a doctor of philosophy and a Fellow of the Royal Society), who paid for two copies in advance. Various private 'book societies' also paid for the translation, including the Book Society of Nottingham and the Book Society of Leicester.

Epictetus was born a slave in the time of Emperor Nero, but he was later exiled to Greece where he became a much-loved teacher of philosophy. He used his experience of owning no material goods and having no personal liberty to teach the way of freedom from material desires. His teachings were preserved by one of his students, Arrian, who recorded them as Discourses, which resemble the conversations Jesus had with his disciples: 'But the Tyrant will chain—What? A leg. He will take away—What?—A head—What is there, then, that he can neither chain, nor take away?' asks Epictetus. 'The Will, and Choice. Hence the Advice of the Ancients—Know thyself.'

Carter shows her independence of mind by sometimes criticising the conclusions of the philosopher with whom she had been closeted for so long. When, for instance, Epictetus takes his stoicism to such an extreme that he tells us it is pointless to mourn the death of a friend and compares the experience to breaking your only cooking pot – 'What if the Pipkin, in which your Meat used to be cooked, should happen to be broken; must you die with Hunger, because you have not your old Pipkin? Do not you send and buy a new one?' – Carter remarks in a tart footnote, 'This is a wretched idea of Friendship.'

Once her translation was published many of the reviewers refused to believe that a woman could have been responsible for such a skilful, frank and robust translation, in spite of her name being clearly announced on the title page as the translator. They suggested that her friend and mentor Thomas Secker, who became the Archbishop of Canterbury, masterminded the edition. In his memoirs, Secker himself writes that he put Carter at first 'into a right manner of translating, which else could have been loose & spiritless'. Her correspondence with him reveals that he had looked over the translation as she worked slowly, page by page, through the discourses, offering some help and advice. But the content, the inspiration, the clear and fluent style of the edition was, undoubtedly, all hers. The Archbishop was far too much of a pedant to have produced anything but an extremely literal translation. On one occasion he tells her, 'Do, dear Madam Carter, get yourself whipt, get yourself whipt. Here are some sheets [i.e. proofs] come down [from London]. I have this moment opened them; and the first thing I have cast my eyes upon is *Epictetus* for *Epicurus*, p. 73.'

Epictetus sold so quickly that a second edition quickly followed, which travelled as far as the furthermost corners of Europe and was read in the court of Catherine the Great at St Petersburg. But the reviewers were still reluctant to concede that Madame Carter had produced such an elegant work. The *Critical Review* declared that it was not just 'a little extraordinary to find a woman mistress of the Greek language', but a bit odd that Mrs Carter was 'sounding the depths of ancient philosophy and capable of giving a faithful and elegant translation of one of the most difficult authors of antiquity'. The *Monthly Review* echoed these reflections: 'The work before us will be no small mortification to the vanity of those men, who presume that the fair sex are unequal to the laborious pursuit of philosophic speculations.'

Carter's translation remains in print and was not surpassed until the Oldfather edition of 1926. Her achievement was to make Epictetus accessible, practical, of relevance to the present moment. Because she was scholarly and down to earth, deeply serious but also playful, she brings Epictetus to life. She was also keenly aware of women's propensity to do themselves down. In November 1742, she teased a friend for playing the martyr:

> It is with the utmost diffidence, dear Miss ——, that I venture to do myself the high honour of writing to you, when I consider my own nothingness and utter incapacity of doing any one thing upon earth. Indeed I cannot help wondering at my own assurance in daring to expose my unworthy performance to your accurate criticisms, which to be sure I should never have presumed to do if I had not thought it necessary to pay my duty to you, which, with the greatest humility, I beg you to accept . . .

Just to make sure her joke was understood, she signed herself, 'Your most devoted, Obsequious, Respectful, Obedient, Obliged, And dutiful, Humble Servant, E. CARTER'. And added a postscript, 'I know you have an extreme good knack at writing respectful letters; but I shall die with envy if you outdo this.'

In some ways Carter did collude with the subtle regulations imposed on women by custom, propriety, rules of etiquette and decorum, suppressing her talents and retreating to Deal. She diverted much of her writing energy into her correspondence, spending hours each day writing long letters to her friends among the bluestockings, filled with literary criticism, entertaining reportage and deeply thought-through moral responses to what was happening in the world. But her legacy is Epictetus as well as these letters, which were published after her death by her nephew, Montagu Pennington (named after Elizabeth Montagu, his aunt's dear friend). Pennington was guilty of editing the letters for publication and then destroying them so that they can never now be restored to what Carter actually wrote. But at least he preserved seven volumes of letters between her and Catherine Talbot, Elizabeth Montagu and Elizabeth Vesey.

In them, Carter's character shines through. When Catherine Talbot sends her a lock of hair, she responds, 'I must be allowed to look on it with delight, as the gift of a person to whom I have the highest obligation, that of having endeavoured to render me wiser and better.' It has sometimes been implied that they were more than just friends, their letters coloured by a sentimentality that we now consider too florid and self-withholding. Catherine, like Elizabeth, never married, living instead a dutiful life caring for her mother and helping to run the household of Archbishop Secker after the death of his wife in 1748. She also wrote essays, reflections, commentaries, but she was too modest to publish. After her death, when Carter ensured that her finished works appeared in print, they were very popular, her *Reflections on the Seven Days of the Week*, in particular, running into several editions until well into the 1800s and selling as many as 25,000 copies.

The letters between the friends are rich with learned allusions but are also full of fun and a delight in the natural world. 'I am now nearly as gay and wild as ever,' Elizabeth writes to Catherine in the middle of winter from a storm-tossed Deal, 'and want to be flying all over the face of the earth, though this weather something cramps my genius, for I cannot meet with any body here romantic enough to take moonlight walks in the snow, and travel as people do in Lapland.'

On reading Aristotle's *Poetics*, Elizabeth witheringly declares that the ancient Greek's critical powers lack 'a single ray of poetic genius' and are 'utterly destitute of the colouring of the imagination'. She could, she says, 'no more judge of the beauties of an author from any of Aristotle's criticisms, than I could of the beauty of Helen, from hearing a Surgeon read a very learned and elaborate lecture upon her Skeleton'. No one was safe from her critical eye.

In April 1751 Catherine tried to persuade Elizabeth to visit her in London, but Elizabeth replied:

I now seem entirely accommodated to a state of inactivity and repose, and grow on faster and faster to my rock, and it must be a violent effort that could draw me from it. And yet besides the particular inducement that there are some very valuable people in the world whom I must be strangely stupid not to wish sometimes to see, there are more general reasons that should make one chuse to mix a little now and then in the hurry of society, in order to keep up some kind of connexion with the universal community of mankind; to enlarge and vary one's ideas, and thus become more useful, and more agreeable to those with whom one is chiefly to converse, than it is possible to be in an absolute regular clock-work kind of life, where one is always moved by the same springs, and perpetually striking the same notes.'

Carter had chanced upon the theme of her life: how to be useful and to make the most of the situation in which you find yourself. She had with-drawn, in the face of the difficulties engendered by being a wit who was not also a wife, but she never shut herself off from experience or the readiness to engage with the whole panoply of life. 'From such considerations,' she writes, 'I should think it right, perhaps, not to live year after year upon the same spot, and the same contracted circle of conversation, if it was in my power to do otherwise.'

'If it was in my power to do otherwise.' Carter recognises the constraints that have been imposed on her. Yet she also insists 'that it is not in my power gives me no uneasiness'. Carter writes about how to live a life of compromise *without* feeling compromised; and how to preserve an inward state of reason and calm in times of external stress.

Carter published one more collection of poetry after *Epictetus*, her *Poems on Several Occasions* in 1762, but after that there is nothing for more than forty years until her death on 19 February 1806. When in 1778 Richard Samuel showed his group portrait of the *Nine Living Muses* (otherwise known as *Portraits in the Characters of the Muses in the Temple of Apollo*) at the annual exhibition of the Academy, he included Elizabeth Carter. She can be seen on the left-hand side of the painting in conversation with her friend, the poet and writer Anna Laetitia Barbauld, and behind the artist Angelica Kauffmann who is shown working at her easel. On the right-hand side of the painting her friend Elizabeth Montagu is seated in pride of place.

Montagu was delighted with the picture, which depicts the nine women as if they are living in a classical paradise, dressed in appropriately long and flowing robes garlanded with sashes and meeting together under a statue of the god Apollo. 'It is charming to think how our praises will ride about the World in every bodies pocket,' she remarked to a friend after discovering that an engraving of the painting had been used as the frontispiece to the 1779 edition of *The Ladies' New and Polite Pocket Memorandum-Book*, a handy notebook, small enough to carry in a pocket but with space to keep a calendar of events. 'I do not see how we could become more universally celebrated.' But Carter, more perceptive than her friend, was less impressed. Although Richard Samuel had done honour to these women by eulogising them on canvas, he had also betrayed them by failing to give them any personality. 'By the mere testimony of my eyes, I cannot very exactly tell which is you, and which is I, and which is anybody else,' Carter declared. Samuel, in attempting to assert the cultural excellence of Britain's women vis-à-vis the rest of Europe, had reduced them to mere cardboard cut-outs.

The painting has nothing remarkable about it artistically but it marks nevertheless a pivotal moment in the fluctuating fortunes of women artists and writers. Just a decade or so later, in the early 1790s, it is unlikely that Samuel would have created such an all-women tableau. In the face of revolutionary times, there was already less freedom of movement between the sexes; fears and insecurities about the future creating a desire for order, convention and stable relations. In such an atmosphere, for an artist to display nine women in a public setting and engaged in professional activities without a man in sight would have broken too many taboos.

By the time she died, aged eighty-eight, Elizabeth Carter's professional accomplishments were less admired than her moral character. In the *Sketch of the Character of Mrs Elizabeth Carter*, published by 'a friend' as a short pamphlet, we are told, 'We have hitherto viewed Mrs Carter as a deep and elegant scholar; but as a proof that knowledge does not necessarily set a female character at variance with its peculiar duties, we shall now consider her as performing every domestic employment, not only with industry, but with perfect propriety and skill.' Carter's skill with puddings was threatening to overtake her genius as a translator.

In 1929, in her book-length essay *A Room of One's Own*, Virginia Woolf gives credit to Elizabeth Carter for paving the way for future writers such as George Eliot: 'For masterpieces are not single and solitary births; they are the outcome of many years of thinking in common.' George Eliot, she says, should have 'done homage to the robust shade of Eliza Carter—the valiant old woman who tied a bell to her bedstead in order that she might wake early and learn Greek'. Woolf recognised Carter's talent but also the debt we owe to her as a woman who achieved her independence, her room of her own, through hard work and a determination to reconcile her domestic obligations with her desire to study, to think, to write.

The success of *Epictetus* in the 1760s earned Carter almost £1,000 (or £75,000), which was more than enough for her to buy her own property in Deal. Even the author of the *Sketch* is willing to acknowledge that 'Mrs Carter was extremely attached to her little habitation at Deal. It is probable this attachment was strengthened by its being a purchase made by herself, with the money produced by her translation of Epictetus.' Elizabeth Carter was proud of her financial independence. She redesigned her house so that from the windows of her sitting room overlooking the sea she could watch the ever-changing fluctuations of the weather and the shipping movements on one of the busiest waterways in Europe. 'A window to the east afforded her all the magnificence of marine scenery,' says the writer of the *Sketch*, 'animated by variety of shipping, continually passing through, or lying at anchor in the Downs. From hence also she enjoyed the glorious sight of the sun rising out of the sea, a sight of which she never failed to be an admiring spectator, both winter and summer.'

Carter's house in Deal still survives, on the corner of South Street and Middle Street, proudly emblazoned by the town council with a placard that declares, 'Mrs Elizabeth Carter, the celebrated Scholar and Authoress, lived in this House from 1762 until her death. Royalty and Society were her friends and visited her here. She died in Clarges St Piccadilly 19th February 1806.' Underneath is displayed in large letters Elizabeth's personal motto, 'Ask it of God'.

In 1948 the house, which for many years was a seaside boarding house, was threatened with demolition, but a petition signed by more than 2,000 residents saved it. When I asked at the town hall if I could see her portrait, which I knew was on display in the council room, I discovered a gracious painting of a thoughtful young woman dressed in a lavish silk gown, amid a gallery of male worthies, including a grand picture of Winston Churchill as Admiral of the Cinque Ports. I asked the commissionaire on duty if he knew anything about the young woman and why her portrait was in the town hall. He told me, 'She wrote poetry. It's really good.'

5

Miss Sainthill and the Female Quixote

'I dined yesterday at Mrs Garrick's, with Mrs Carter, Miss Hannah More, and Miss Fanny Burney,' Johnson told his friend and biographer James Boswell in May 1784, with some pride at having been the only male guest. He had befriended Garrick's widow after the death of the great actor and his former pupil in 1779. Her dinner parties were frequented by many of the bluestocking writers, whose company and conversation Johnson always enjoyed. 'Three such women are not to be found,' he assured Boswell afterwards. 'I know not where I could find a fourth, except Mrs Lennox, who is superior to them all.'

Johnson's provocative assertion surprised many readers of Boswell's *Life*, especially Miss Fanny Burney, the best-selling novelist who became a close friend of Johnson in his later years. 'The small party to whom Dr Johnson was known,' she insisted in a letter to her sister Susan, know 'how little of his solid opinion was to be gathered from his accidental assertions'. He was just joshing Boswell, she preferred to think. The bluestocking circle begrudgingly admired Charlotte Lennox's talent but they did not approve of her. She once received an anonymous letter from 'a friend', who told her, 'Several ladies . . . were astonished to see a Gentlewoman's hands in such horrid condition. For God's sake wash them & rub back the skin at the roots of the nails.'

Burney could not believe that Johnson really meant what he said. Lennox superior to them all? But Johnson saw something of himself in

Lennox. He also hugely respected her gifts as a writer – including a quotation from her not-long-published novel *The Female Quixote* in his *Dictionary of the English Language*. Lennox was one of very few living authors to have been given such a tribute by Johnson, who preferred to quote only from those books whose immortality was assured. Under his second definition of 'Talent' meaning 'Faculty; power; gift of nature', he adds, from book VII chapter VI of *The Female Quixote*, 'Persons who possess the true talent of raillery are like comets; they are seldom seen, and all at once admired and feared.'

Lennox was both admired and derided in her lifetime, experiencing huge success and dire poverty. In her professional life, she published not just poetry and novels, but also translations from French and Italian, a study of Shakespeare and a female version of the *Gentleman's Magazine*. As an unhappily married woman, she narrowly escaped debtors' prison and was brought before the magistrates accused of assault. 'She has many fopperies,' Johnson told a mutual friend, 'but she is a great Genius, and *nullum magnum ingenium sine mixtura*.' ('No great genius has ever existed without some touch of madness.') 'Do for her what you can,' he asks. 'You were perhaps never called to the relief of a more powerful mind.' Yet Lennox is now virtually forgotten, her novels read only by scholars.

Her origins were always uncertain – she liked to keep it that way – and no one knew whether she spent her childhood in New York or Gibraltar, or even when she was born. At the end of her life she claimed that her father, an army officer, was once the governor of New York, but researchers have since discovered this cannot be true, since no one of the right name is listed in the army records. All we can know for sure is that Lennox arrived in London in about 1745 as Barbara Ramsay, a young woman without family or income, aged probably between sixteen and seventeen. At some point she adopted the name 'Charlotte', perhaps when she took up acting.

Horace Walpole saw her on stage in Richmond on 2 September 1748, billed as Charlotte Ramsay, afterwards declaring that her performance was 'deplorable'. A year later she was still acting, but was now married, becoming Charlotte Lennox. She could not have been all that bad an actress because on 6 February 1749 the *General Advertiser* announced a benefit evening for 'Mrs Charlotte Lennox' at the Little Theatre in the Haymarket, managed by Samuel Foote, an impresario noted for his wit and gift for mimicry. Charlotte, who played Almeria, the starring role in Congreve's Restoration tragedy *The Mourning Bride*, would have been given all the receipts from the house.

Soon afterwards, though, she abandoned the stage, cashing in on the publishing boom. She had already appeared in print, in October 1747, with her *Poems on Several Occasions, Written by a Young Lady*, printed and sold by S. Paterson at Shakespear's Head, opposite Durham Yard, in the Strand, for the price of one shilling and sixpence. No name was given on the title page, but Charlotte dedicated the volume to the Right Honourable Lady Isabella Finch, First Lady of the Bedchamber to their Royal Highnesses the Princesses, and signed the dedication under her maiden name, Charlotte Ramsay. Unlike Elizabeth Carter, Lennox had no intention of remaining anonymous.

This debut collection caused such a stir that some of the thirty poems were still being reprinted in the *Gentleman's Magazine* three years later. Lennox was a distinctive new 'voice' as a writer, cheeky, teasing, veering on the risqué, yet always easy on the ear. 'The Art of Coquetry', in particular, shows off her wit and effortless style:

> Ye lovely maids, whose yet unpractis'd Hearts
> Ne'er felt the Force of Love's resistless Darts;
> Who justly set a Value on your Charms . . .
>
> Attend my Rules to you alone addrest,
> Deep let them sink in every female Breast.
> The Queen of Love herself my Bosom fires,
> Assists my Numbers, and my Thoughts inspires.
> Me she instructed in each secret Art,
> How to enslave and keep the vanquish'd Heart.

The poem includes a list of rules on how the coquette should entrap her chosen victim, ending with the warning:

> Not for the tender were these Rules design'd,
> Who in their Faces show their yielding Mind:
> Eyes that a native Languishment can wear,
> Whose Smiles are artless, and whose Blush sincere;
> But the gay Nymph who Liberty can prize,
> And vindicate the Triumph of her Eyes . . .

Many of the 'gay Nymphs' of London were shocked by Lennox's saucy jibes at their artful behaviour but they could not resist the poet's skill. Elizabeth

Carter, by then a mature thirty-three-year-old, thoroughly disliked the tone of the poem but was intrigued by the sophistication of its wit. She asked her friend Catherine Talbot if she knew anything about this 'Charlotte Lennox', and then remarked, 'It is intolerably provoking to see people who really appear to have a genius, apply it to such idle unprofitable purposes.'

Lennox never did profit from her pen, but Carter was wrong to accuse her of idleness. Just a month after 'The Art of Coquetry' was reprinted in the *Gentleman's Magazine* on 13 December 1750, Lennox published her first novel, cleverly cashing in on the poem's notoriety. *The Life of Harriot Stuart, Written by Herself* was published by John Payne and Joseph Bouquet of Paternoster Row for the price of five shillings; expensive for a first novel, but Payne and Bouquet had confidence in Lennox as a writer and gave her first novel every chance of succeeding by selling it as a finely bound copy rather than in unstitched sections. It stars a teenage girl, Harriot Stuart, whose experiences were inspired, it is tempting to believe, by those of Lennox herself.

Harriot moves with her family from London to New York, a small town in America described by her as 'the seat of love and gallantry'. When her father dies, the family is left without an income and Harriot is sent home to England to live with an aunt. But by the time she arrives in London, after a thrilling three-week passage across the Atlantic (during which her ship is captured by privateers and then rescued by a British man-o'-war), her aunt has become ill and helpless with dementia, leaving Harriot with no financial support and no introduction to polite circles. At just fifteen, Harriot has to learn how to fend for herself in the treacherous social whirl of metropolitan life, living by her wits until she finds a suitable husband.

The novel was an instant success, although Lennox herself barely made £10 from it, the publishers holding on to the copyright and printing new editions without her approval. (Copyright law, protecting writers from pirated editions of their work, especially those printed in Dublin and sold in England, was not established until 1773.) Johnson was so impressed by Lennox's wit, and also no doubt by her willingness to affront the very people on whose patronage she depended, that he called a special meeting of his Ivy Lane Club to celebrate 'the birth of Mrs Lennox's first literary child' to which Charlotte was invited (along with her husband). She was the only woman present at the feast.

An account of the evening was published by Sir John Hawkins, who witnessed the party, in his biography of Johnson. Hawkins tells us:

> The place appointed was the Devil tavern, and there, about the hour of eight, Mrs Lennox and her husband, and a lady of her acquaintance, now living, as also the [Ivy Lane] club, and friends to the number of near twenty, assembled. Our supper was elegant, and Johnson had directed that a magnificent hot apple-pye should make a part of it, and this he would have stuck with bay-leaves, because, forsooth, Mrs Lennox was an authoress, and had written verses; and further, he had prepared for her a crown of laurel, with which, but not till he had invoked the muses by some ceremonies of his own invention, he encircled her brows.

Looking back, Hawkins, whom Johnson once described rather cruelly as 'unclubable', took no pleasure in his memories of the night. He was suffering from toothache, and drank too much to mask the pain:

> About five, Johnson's face shone with meridian splendour, though his drink had been only lemonade; but the far greater part of us had deserted the colours of the Bacchus, and were with difficulty rallied to partake of a second refreshment of coffee, which was scarcely ended when the day began to dawn. This phenomenon began to put us in mind of our reckoning; but the waiters were all so overcome with sleep, that it was two hours before we could get a bill, and it was not till near eight that the creaking of the street-door gave the signal for our departure . . . and I well remember, at the instant of my going out of the tavern-door, the sensation of shame that affected me, occasioned not by reflection on any thing evil that had passed in the course of the night's entertainment, but on the resemblance it bore to a debauch.

Why, though, did Hawkins remember the evening so clearly, and write about it in such detail in his life of Johnson? He did not approve of Lennox, a view shared by his daughter, Laetitia Matilda, who recorded in print that although Charlotte was a favourite with Johnson she was 'as little entitled to favour as most women'. Yet by giving us such a vivid account of the celebration party Hawkins affirmed Lennox's significance in Johnson's life and her stature as a writer.

Unfortunately for Lennox, Hawkins's biography (which he published in

1787) was soon surpassed by Boswell's *Life*, which appeared four years later and makes no mention of the evening. The story of her night of triumph languishes in a book that hardly anyone reads.

Harriot Stuart, too, is virtually unknown. Those who have delved into it might well be puzzled by Johnson's enthusiasm. Harriot declares at the beginning of the novel, 'I was born a coquet, and what would have been art in others, in me was pure nature.' When she is taken to the theatre for the first time, she cares nothing for what is happening on stage; instead her eyes are riveted on a group of boys who have just arrived at the theatre from Westminster School:

> I first discovered my propensity to gallantry upon this occasion; for I managed my looks with such art, that I soon had the eyes of some of these young gentlemen upon me. Among the rest a youth about fifteen, drest in deep mourning, considered me attentively. He was lovely, I may say, to a fault; for his beauty had something too sweet and delicate in it for one of his sex. However, I found a secret pleasure in meeting his glances; and could not forbear enquiring of a young lady, who sat next me, and seemed to know him, who he was. She told me he was called Lord S—. My heart bounded at the knowledge of his quality, and I felt an increase of transport whenever I surprised him gazing on me, which he did almost every moment.

Was Johnson being truthful when he claimed to enjoy reading such stuff? The critic in the *Monthly Review* dismissed the novel as lacking 'anything great, or noble, or useful or entertaining . . . Here are no striking characters, no interesting events, nor in short anything that will strongly fix the attention, or greatly improve the morals of the reader.'

Harriot is a lively heroine, and the scenes in America when she is captured by Native Americans and travels with them by canoe up the Hudson River are vividly evoked. But there is no psychological depth to Harriot's vivacious character and in spite of her adventures and Lennox's highly inventive plotting the novel lacks suspense. The *Gentleman's Magazine*, by 1751 regarded as the acme of taste and literary excellence, mentioned the novel only briefly (in a list of ten new books that also included *The Secret History of Pythagoras* and *Robin Hood*). Lennox's debut was described in the magazine as 'a series of love-affairs from 11 [*sic*] years of age, attended with a number of her adventures and misfortunes'. But then the reviewer added, 'which were borne with the patience, and are penn'd with the purity of a *Clarissa*'. Lennox was already being compared to Samuel Richardson, whose novel *Clarissa* in just three years had become the standard to which all serious novelists aspired. Why, then, was her reputation so short-lived? Who was she, and why did Johnson think she was superior to Burney, to Carter and to Hannah More?

There is no surviving portrait of Charlotte Lennox. She sat for Sir Joshua Reynolds in 1761, but the finished portrait has been lost. Perhaps the disappearance was no accident? Charlotte overheard Horace Walpole declaring after seeing it that 'Mr Reynolds seldom succeeds with women'. Engravings taken from the picture in 1793 and 1813 (and used as illustrations for an edition of Lennox's edition of Shakespeare, *Shakespear Illustrated*, and a magazine obituary after her death) are not flattering. There's no spark, no character. Her face has been flattened out; her vitality squashed. Her hair is dressed in a fashionable coiffure, brushed high on the head and with elaborate rolls on top like a halo, or a laurel wreath. But where are the flashing eyes of the coquet? Or the pert smile of the young woman who in such a short time established herself as a poet and a novelist compared to Richardson and celebrated by Johnson?

Lennox was not just a skilful and original writer, she was also a consummate professional. Of her surviving correspondence, most of it concerns her working life and is addressed to either male writers or theatrical agents, including Samuel Richardson, Oliver Goldsmith, David Garrick and George Colman, asking for their help and advice on how to maximise her earnings. She also had dealings with all the major printers in London at the time, including the Dodsley brothers, William Strahan, Andrew Millar and John Payne. Most frequent among these supportive correspondents was Sam. Johnson.

They most probably met for the first time in the offices of William Strahan, who was part of the consortium of printers who had contracted with Johnson to produce the *Dictionary*. Strahan's print shop and works was in Wine Office Court, just a couple of alleys away from Johnson's house in Gough Square. Charlotte's husband, Alexander Lennox, worked as a printer for Strahan. He might well have arranged for Charlotte to be at Wine Office Court when he knew the author of the *Dictionary* was likely to turn up with a new batch of manuscript sheets ready for setting up as blocks of type on the stone.

Perhaps Charlotte married Alexander not for love but because of his connections with these printers and publishers. Her plotting, if this is what it was, succeeded remarkably well for within a few months she had become part of a friendship and professional network that included Johnson and Richardson. The creator of *Clarissa* was not only a compulsive writer; he also took a great interest in nurturing new writers, especially if they were female, by promoting their work in his other guise as a printer and publisher.

Johnson took his new young friend to meet Richardson, according to Frances Burney, who recorded the story in her diaries after hearing it straight from Johnson many years later. Burney was intrigued by what she knew of Lennox's skilful and confident manoeuvring as a woman wanting to make her name (and her living) as a writer, and she led Johnson to tell her over dinner at Streatham Park (with Henry and Hester Thrale) the story of his involvement in Lennox's career. Lennox, writes Burney, 'waited upon Dr Johnson upon her commencing writer, and . . . at her request, he carried her to Richardson'. But when they arrived at Richardson's house in North End Road, west of London in the village of Kensington, Lennox asked Johnson to leave, 'for, says she, "I am under great restraint in your presence, but if you leave me alone with Richardson I'll give you a very good account of him"'.

Johnson told Burney, 'However, I fear poor Charlotte was disappointed, for she gave me no account at all!' In fact, Lennox had secured a deal with Richardson to print her next novel, but she saw no reason to thank her benefactor, Johnson, or to explain to him what had occurred at the meeting he had helped to set up. She operated on her own terms and for her own benefit.

The most impressive aspect of Lennox's character is her industry, her refusal to give up or to follow the rules established for women. She needed to make money; she had talent as a writer; she ensured that her second novel, *The Female Quixote*, was accepted and published by the best operators in the business. By November 1751 she was deep in correspondence with Richardson regarding its publication. Initially, she had arranged for it to be published by Andrew Millar, who also published both Johnson and Richardson. Millar had seen the manuscript of the first volume and had already sent it off to his printer for typesetting, but he began to have doubts about its quality after receiving negative feedback from his advisory readers. His printer, though, was Richardson, who read the first volume while setting up the type.

Richardson appreciated Lennox's wit and her originality and he insisted to Millar that the novel would be a great success. Lennox, hugely grateful, wrote to Richardson on 21 November:

> Mr Johnson has inform'd me of the generous concern you exprest for the severity of my Criticks and your intentions to rescue my Book from their censures and restore me to Mr Millar's good opinion, which in my present dependant situation it much concerns me to preserve. I am not able to express how much I am affected with this instance of your goodness, but I beg you to believe that I shall always preserve the most grateful remembrance of it . . . I would not appeal from your Judgment and Mr Johnson's to that of any Person living, and since your praise might flatter the ambition of any author whatever surely I have reason to be perfectly happy in it . . .

Lennox had only just turned twenty-one (if her date of birth in 1729/30 is correct) and yet she, not her husband, was negotiating terms with the most influential figures in publishing in the capital.

She also reveals that in spite of her appearance of coquettish confidence, she was very fearful that she might fail:

> I have taken the liberty to send the second volume of my Book, and shall with the utmost anxiety expect your opinion of it. I must beg leave to acquaint you that it being transcribed from my first Copy, it has yet received no Corrections, and is therefore indeed unfit for your perusal, but if with the allowance you will be pleased to make on that account, it should be so fortunate to meet with your approbation I shall go on with redoubled Spirit.

Would a desperately ambitious young man have dared to be so frank? Many years later Lennox admitted to a friend, 'I have been a wretch since I was thirteen years old when I lost my father—adversity is habitual to me.' Lennox, like Johnson, suffered from inner doubts, those niggling fears about her true worth and the real value of her work.

Andrew Millar advised her that she should delay the publication of *The Female Quixote* until the autumn. He was 'apprehensive' that the book would not be ready in time to maximise sales before everyone left town to spend the summer on their country estates. Lennox again feared that he was delaying work on her manuscript because he did not believe in it. She had just spent the last couple of months furiously struggling to revise the second volume, and was exhausted by her efforts. She also could not afford to wait another nine months before receiving the profits of her labours (she appears never to have relied on her husband for money). On 3 February 1752 she wrote to Johnson for advice on what to do.

In an act of genuine friendship, he took the trouble to reply immediately, writing his letter from the garret in Gough Square even while his wife Tetty was lying downstairs in bed close to death:

> Madam
>
> I am extremely sorry to hear that your Book suffers such delays, and think you unkindly treated by Mr Richardson. You see how ill we judge of our own advantages, I wish Strahan had it even now, for I am afraid you will be greatly injured by so long a delay. What can be done? It is already sent to Mr Millar, and you cannot decently make any warm remonstrance. I wish I could help it. But if you can stay till next year the prospect of success will be better, and I will try to speak to . . . others for employment in the mean time . . . I am much concerned for you.

Johnson believed that his friend and publisher William Strahan, who had more presses than any other printer in London, would have been able to set the text more quickly than Richardson, who printed as a hobby rather than a profession. But he did not see how Lennox could withdraw the book from Richardson's presses, since so much of it had already been set by him.

In the end *The Female Quixote* was published in March 1752 just as Lennox wanted, with the second volume being printed by William Strahan rather than Richardson. How she managed to persuade Millar to swap printers and to bring forward publication we do not know since the correspondence has been lost. She sent a complimentary copy to Johnson who wrote to her on 12 March, thanking her for her 'kind present' and 'wishing it the Success which it deserves'. He added, 'Poor Tetty's illness will not suffer me to think of going any whither, out of her call.' His wife had spent the last few months confined to bed in Gough Square, dosing herself with opium and drink to mask the pain. Five days later she was dead. There would be no all-night party in celebration of the latest novel from Johnson's protégée.

Lennox, though, was on the ascendant. *The Female Quixote* was an immediate success with readers and critics, the novelist Henry Fielding declaring in the *Covent Garden Journal* on 24 March, 'I do very earnestly recommend it, as a most extraordinary and most excellent Performance. It is indeed a Work of true Humour, and cannot fail of giving a rational, as well as very pleasing Amusement to a sensible Reader.' In his opinion, Lennox's book was superior to Cervantes's *Don Quixote*, which inspired it, because her heroine, Arabella, was more endearing than Quixote, and in some ways more believable.

By June a second edition had been printed, plus a pirated Dublin version. It was translated into French, German and Spanish and was never out of print until well after Lennox died in 1804. Jane Austen read it several times and found it highly entertaining, Arabella providing an inspiration for Catherine Morland, the precocious but susceptible heroine of *Northanger Abbey*. Shortly afterwards it fell out of fashion and has never been revived, except in academic circles intrigued by its original conceit and its feminist credentials.

The fiction itself was not just a clever allusion to Cervantes's classic parody of chivalric adventure. Lennox was developing her artistry as a writer and in *The Female Quixote* she set out to satirise the kind of romantic folly she had herself written in *Harriot Stuart* while at the same time creating an original new style of comic fantasy. Her heroine Arabella has been brought up in isolation after the death of her mother and has had nothing else to read but books written in the French romantic tradition. Her obsession with the search for perfect love is deconstructed by Lennox in exquisite detail.

Arabella believes that every man she sees is either a potential prince in disguise, pining for love of her, or a rapist with wicked designs on her virtue. We, her readers, are let into a secret – Arabella is deluded – and although we do not laugh at her, for that would mean laughing at ourselves for being similarly taken in, the joke lies in all the ridiculous fictions she has been forced to read. When, for example, the fantastically adorned Arabella goes to church she believes she has attracted the attention of a stranger to the village:

> Mr Hervey, for that was the Stranger's Name, was no less surprised at her Beauty, than the Singularity of her Dress; and the odd Whim of being followed into the Church by three Women-Attendants, who, as soon as she was seated, took their Places behind her.

Her Dress, tho' singular, was far from being unbecoming. All the Beauties of her Neck and Shape were set off to the greatest Advantage by the Fashion of her Gown, which, in the Manner of a Robe, was made to fit tight to her Body; and fastened on the Breast with a Knot of Diamonds. Her fine black Hair, hung upon her Neck in Curls, which had so much the Appearance of being artless, that all but her Maid, whose Employment it was to give them that Form, imagined they were so. Her Head-dress was only a few Knots advantageously disposed, over which she wore a white Sarsenet Hood, somewhat in the Form of a Veil, with which she sometimes wholly covered her fair Face, when she saw herself beheld with too much attention . . .

Arabella goes out riding, and happens upon Mr Hervey:

Arabella, suddenly seeing him, and observing he was making up to her, her Imagination immediately suggested to her, that this insolent Lover had a Design to seize her Person; and this Thought terrifying her extremely, she gave a loud Shriek; which Mr Hervey hearing, rode eagerly up to her to inquire the Reason of it . . . Arabella, upon his coming close to her, redoubled her Cries. If you have any Valour, said she to her Servants, defend your unfortunate Mistress, and rescue her from this unworthy Man.

The Servants, believing him to be a Highwayman, by this Exclamation, and dreading lest he should present his Pistol at their Heads, if they offered to make any Resistance, recoiled a few Paces back, expecting he would demand their Purses when he had robbed their Lady: But the extreme Surprise he was in, keeping him motionless, the Fellows not seeing any Pistols in his Hand, and animated by Arabella's Cries, who, calling them Cowards and Traitors, urged them to deliver her; they both, in a Moment, laid hold of Mr Hervey, and forced him to alight . . .

In the ensuing eighty-five chapters Arabella encounters numerous hazards in the pursuit of love until eventually she throws herself into the Thames at Richmond while escaping from a group of horsemen whom she fears are brigands in disguise intent on carrying her off to a dreadful castle to have their wicked way with her.

At last, in this penultimate chapter of the novel, Lennox's mock fantasy turns into an intellectual argument as Arabella encounters an elderly clergyman. He tries to educate her about the difference between fantasy, fiction and real life. 'Has it ever been known that a Lady of your Rank was attack'd with such Intentions, in a Place so publick?' he asks Arabella. 'Does there in the Records of the World appear a single Instance of such hopeless Villainy?' In any case, he tells her, your attackers will not be able to carry you away to 'any of these dreadful Places' because 'there is no such Castle, Desert, Cavern, or Lake'.

Arabella, having miraculously acquired the intellectual rigour of a political philosopher, replies, 'Universal Negatives are seldom safe . . . That there is a Castle, any Man who has seen it may safely affirm. But you cannot with equal Reason, maintain that there is no Castle, because you have not seen it.' She's no flighty female, hooked on fantasy because of the superficiality of her mind. She's a genuine inquirer into the meaning of things. What can we be sure of? How much reality is there in fiction, and vice versa?

The change of tone is surprising and is so Johnsonian in flavour that it has been suggested Johnson must have written it. This is a ruse that has often been adopted to belittle female achievement. But Johnson was preoccupied in February 1752 with his wife's grave illness and was struggling to fulfil his obligation to write his own twice-weekly *Rambler* essays. He ended the series a month later, just as Tetty died. We also know that Lennox was writing furiously in these weeks, anxious to have the novel published as soon as possible. Surely she would not have risked waiting for the notoriously dilatory Johnson to come up with such a crucial chapter and thereby miss the chance of publishing her novel before the spring exodus to the country of the rich and fashionable? Lennox wrote purely for money, not the luxury of her own amusement. She needed to maximise her earnings from the book by publishing at the best time.

Charlotte Lennox was always looking for new ways to profit as much as possible from her endeavours, and on this occasion she negotiated with the Earl of Middlesex for permission to dedicate her novel to him. Her request ensured his patronage, and that of his wealthy and influential friends, too. But this willingness to market her own work, to deal in commerce, alienated her from most of the other women writers of her time, who either found such dealing in public difficult, or thought it unseemly. Johnson was almost alone in his loyalty to Lennox's talent, his appreciation of her wit. His relationship with her shows him in quite a different light – fatherly, supportive and always prepared to listen and encourage – so different from his wary acknowledgement of Elizabeth Carter's achievement.

Lennox was young enough to be his daughter. On their first meeting he is supposed to have taken her on his knee, 'as if she were a mere child; after which he carried her in his arms, to shew her his library; and . . . sent his servant to a pastry-cook, to purchase some cakes for the young lady'. It's an unsettling story about Johnson, infantilising Lennox who was already married, and somehow diminishing Johnson's stature, making him appear slightly ridiculous. Would he really have carried in his arms an eighteen-year-old married woman whom he had only just met? Charlotte, too, was no ingénue. She was born an adult, at least in her self-possession and innate understanding of the ways of the world. By the time she met Johnson, she had travelled to and fro across the Atlantic with her family, tried and failed to be an actress, and experienced a fair share of life's cruelties. After the death of her father in America, probably garrisoned north of New York in the fortress towns of Albany and Schenectady, she was sent back to England to make her own way in life (if the stories she later told about herself are true). At eighteen, she had experienced so much of life that she would surely have appeared more like a mature woman in her thirties.

Maybe there was something of the parent-and-child about the friendship between them, Lennox looking up to Johnson as the father-figure she lost when young, Johnson regarding Lennox with the concern of a parent for the daughter he never had (or out of guilt that he had abandoned his step-daughter)? Perhaps when he met Lennox, just as Tetty was becoming so ill, he was looking for 'family' among his acquaintances on Grub Street? Throughout the letters that have survived between Johnson and Lennox he writes not just with advice about her publishing career but also with concern about her unhappiness, her struggles to establish a settled life, her repeated illnesses. He tells her to consult the doctor when she is ill, and advises her not to be so hasty in her dealings with people, but to exercise a little cool judgement.

'The letter which you sent me some time ago, was rather too full of wrath for the provocation,' he writes to her on 30 July 1756. 'I read both the reviews [of her latest translation], and though the Critical Reviewers, according to their Plan, showed their superiority of knowledge with some ostentation, they mentioned you with great respect, and the other Reviewers, though less ceremonious, said nothing that can excite or justify such resentment.' He adds, 'I do not believe that either of the Reviews, intended you any hurt.' Like an anxious parent, he tries to reassure her: 'It is certain that if they meant to hurt you they will be disappointed, and if you were not too proud already, I would tell you, that you are now got above their malice, and though you cannot expect to be always equally successful, have such a degree of reputation as will secure you from any neglect of readers or Stationers.'

Perhaps most tellingly after the death of Tetty in 1752 Johnson took on the role of the female confidante which Charlotte never had, falling out with her on occasion but always ensuring that they were soon reconciled. 'Dear Madam,' he begins a letter:

> I wish you would for once resolve to use any method of transacting with your friends, but that of letters. You will, in whatever part of the world you may be placed, find mankind extremely impatient of such letters as you are inclined to favour them with. You can send your letters, such as the last but one, only to two sorts of people, those whom you cannot pain, and those whom you can, and surely it is not eligible either to give mirth to your enemies or to raise anger in your friends.

Ever sensitive, though, to the importance of keeping his friendships in good repair, he adds, 'I have no Pleasure in saying this, and am glad that I have delayed beyond the time in which I might have been inclined to say more . . .'

On another occasion he warns her that too much eagerness in soliciting help from your friends can be counterproductive. 'By telling your friends how much you expect from them you discourage them, for they finding themselves unequal to your expectations, will rather do nothing and be quiet, than do their utmost, and yet not please.'

Johnson's friendship with Lennox was thrown into sharp relief by his connection with another woman to whom he began sending letters in 1753, just as he was becoming closely involved in Lennox's publishing career. Hill Boothby, unlike Charlotte Lennox, was so far above reproach that she was supposed to have been the model for the character of Miss Sainthill in a long-forgotten novel by Richard Graves entitled *The Spiritual Quixote*. This fiction is both a spoof of Cervantes and inspired in part by Lennox's *The Female Quixote*.

The plot focuses on the quixotic adventures of Geoffrey Wildgoose and his sidekick Jerry Tugwell. They travel the country on horseback in the spirit of George Whitefield and the evangelical reformers looking for unbelievers to convert. Their spiritual credentials are comically undone by Miss Sainthill, whom they encounter while staying at Ashbourne Hall in Derbyshire. 'To be sure,' says Miss Sainthill, 'people might say their prayers in any place, or in any posture, and even in a warm bed; but she could not but think, there was a natural decency of behaviour due to the Supreme Being . . . and she was afraid those who deferred their prayers till they lay down upon their pillows very frequently fell asleep without saying them at all.'

Johnson first met Miss Sainthill, or rather Hill Boothby, while staying in the market town of Ashbourne in Derbyshire with his old schoolfriend, the Revd John Taylor, in the winter of 1739–40; those months when he left Tetty alone and desolate in London. The daughter of a genteel family, Hill's unusual Christian name came from her grandmother, 'Dame Hill', who had a formidable reputation for saintliness. Her granddaughter inherited both this devotional spirit and a sharp, intelligent, pious mind, compiling her own Hebrew dictionary so that, like Elizabeth Carter, she could read the Old Testament in its original language.

Such was Hill Boothby's sense of duty that when her great friend Mary Fitzherbert died in February 1753, leaving six young children without a mother, she willingly took on responsibility for them. At the time the eldest child was only eight and the youngest still a baby. Hill Boothby became a full-time carer, living in at the Fitzherberts' manorial home, Tissington Hall. Shortly afterwards Johnson began writing to her, partly to assuage the deep loneliness he experienced after his wife's death, partly for spiritual guidance in the hope that if he improved his Christian faith he might stave off the depression that was once again threatening to overwhelm him. Hill Boothby replied by quoting passages of the Bible and encouraging Johnson to seek a religious conversion.

'We are all alike bad, my dear friend,' she tells him in a letter. 'Depend upon it, till a change is wrought upon us, not by our own reasoning, but by the same Divine Power, who first created, and pronounced all he had made, *very good.* From this happy state, we all plainly fell, and to it we can only be restored by the second Adam, who wrought out a full and complete redemption and restoration for us.' She is worried that Johnson will accuse her of Wesleyan enthusiasm (he defines 'enthusiasm' in the *Dictionary* as 'A vain belief of private revelation'), and so she adds, 'Is this enthusiasm? Indeed it is truth: and, I trust, you will some time be sure it is so; and then, and not till then, will you be happy, as I ardently wish you.'

Hill Boothby was well educated with an independence of mind nurtured by her comfortable, financially at-ease way of life. Tissington Hall, which is still occupied by the Fitzherbert family, is a beautifully preserved Jacobean manor at the heart of a village of identical stone-built cottages in a lush, green valley with fields of grazing sheep. There could not have been a greater contrast to the money-grubbing grind endured by Johnson and Lennox in the crowded dark heart of the capital.

'Sir, I assure you I esteemed your request to write to and hear from me,' Hill Boothby replied to Johnson on 30 July 1753. 'Most people, and particularly a lady, would tremble at taking up the pen to reply to a letter from Mr Johnson.' She, however, was no coward, and instead of being intimidated by his 'eminent genius' and 'extensive learning' she was prepared to admonish him: 'How should I rejoice to see your pen wholly employed in the glorious Christian cause.' Johnson looked to Hill Boothby for affirmation and advice, much as Charlotte Lennox depended on him for guidance and faith in her abilities. He preserved all of Hill Boothby's letters to him in an expensive leather-bound volume, reading them often after her death, still seeking the encouragement she had given him while she was alive.

Some scholars and biographers have argued that Johnson began writing to Hill Boothby because he wished to marry her. There is certainly a coincidence in the timing. On Easter Day, 22 April 1753, just over a year after his wife's death, he resolved, 'As I purpose to try on Monday to seek a new wife without any derogation from dear Tetty's memory, I purpose at sacrament in the morning to take my leave of Tetty in a solemn commendation of her soul to God.'

Johnson's resolution, recorded by him in his private diary (since destroyed) but not published by Boswell in his *Life of Samuel Johnson*, was not known of until 1936 when it turned up among the cache of Boswell's papers discovered in the attics of Malahide Castle in Ireland. Boswell must have caught sight of Johnson's diary while waiting for him at his home one afternoon.

He quickly copied into his notebook as much as he could before Johnson was ready to greet him, hoping to use the diary entries in the book of Johnson's life he intended later to write. But in the end his scruples must have got the better of him, and the hurried copies he took in secret were never published by him. He took care, though, to ensure that, although well hidden, his notebooks were never destroyed and their discovery so many years later has given scholars puzzling new information about previously unknown areas of Johnson's life. Did Johnson intend to embark on a second marriage? And, if so, whom did he have in mind as a possible candidate?

On the following day, Easter Monday 1753, Johnson travelled down to Bromley in Kent to see Tetty's grave. It was his first visit since her death. He took communion and later noted in his diary, 'During the whole service, I was never once distracted by any thoughts of any other woman or with any design of a new wife which freedom of mind I remembered with gladness.' Then, confusingly, he added, 'God guide me.'

What did he mean? Was he asking God to help him remain celibate in Tetty's memory, or to guide him in his choice of a new wife?

Very soon afterwards he began writing to Hill Boothby. Most of his letters to her have not survived; only those she wrote to him. 'Treat me as a Friend, dear Sir,' she tells him. 'Exercise the kindest office of one towards me; tell me my faults, and assist me in rectifying them.' In return she promises to write as frankly to him: 'As I think, I write: and express my thoughts in words that first offer, sans premeditation, as you see. As I have told you before, I write to the friend, not to *the* Mr Johnson who himself writes better than any man.'

She had heard rumours that Johnson was behind the new series of essays published as the *Adventurer* on Tuesdays and Saturdays from 3 March 1753. She had not yet read any of them but asked Johnson, 'Pray tell me if I must; for, if your pen has any share in them, I shall take it ill to be deprived of the benefit.' Unlike the *Rambler* or the *Idler* essays, Johnson was not the driving force behind the *Adventurer* but merely one of several contributors, whose essays were distinguished by a series of coded 'initials'. Johnson told Hill Boothby to look especially at those that have been signed 'T' for they were by him. She responded, 'I wonder not at your hesitating to impart a secret to a woman; but am the more obliged to you for communicating it as a secret, after so hesitating. Such a mark of your deliberate confidence shall be strictly regarded; and I shall seek for letter "T", that I may read with *redoubled* pleasure.' Coded letters, secrets, confidential information: Hill Boothby and Johnson enjoyed an intimate correspondence.

She took an unusual degree of interest in his work, rushing out to purchase the latest edition of the *Gentleman's Magazine* after discovering that Cave had reprinted one of his *Adventurer* essays. 'I beg you never to let me lose one of your reflections upon life,' she writes to him on 1 July 1754. 'Drop them on the paper just as they arise from your mind; I love them, and profit by them; and I am pleased particularly to find one of my own, brightened and adorned with your strong and masterly colouring, which gives me back the image of my mind, like the meeting of an old acquaintance after absence, but extremely improved.'

She reassured him after the *Dictionary* was eventually published in April 1755, 'The great Dictionary is placed in full view, on a desk in my own room.' (Johnson had presented her with a first edition.) She flattered Johnson by asking him for advice on suitable schools for the eldest boy in her charge, now aged six, who was to be sent away to school on his father's instructions, 'the sooner the better'. Johnson replied by recommending one in Kensington run by his friend James Elphinston, who was also a publisher and who had earlier printed an edition of the *Rambler* essays in Edinburgh. 'I shall be much obliged to you for a more particular account of your friend; as—how many boys he takes—his rules and rates—and also if he has a French and dancing-master,' she asked.

There were responsibilities for which the son and heir to the Tissington estate would have to be prepared – a social whirl of hunting, county balls and the races, followed by quadrilles and game pie. In the future he would be expected to visit the family's sugar plantations in Barbados upon which a good deal of their wealth depended. 'To some proper place I hope I shall be permitted to take this dear boy this Summer,' she tells Johnson, 'when I also hope for the pleasure of seeing you.' Johnson's suggestion was not taken up, but the boy was eventually sent to an establishment in Fulham, where Johnson visited him occasionally on behalf of his parents.

Hill Boothby was confident enough of their friendship sometimes to tick off Johnson, reproving him for his habitual and not entirely honest self-deprecation: 'Ask yourself why I value your affection; for you cannot be so much a stranger to yourself, as not to know many reasons why I *ought highly* to value it . . . Do not treat me with deference. I have no claim to it; and, from a friend, it looks too much like ceremony.'

But their epistolary relationship was short-lived. Not long after it began Hill Boothby showed symptoms of the illness that would cause her death and by the end of 1755 she was seriously unwell. 'Dear Sir,' she wrote to him in August 1754 from Holborn Bridge in London, 'Do you think I would have been almost two days in town without seeing you, if I could either have been at liberty to have made you a visit, or have received one from you? No: you cannot think so unjustly of me. The truth is, I have been in a hurry ever since I came here, and am not well.'

As the mistress of Tissington Hall, she not only cared for six children not her own, she was also required to educate the girls, prepare the boys for boarding school, and play the role of 'lady of the manor' at the dances and picnics around which county life in England revolved. There was precious little time for her to write letters to Johnson, let alone arrange to meet him when the family were in London for the season.

In his *Rambler* essay for 31 July 1750, Johnson begins by saying, 'The condition of the female sex has been frequently the subject of compassion to medical writers; because their constitution of body is such, that every state of life brings its peculiar diseases . . . and whether they embrace marriage, or determine upon single life, are exposed, in consequence of their choice, to sickness, misery, and death.'

While Hill Boothby fell ill with exhaustion, after taking on the responsibility of so many children, Charlotte Lennox also experienced many periods of debilitating weakness. Although she married young, she did not have children until the birth of her daughter Harriet Holles in 1765 and her son George Louis in 1770. Perhaps some of her unexplained illnesses were miscarriages. She also suffered from the constant harassment of financial worry.

Her semi-permanent state of exhaustion can also be explained by her phenomenal industry: from her first collection of poetry in 1747 until the birth of Harriet almost twenty years later Lennox published a major work of fiction, translation or literary criticism almost every year. She turned herself into a remarkably versatile writer, swapping genres according to whatever she hoped might make money; dropping poetry when it became unfashionable and turning to the latest craze for fiction, before exploiting the new wave of enthusiasm for Shakespeare with a three-volume selection of the original stories on which his plays were based. She translated memoirs from French and Italian, wrote and adapted plays, and from March 1760 to

February 1761 single-handedly created an illustrated magazine, the *Lady's Museum*, which ran for eleven issues. She invented a new literary form, the serialised novel, publishing one excerpt from her latest fiction *The History of Harriot and Sophia* in each issue of her magazine. When the novel was ended, she killed off the magazine.

Although some might argue that she never excelled in a single genre, Lennox was gifted with an extraordinary ability to adapt, to write on demand, to come up with something new to suit changing literary tastes. She was like the 'comet' in her own description of 'talent' from *The Female Quixote*: the likes of Lennox are seldom seen, but are always admired and feared. Even the fusty academic, Thomas Birch, the colleague of Johnson and Elizabeth Carter on the *Gentleman's Magazine*, must have written a favourable review of her latest translation: three volumes of the most important French text on the theatre of the ancient world, *The Greek Theatre of Father Brumoy*. A letter from her, dated 16 March 1759, thanks Birch for 'the favourable mention you are pleased to make of me, and my little writings'.

Her magazine, the *Lady's Museum*, was closely modelled on Edward Cave's *Gentleman's Magazine*, but with the exception that virtually all of the items were written or translated by Lennox herself. The first issue began with an essay by 'The Trifler', inspired by Johnson's *Idler* but written very much from a female point of view. 'Cast your eyes upon paper, Madam,' Lennox begins her tale of trifling flirtation:

> there you may look innocently, said a polite old gentleman of my acquaintance to me, one day, in the words of a wit to a fine lady. A compliment is no unpleasing way of conveying advice to a young woman and when that advice may be so construed, as to become perfectly agreeable to her own inclinations, it is certain to be well received, and quickly complied with. It is indeed very clear to me, that my friend in this borrowed admonition recommended reading to eyes which he probably thought were too intent upon pleasing; but I with a small deviation from the sense applied it to what is I freely own my predominant passion; and therefore resolved to write, still pursuing the same darling end, though by different means.
>
> So frankly to acknowledge the desire of pleasing to be my predominant passion, is in other words, to confess myself, one of that ridiculous species of beings, called a coquet . . .

She was tapping here into her old notoriety as the author of 'The Art of Coquetry' in the hope that this would ensure the success of her latest venture. But she also included in her first issue a translation from French 'Of the Studies Proper for Young Ladies' in an attempt to broaden the magazine's appeal, finding readers among the daughters of the genteel as well as the newly rich merchants and traders.

Her inventive translation of the text advocated an education for young women that would prepare them not just to flaunt their feminine skills but also develop their independence of thought. 'To prohibit women entirely from learning is treating them with the same indignity that Mahomet did, who, to render them voluptuous, denied them souls,' she declared. Lennox proposed an education beyond needlework, the spinet and the finer points of quadrille; ideas that were later taken up by Mary Wollstonecraft in her *Thoughts on the Education of Daughters*.

The main purpose of Lennox's magazine, though, was to market her latest novel, *The History of Harriot and Sophia*, in an entirely new way – as a series of episodes published at intervals. The novelist Tobias Smollett also at the same time began publishing his latest fiction, *Launcelot Greaves*, as a series of monthly episodes. But Lennox completed her novel first, in just eleven episodes, and could rightfully claim the credit as the first writer to publish a serialised novel, the fictional form later beloved of Mrs Gaskell, Dickens and Dostoevsky.

Lennox also splashed out on the design of her magazine, commissioning two illustrations relating to the adventures of Harriot and Sophia (creating also the first illustrated novel) and an intriguing frontispiece for the first issue. This engraving depicts a female writer at centre stage, seated at her desk in what is obviously meant to be the Temple of Parnassus. She is surrounded by cherubic-looking gods and a figure representing Cupid, whose love dart is deflected just in time by the formidable female guard who stands on the right of the writer, protecting her. The guard holds a garland of laurel leaves destined for our female hero *if* she successfully foils Cupid's attempts to divert her attention from the task in hand: to write, to publish, to attain literary acclaim.

Lennox was an innovator, and an inspiration to others. When Smollett compiled a catalogue of those artists and writers who had contributed to 'The Progress of the Arts and Sciences under the Reign of George II', he included Lennox. The only other woman writer to whom he paid such tribute was Elizabeth Carter. In 1778, Lennox was portrayed by Richard Samuel as one of the *Nine Living Muses* in his group portrait of the bluestocking women. Lennox is seated on the right-hand side of the portrait, alongside Elizabeth Montagu, with a scroll in her hand as if she is writing, in mid-flow. By then, however, Lennox had virtually stopped writing and publishing and her last twenty or so years were spent in penury and disappointment.

Her husband Alexander Lennox never played much of a role in her life. On the contrary, it was usually Charlotte who bailed them out of debt. In July 1755 she had been forced by lack of money to write to her publisher, Andrew Millar:

> Mr Lennox has been obligd to keep the house for this fortnight past. I want to remove to some place of security, till I can satisfy those persons he is most apprehensive of. When they know he is out of their reach, we can offer, and they will accept easier terms, than they will now hear of. But it is not in my power to go till you are so good as to settle with me for Sully—I am grieved to the soul about the [money?] I owe you, but what can I do so unhappily circumstanced as I am. Do not imagine I want to importune you, but let me say this once that if you will allow me to pay you by the Work I proposed, which I am sure will be an advantageous one to you, I will undertake it with more chearfulness than ever I did any thing in my life for however you may be prejudiced against me, yet it is a most certain truth that I have ever looked upon you as one of the sincerest of my friends.

The Lennoxes were so much in debt that they were confined to the house for fear of meeting with their creditors, who would then have had the right to send them to one of the many private sponging houses (or jails) that surrounded Grub Street until their debts were paid off.

With resourceful spirit and aptitude, typical of her throughout her life, Charlotte suggested to Millar that she would apply herself to a new and lucrative literary challenge: translation. She was fluent in French and Italian, and with so many excellent books to translate from Europe there was an almost endless supply of books not available in English but with readers keen to read them. She asked Andrew Millar for an advance in cash and in return she would supply him with a translation of the memoirs of Maximilian de Béthune, the Duke of Sully, which she knew had been a bestseller in France.

Millar agreed terms, and in just three months she had ready for publication the *Memoirs*, three volumes of them, which were published on 1 November. Her translation was an immediate success, and two years later she completed two more volumes.

Maximilian de Béthune was the French prime minister under Henry IV in the early seventeenth century, a Huguenot prepared to work under a Catholic king, restoring the nation's finances after thirty years of civil war. Lennox, with her popular touch, had sensed the potential market for such a work. Although by now it was almost 100 years since the Restoration, the wounds of England's civil war were not completely forgotten, nor the devastation it caused to the national economy. Her 'easy, spritely, and elegant style' was well suited to the task, as the critic in the *Literary Magazine* wrote:

> This translation has already [in September 1756] been so well received by the public that we can add little to its reputation by the addition of our suffrage in its favour. But as the copies are about to be multiplied by a cheaper edition; it is not yet too late to remark, that those memoirs contain an account of that time in which France just began to assume her superiority in Europe . . . There can be no age or people to which such a history may not be useful or pleasing, but it must more particularly invite the attention of those who like us are now labouring with the same distress, and whose duty it is to endeavour at the same relief.

Lennox, though, was unlucky in her choice of publisher. Millar went bust in 1759 and she was never able to capitalise on the success of her work. Editions of the *Memoirs* were pirated in Dublin and Edinburgh and reprinted without her permission so that she never made any money from them.

Charlotte was also unfortunate in her choice of husband, or else too independent-minded to make a success of marriage. When Johnson wrote in the *Rambler* on Saturday 19 May 1750, 'There is no observation more frequently made by such as employ themselves in surveying the conduct of mankind, than that marriage, though the dictate of nature, and the institute of Providence, is yet very often the cause of misery,' he could have been writing about the Lennoxes.

Alexander never seems to have made much of his life. He did not work as a printer for long, but later turned up as a tide waiter in the Customs House (which entailed supervising the excise on incoming cargoes). Little is known about him, and he rarely appears in Lennox's letters. In her last published work, *Euphemia*, published in 1790, however, she created a very strong portrait of a feckless, difficult husband.

Euphemia, Lennox's sixth novel, is a very different read from those first indulgent chapters of *Harriot Stuart*, yet Mary Wollstonecraft was not impressed. She was disappointed that a writer with such 'a respectable name' as Lennox should have produced a work in which 'so many cold romantic flights struck us in the main story, and still more in the episodes, that we could not avoid ranking it with those novels which, perhaps, tend to lead the female mind further astray from nature and common sense, than even the tales of chivalry to which Mrs L. has allowed no quarter . . .' Wollstonecraft, though, was perhaps too harsh a critic. Although *Euphemia* is too long and loses pace in the middle chapters, it is a far more memorable, though less worthy, fiction than Wollstonecraft's own *Maria; or The Wrongs of Woman*.

With hindsight, Lennox's *Euphemia* appears both sophisticated and transitional, paving the way for the elegance and acuity of Jane Austen. The novel glides along with effortless fluency, exploring the fate of two women, Euphemia and her friend Maria, both of whom lose their parents but whose fortunes thereafter diverge. It's unusual in the way that it does not follow the fortunes of these young women as they look for love and happiness, but rather shows us how they survive marriage and all its compromises.

Euphemia is persuaded to marry Mr Neville by her widowed mother after she discovers she is close to death. Without a husband, her sick mother worries, Euphemia will be left defenceless and with no money. Neville at first appears eminently suitable but soon shows his true colours as irascible and incompetent. He takes Euphemia to America, after buying a commission in an independent company of soldiers, stationed first at the fort of Albany in upstate New York and then in the remote settlement of Schenectady. Here Euphemia lives a simple rural life alongside the native Mohawks and Hurons, who think nothing of strolling into the house and making themselves at home. One of them wanders into her kitchen and sits down to smoke his pipe:

> He had a fierce and menacing look; his copper-coloured face was painted in round spots of red, yellow, and black; his hair strewed with some kind of powder of a deep red, which looked like blood streaming from

different wounds in his head; his ears were stretched to an enormous length by the weight of the strange ornaments he wore in them, pieces of tin, glass, strings of shells, brass rings, and even slips of woollen cloth of several colours, which hung down to his shoulders . . . He had a large knife hanging at a kind of girdle, unsheathed, ready for mischief, as I thought.

These scenes in America capture the sense of frontier life, far from the 'civilised' society of New York, fearful of the native people and battling against the harsh conditions of winter when even the ink in Euphemia's pen freezes so that flakes of black ice fall from it on to the letter she is writing. Euphemia describes the natives as 'savages' but she also recognises the virtues of their way of life. These are inborn, she says, and their vices are 'often copies from their enlightened allies'. She understands that drinking is something they have been introduced to by the settlers, and it has become 'the principal end of all their treaties with us, and from this they suffer inexpressible calamities; for having once begun to drink, they observe no measure but continue a succession of drunkenness as long as the means of procuring liquor lasts'.

Euphemia's letters to Maria from fortified America have the liveliness and telling details of actual memory, suggesting that Lennox is drawing on her childhood for inspiration and local colour. But the most unconventional aspect of *Euphemia* is its portrait of an unhappy marriage. Although Maria's story follows the traditional fictional pattern of falling in love with a suitor at first deemed unsuitable but then won over, Euphemia is married almost from the outset and we follow her story not on the usual trajectory from testing courtship to happy outcome but through the travails of living with a feckless and unlovable man.

'I have often experienced the truth of that observation,' Euphemia tells Maria, 'that with some persons it is not safe to be reasonable. Whenever it happens that my arguments press home upon him, he has recourse to an expedient that never fails to silence me – he falls into a passion . . .' On another occasion, she says, 'It has been observed that obstinate persons are ever most obstinate in error. Unhappily I experience the truth of this observation every day, on some occasion or other. When Mr Neville has once given his opinion, however erroneous it may be, it is impossible by argument to set him right, for reason itself would seem to be wrong if it is not of his side.'

In the late 1770s, when deciding what to do about her daughter Harriet's education, Charlotte wrote, with similar unhappy expectations, to her husband. Alexander had suggested that their daughter should be sent to Boulogne, probably to a convent run by Ursuline nuns, because it would be cheaper than an English boarding school. (Boulogne was at that time a haven for those escaping their debts, and had a number of schools offering a good education at much cheaper rates than anything available in England.) It would mean, though, a lengthy separation. Charlotte told him that she had discussed her concerns about Harriet with Johnson and 'other persons of good sense and experience' (a comment surely designed to irritate Alexander) and had concluded it would be much better to find a boarding school for their daughter close to London. 'Their reasons have convinced me,' she writes, 'and that is the cause that they will never convince you—therefore I submit to your despotick will, with this condition only, that I go with her, and see her settled—this point I never will give up . . .' Charlotte won her battle and Harriet was not sent away, but the tone of her letter suggests that confrontation was the usual mode of communication between the Lennoxes.

Euphemia has its flaws as a novel. Lennox was always writing in great haste because she needed the money urgently. She could usefully have employed the help of an editor for advice on how to tighten up the plot. But her portrait of Euphemia as an unhappy wife is not a monotonous complaint about the plight of women in a world dominated by difficult husbands. Lennox is far too clever a writer to be so predictable. She creates a terrible, and terrifying, woman in the character of Lady Jackson who bewitches Maria's wealthy guardian and seeks to marry him: 'She is a perfect homicide. There was no end to the murders of her eyes . . .' She also ruefully acknowledges the perils lying in wait for older women in her portrait of the merry widow, Mrs Mountfort:

> I have been young and handsome; I forget that I am no longer so; I have lost the power of pleasing, but the inordinate desire of it remains. I am surprised to find myself practising those coquet airs, which are excusable in youth and beauty, but which are ridiculous in one of my age; I blush at my folly one minute, and the next, dragged on by habit, I fall into it again. Among the young and gay, I am overlooked, and I am ready to die with vexation.

Her writing here is so vivacious, so strong it could well be Lennox confessing her own vexation. It had been fifteen years since she had published anything, and it was much longer since her work had been appreciated, and longer still since she had made any real money from it.

On 17 June 1777 she wrote a self-mocking letter to Johnson from her 'cottage' on Nottingham Street, just off Marylebone Lane, perhaps because she had heard tales of Elizabeth Carter's prowess as a pudding-maker:

> Sir, You cannot imagine the pleasure it gave me to hear you say you would come and eat apple dumplings of my making. You may be sure I will hold you to your promise, but alas! apples will not be ripe this long time, and I am impatient for your company. Suppose you were to try my hand at a gooseberry tart—if I might venture to say it without being thought vain, I could tell you that my tarts have been admired.

Even the witty, spirited Charlotte Lennox felt obliged at times to show off her domestic accomplishments rather than her intellectual gifts.

Lennox was writing at a time when women's achievements in the literary world were being celebrated by artists like Richard Samuel and by publishers, too, cashing in on the burgeoning audience of women readers, wives of the new trading and shopkeeping classes. But Lennox's comet had been too bright for some. When in 1753 she dared to criticise Shakespeare in her two volumes of *Shakespear Illustrated; or the Novels and Histories, on which the Plays of Shakespear are founded, Collected and Translated from the Original Authors. With Critical Remarks*, the actor David Garrick (who later organised the Shakespeare Jubilee in 1769) was not amused. You have 'betray'd a greater desire of Exposing his Errors than of *illustrating* his Beauties,' he writes to her. 'There appeared to me a kind of severe Levity & Ridicule.'

Johnson had encouraged Lennox to embark on this project, after the success of *The Female Quixote*. He was planning to produce his own commentaries on the plays, but was too tied up with the *Dictionary* to begin work on them and knew he would not be able to do so for several years. He advised Lennox instead to take advantage of the new wave of enthusiasm for the playwright, which had been generated by Garrick's productions of the plays and especially by his galvanising performances as Richard III, Hamlet and Macbeth. Johnson also suggested the form her book should take:

collecting the original stories on which Shakespeare had based his plays and providing 'critical remarks' on his use of them.

Lennox proved herself equal to the task, confident enough to criticise the Bard and to suggest improvements in the dramatic content of his plays. She wonders, for example, why Shakespeare used such a feeble story as his inspiration for *The Winter's Tale,* and then asserts boldly that his alterations are absurd. We cannot but laugh at the Bear, which rushes out of the woods to devour the trusty servant Antigonus, creating the stage direction that is so unbelievably difficult to pull off without provoking spontaneous laughter: 'Exit. Pursued by a Bear.' Lennox also argues that the 'Rise and Progress' of Leontes's jealousy is too sudden to be believable: 'The Legerdemain, who shews you a Tree that buds Blossoms and bears ripe Fruit in the space of five Minutes, does not put so great a Cheat on the Senses, as Shakespear does on the Understanding.'

Hamlet, too, is deconstructed by Lennox in ways that are not always complimentary to Shakespeare. The hero's feigned madness, she says, is an unnecessary complication: 'But since the King's conscious Guilt and Terror might reasonably have created a Distrust of Hamlet, and that Distrust, and a Desire of Security induced him to seek his Death, what need had Shakespeare to make his Hero's Sense and Discretion appear doubtful, by shewing him feigning a Madness, destructive to his Safety, and which he himself knows to be so, and yet persists in.'

Lennox dared to assert that Shakespeare's psychological development of character does not always work. She also criticised him on moral grounds, disapproving of the ambiguous ending to *Measure for Measure.* How much better it would be, she suggests, if Isabella entered a convent while her persecutor Angelo stabbed himself in despair, having at last understood Isabella's true value? The rest, she says, 'is all Episode, made up of the extravagant Behaviour of a wild Rake, the Blunders of a drunken Clown, and the Absurdities of an ignorant Constable'.

Her title, *Shakespear Illustrated,* suggests a dusty academic tome, or perhaps a picture book for children. On the contrary, it is a revelation, proving that Shakespeare had drawn on earlier stories for his plots. Lennox's irrepressible irreverence, her ability to identify weaknesses in the dramatic arc of Shakespeare's plays, should have ensured her fame long after her death. But, like so many of the women writers of the period, Lennox's reputation was singed, not burnished, by success.

Johnson was impressed by the way she had taken up his idea for a book on Shakespeare and had produced such an original work, and he tried to persuade her to do more, inciting her to attack Milton:

Madam

I hope you take great care to observe the Doctor's prescriptions, and take your physick regularly, for I shall soon come to enquire. I should be sorry to lose Criticism in her bloom. Your remarks are I think all very judicious, clearly expressed, and incontrovertibly certain. When Shakespeare is demolished your wings will be <u>full summed</u> and I will fly you at Milton; for you are a bird of Prey, but the Bird of Jupiter.

I am, Madam, Your most obedient Servant

Sam Johnson.

He enjoyed inciting Lennox to tilt at windmills, knowing full well that she needed very little encouragement to do so.

Charlotte's impulsive character led her into all sorts of practical tangles. She was the kind of person who was never out of trouble. But rather than tiring of her endless difficulties and requests for help, Johnson always stood by her, even when she ended up in court. On 23 September 1778 she was called to appear before Sir John Hawkins (a magistrate as well as a writer) at the Quarter Sessions in Hick's Hall in Clerkenwell. Ann Brown had accused her of 'assaulting and striking her and pulling her about against the peace'. Also accused were Charlotte's daughter, Harriet Holles, and another woman, Hannah Davis, who was perhaps their maidservant.

Charlotte, Harriet and Hannah pleaded not guilty and were bailed out by a Robert Armitage, Esquire, of Parson's Yard, Kensington, and Edmund Allen 'of Bolt Court, Fleet Street', a printer and friend to Johnson. It seems very likely that Johnson arranged for Allen to help them out.

Hawkins's daughter, Laetitia Matilda, happened to be at Hick's Hall on the day of Charlotte's appearance and took great delight in recording the incident in her *Memoirs*. She claims that Charlotte was brought to court by 'a low female servant' who had 'endeavoured to obtain a compensation for ill words and hard blows received from her mistress'. Perhaps she did not know that in the same sessions roll Ann Brown is accused by Harriet Holles Lennox of 'assaulting and beating her', also on 23 September 1778. Who then struck the first blow?

Quite what happened and who was to blame is not clear, but the incident revealed just how rackety, distressed and unconventional Lennox's life had become, and in Laetitia Matilda's catty reaction we discover how few friends Lennox had in literary circles. In 1769, when she attempted to stage a new play, *The Sister* (adapted from her third novel, *Henrietta*), at the Covent Garden Theatre, the production was booed off the stage by a professional band of hecklers employed by an anonymous rival (probably the curmudgeonly playwright Richard Cumberland, who was always attacking women writers in print). Lennox was never without her enemies, whether it be other women shocked by her lack of respect for the conventions, or other writers jealous of her success.

The Sister was withdrawn by Lennox and never again performed, although she was at the time desperate for money. Undaunted, she had another go at writing for the stage. Garrick asked her to update an old comedy by Ben Jonson, *Eastward Hoe*, for his Drury Lane Theatre. *Old City Manners* was staged on 9 November 1775 and this time suffered no heckling. It ran for several nights and the full text was published later that month, but Lennox made little money from it. Thereafter she appeared to have lost her creative drive, and she published nothing more until *Euphemia*.

By then, Johnson had died and Charlotte had lost her most steadfast supporter and adviser. In one of his last letters to her he tells her:

> When friends fall out the first thing to be considered is how to fall in again, and he is best that makes the first advances, I have designed to come to you ever since half an hour after you ran from me but I knew not whither. I did not when I began intend to say more [than] the first sentence, nor when I left off, to have a final quarrel. Pray, my dear, think no more of it, but come to me or let me know when I can come to you, for the thought of driving you away will be very painful to, Dearest Partlet, Your most obedient &c Sam. Johnson.

No matter how demanding and unreasonable her behaviour, Johnson never gave up on Lennox. 'Dearest Partlet' (or 'poulet', chicken) was a term of affection, not condescension. He wished to protect and cheer her. In a postscript, he tells her that he has not read her letter, 'nor will read it, till I know whether it is peevish or no'. He will not fall out with her.

In return Lennox paid Johnson the ultimate compliment of keeping private her friendship with him. In this, she showed her true nature and her strength of character. After his death in December 1784, she was always short of money and was suffering the distress of her daughter's death, from unknown causes, and her son's emigration to America in search of work and the chance to make money. She never saw him again. Alexander, her husband, was no longer living with her. We do not even know his date of death, although scholars have suggested that he died in Scotland in 1797.

Charlotte could well have made much-needed money by publishing her recollections of her friendship with Johnson. She had known him long before he had become such an important figure and could have written an insightful and entertaining account of him. But she refrained, too respectful of his memory, their friendship, and what he had done for her.

From that time, though, her life descended into even greater chaos. Her letters reveal a peripatetic existence, moving constantly between lodgings. Between 1751 and 1802 she is thought to have lived at twenty different addresses, dotted around the capital from 'the first House on the right hand on Camberwell Green with a Basket' to Great Tower Hill, on the corner of Muscovy Court, and the house in Queen Square, just off St James's, which she shared, briefly, with Frances Reynolds. She also for a few years in the 1760s lived in grace-and-favour lodgings in Somerset House because of Alexander's work for the Excise. In 1792 she applied to the newly created Royal Literary Fund for financial assistance, ostensibly for money to send her son George Louis to America but in reality to stave off her own debts. When she died, on 4 January 1804, she was penniless and without family to support her in her old age. She was buried in an unmarked grave in the burial ground of Broad Chapel, Westminster, long gone but now part of Broad Sanctuary, the open area between Westminster Abbey and Middlesex Guildhall (now the Supreme Court).

Hill Boothby's fate was very different. Never financially threatened, or lacking family support, she was buried close to home in the church of St Oswald's at Ashbourne, marked by a stone that acknowledges her virtue, her talents, 'friendship's chaste flame'. With her, Johnson also shared a deep, but very different friendship. She addressed him as 'My good friend'; he told her that she was constantly in his thoughts 'at Oxford—in town' and wrote to her as his 'Dearest dear' and 'My sweet Angel'. He sent her a copy of his verse tragedy, *Irene*, to which she replied, 'Perhaps you are the only author in England, who could make a play a very acceptable present to me.' (Most plays of the time would have been too frivolous, or risqué, for Hill Boothby's sublimated tastes.) She advised him on books that he should read to 'improve' his mind; and biblical texts that would comfort his soul: 'I can only be sorry that the text in Corinthians does not prove to you what I would have it, and add to my prayers for you that it may prove it.'

While Johnson fed oysters to his cat and ate his dinners at various chop-houses in the vicinity of Gough Square, Hill Boothby entertained her friends and neighbours in the county set to dinners of turtle soup (the turtle brought up from London) and game shot on the Tissington estate. (Her nephew was Sir Brooke Boothby, painted by Joseph Wright of Derby lounging in a wood beside a brook in a portrait now in Tate Britain.) 'You have often declared you cannot be alone,' she reminded Johnson. 'And I, as often, that I could not *be* long, unless I was some hours in every day alone. I have found myself mistaken; for yet I am in being, though for some time past I have seldom had one half hour in a day to myself; and I have learned this profitable lesson, that resignation is better than indulgence; and, time is too precious a thing for me to have at my own disposal.'

He recommended a remedy for indigestion and 'lubricity of the bowels': 'Take an ounce of dried orange-peel finely powdered, divide it into scruples, and take one scruple at a time in any manner; the best way is perhaps to drink it in a glass of hot red port, or to eat it first, and drink the wine after it. If you mix cinnamon or nutmeg with the powder, it were not worse; but it will be more bulky, and so more troublesome.'

Johnson took a great interest in medicinal remedies:

This is a medicine not disgusting, not costly, easily tried, and if not found useful, easily left off. I would not have you offer it to the Doctor as mine. Physicians do not love intruders; yet do not take it without his leave. But do not be put off, for it is in my opinion very likely to help you, and not likely to do you harm; do not take too much in haste; a scruple once in three hours, or about five scruples a day, will be sufficient to begin; or less, if you find any aversion. I think using sugar with it might be bad; if syrup, use cold syrup of quinces, but even that I do not like. I should think better of conserve of sloes . . .

He had no idea, though, of the severity of Hill Boothby's illness until December 1755 when she was unable to travel from Tissington to London.

He had been very ill himself, exhausted by his efforts to finish the *Dictionary*, and there had been gossip in the newspapers that he was close to death. He wrote to her on 30 December:

> Dear Madam. It is again midnight, and I am again alone. With what meditation shall I amuse this waste hour of darkness and vacuity? If I turn my thoughts upon myself, what do I perceive, but a poor help-less being, reduced by a blast of wind to weakness and misery? . . . This illness, in which I have suffered something, and feared much more, has depressed my confidence and elation; and made me consider all that I have promised myself, as less certain to be attained or enjoyed. I have endeavoured to form resolutions of a better life; but I form them weakly . . . Consider, my dearest, your prayers for me, that no good resolution may be in vain. You think, I believe, better of me than I deserve. I hope to be, in time, what I wish to be, and what I have hitherto satisfied myself too readily with only wishing . . . There has gone about a report that I died to-day; which I mention lest you should hear it and be alarmed. You see that I think my death may alarm you; which, for me, is to think very highly of earthly friendship. I believe it arose from the death of one of my neighbours. You know Des Cartes's argument, 'I think, therefore I am.' It is as good a conse-quence, 'I write, therefore I love Miss Boothby,' but that I hope our friendship may be of far longer duration than life. I am dearest Madam, with sincere affection, your, etc.

Johnson uses 'I' twenty-one times in this excerpt alone, but it was not he who was in such mortal danger. Hill Boothby, though, *was* close to death and too weak to write a reply. We do not know what she made of Johnson's morose epistle. A fortnight later, on 16 January 1756, she died, aged forty-seven.

Johnson was for a time so 'distracted with grief' that his friends feared for his sanity. Did he ever intend to marry her, as his own triumph of hope over experience? Would he not soon have tired of her moralising strictures? In *The Spiritual Quixote*, Miss Sainthill is depicted as knowing the Bible well enough to quote from it in everyday conversation. '"Well prayed! Miss Sainthill," cries the Colonel. "Why Lady Forrester has no occasion for a Chaplain; you quote Chapter and Verse as well as the best Divine in Christendom."'

Johnson once accused Hill Boothby of being 'too abstracted from common life', believing that her religious focus, her high-flying spirituality, was a luxury possible only for those with money enough never to be brought low by indigence and chaotic cash-flow problems. His friend Charlotte Lennox, on the contrary, could never afford to be 'abstracted' from life. Yet both women played a valuable part in Johnson's life. While Hill Boothby gave him Christian solace and intellectual friendship when he most needed it after Tetty's death, Lennox's friendship allowed him to adopt a nurturing, guiding, almost fatherly role, so that she in turn had the opportunity to flex her innate skills as a writer, her talent for raillery.

6

A Stifled Sigh

'How many times has this great, this formidable Doctor Johnson kissed my hand, ay & my foot too upon his knees!' Hester Thrale confided to her diary in December 1779. She did not meet Johnson until he was fifty-five, while she was just twenty-three, married and with a young child. But they soon became friends, so close that rumours began circulating there was something more between them than mere friendship. In 1772 the *London Packet* reported that Johnson, codenamed 'a great folio', was being sued by a certain brewer for making love to his wife. Other gossip columnists made mischief with stories about 'Dr Samuel Positive' and the 'great sow of Streatham', picking up a reference to the country estate, about eight miles south of the capital, where Johnson spent several days each week entertained by the Thrales and their children.

Hester Thrale only met Johnson after he had become the celebrated writer, the successful scholar, admired for his *Dictionary* and loved for his *Rambler* and *Idler* essays. His physical proportions, too, had altered greatly. He was no longer the gangly young man whom Tetty knew, but the imposing figure of the portraits, large, solid and filled with confidence. Johnson was tall, and especially when standing next to Hester who was just four foot seven. In her diary Hester wrote up a precise description: 'His Height was five Foot eleven without Shoes, his Neck short, his Bones large & his Shoulders broad.'

She also attempted in her diary an accurate, impartial description of his unprepossessing and often intimidating character, which surely she must have intended for others to read after her death. 'His leg & Foot' were 'eminently handsome, his hand handsome too', she writes, 'in spite of Dirt, & of such Deformity as perpetual picking his Fingers necessarily produced'. His countenance, his expression, she says, was 'rugged', but she adds, with sharp insight, 'tho' many People pretended to see a benignity of Expression when he was in Good humour'. His eyes were light grey in colour (although sometimes Hester refers to them as light blue) and were 'so wild, so piercing and at Times so fierce; that Fear was I believe the first Emotion in the hearts of all his Beholders'.

Their first meeting was not auspicious. On the second Thursday in January 1765, Johnson was brought by his friend, the playwright Arthur Murphy, to be entertained by the Thrales at their town house attached to the family brewery in Borough, south of London Bridge. Hester regarded her new guest as rather a coup; the man who created the *Dictionary* crossing the river to the insalubrious south bank to have dinner at an address in Dead Man's Place. But Johnson misbehaved, winding up another guest whom Hester had invited specially on his behalf. James Woodhouse was a poet whose latest collection had just created a bit of a sensation. Johnson said nothing complimentary about his poems but told him he should read Addison, 'if you mean either to be a good writer, or what is more worth, an honest man'.

Hester was hoping to create for herself a literary salon to equal that of the prestigious Elizabeth Montagu. She wanted Johnson to know that her circle of acquaintance included the latest literary star. Impressed herself, she was too young and too inexperienced a hostess to perceive Johnson's disdain for such social manoeuvring. All that she could later recall of that first meeting was her embarrassment as she witnessed one of her guests being so rudely put down by another. Yet, undaunted, she and Henry invited Johnson back the following Thursday, and then again the next Thursday and so on throughout the winter and into the spring, determined that through Johnson they would access the most elevated *and* literary social circle in London.

No expense was spared in the laying out of meats, pies, puddings and tarts to tempt Johnson to come again. Other guests were invited to stimulate the conversation, which veered wildly from the politics of Wilkes to the price of hops at the Borough market. The patience of the Thrales paid off and when in August they decamped to Brighthelmston (as Brighton was then called), Johnson was so disappointed to lose his weekly visit to the Borough that he wrote to Hester, 'When business is done what remains but pleasure? and where should pleasure be sought but under Mrs Thrale's influence?'

Boswell suggests in his *Life of Johnson* that 'a false notion has prevailed that Mr Thrale was inferior, and in some degree insignificant, compared with Mrs Thrale'. He quotes Johnson as having once said, 'It is a great mistake to suppose that she is above him in literary attainments. She is more flippant; but he [i.e. Henry Thrale] has ten times more learning: he is a regular scholar; but her learning is that of a schoolboy in one of the lower forms.' Boswell disliked Hester, jealous of her intimacy with Johnson, her access to his most confidential conversation. He wanted to discredit their friendship. Hester had received no formal schooling, but she prided herself on her wit – in the eighteenth-century sense: 'The powers of the mind; the mental faculties; the intellects'. Her husband had the advantage of an Oxford degree, but she had been taught by private tutors who themselves had degrees from Oxford. She knew Latin, although not Greek, but also French, Italian and Spanish. She wrote poetry and corresponded with scholars such as Dr Oliver of Bath (the physician after whom the famously dry biscuits were named), discussing the latest discoveries in astronomy, metaphysics and medicine.

When Johnson suggested to Hester that she should begin a journal in 1776, to help her recover from the sudden death of her son Harry, she took to the task with relish, filling page after page with her own poems and translations, with nature notes and weather reports, a dense thicket of facts and figures, thoughts and observations. In these leather-bound volumes of neatly handwritten pages, fair copies rather than rapid drafts, she preserved not just the bare bones of her life story but also the fleeting passage of thoughts through her mind. She never published them, nor did her descendants, but she must somehow have ensured their survival, and in the 1930s an American scholar, Katharine C. Balderston, laboriously transcribed and edited them. The publication of the two-volume *Thraliana* provided new insights into Hester Thrale's personality: always curious, sometimes shockingly insightful, at others wilfully blind to the ebb and flow of human feeling.

Her conversation, if it in any way resembled what she wrote in her diaries, must have constantly flitted from subject to subject, teasing, provoking, entertaining. She was brilliant in her way, and from the *Thraliana* it is easy to see how and why she fascinated Johnson:

Johnson among the ladies:
detail from Thomas Rowlandson's *Madame Weischel Singing at Vauxhall Gardens* (1784)

The 'most authentick witness' of Johnson's character:
Tetty Johnson

'A pattern for sitters':
Johnson in 1775, possibly by Frances Reynolds

Battling for the right to knowledge:
Elizabeth Carter as Minerva (c. 1735–41), by John Fayram

Greek scholar and baker of exceedingly fine puddings:
Elizabeth Carter in middle age (c. 1765), by her friend Katharine Read

'He see-sawed at such a violent rate as to excite the curiosity of
some people at a distance to come and see':
a sketch believed to be of Dr Johnson, attributed to Paul Sandby

Frontispiece to *The Lady's Museum* (1760),
the magazine edited by Charlotte Lennox

The Nine Living Muses of Great Britain (1778), by Richard Samuel: Elizabeth Carter with Anna Laetitia Barbauld, standing behind Angelica Kauffmann who is seated at her easel. Elizabeth Linley is centre-stage, with Charlotte Lennox on the right holding a scroll and Hannah More bearing the cup of knowledge. Elizabeth Montagu is seated in the middle, Elizabeth Griffith plays the lute and Catherine Macaulay, the historian, deciphers a writing tablet

'I am a good writer too':
Hester Thrale in 1773, by Richard Cosway

At first the proud mother:
Hester Thrale with her daughter 'Queeney'
in 1781, by Sir Joshua Reynolds

The female wit at work:
Hannah More (1780), by Frances Reynolds

Her love of painting 'clashed with the honourable province of family duties':
Frances Reynolds's self-portrait, with her sister Mary

'A grimly ghost':
Johnson in 1783, probably by Frances Reynolds

'The doctor [Johnson] treated her with particular kindness':
Mary Wollstonecraft (1790–91), by John Opie

The good times are over:
Thomas Rowlandson's *Breaking Up of the Blue Stocking Club* (c. 1815)

On the sixteen of April 1771 it froze exceedingly hard, there was Ice in all the Channels and no appearance of Spring even in the neighbourhood of London . . .

When Fordyce broke in the Year 1772, and so many people were ruined by his and many other Bankruptcies—the great Noise did not begin till a Month or more after the Mischief was done, Oh says I this is only the Thunder after the Lightning.— . . .

It is observable that even Brutes cannot be happy in Solitude. When a Cat is alone she never purs.

Says Johnson to me I have been thinking this Morning what Creature you most resemble & 'tis the Rattle Snake; I am sure you have its *Attractions*, I think you have its *Venom* too, and all the World knows you have its *Rattle*.

On the 2d of April 1774, the Trees are bursting out—not into Bloom but into Leaf, one cannot bear a fire in the Room and London is as disagreeable from Heat & Dust as in July.—

The 2d of April 1775 was a Day remarkably warm & fine; The Trees are all in Bloom, some in Leaf, & Summer seems already far advanced . . .

21st of April 1775 I returned *home* from Southwark to Streatham to lye in: I think it something remarkable that I should fix this day six months ago & be able to keep it so exactly. The Cuckoo sung all the way home . . .

The largest Ivy I ever saw was at Caernarvon Castle—it measured as thick in Timber as Mr Johnson's Thigh.

She takes us from the weather to her observations on cat behaviour via Johnson's description of her as a rattlesnake in just couple of pages.

Hester's intention in writing up the intimate moments and casual thoughts of daily life was also to record her conversations with Johnson, which she soon began to understand would be of immense interest to posterity. 'All my Friends reproach me with neglecting to write down such Things as drop from him almost perpetually, and often say how much I shall some Time regret that I have not done it with diligence ever since the commencement of our Acquaintance,' she wrote at the beginning of her second manuscript volume, on 18 September 1777, Johnson's birthday (using the new post-1752 calendar). Her *Thraliana*, though, is not a catalogue of Johnson's conversations; she left that task to Boswell: 'Mr Boswell however is the Man for a Johnsoniana: he really knows ten Times more Anecdotes of his Life than I do who see so much more of him.' Hester instead wanted to preserve Johnson unbound; the man she knew at leisure amid the hubbub of family life, and indulging his passions for chemistry, sport and wordplay.

'Mr Johnson & I were distilling some Pot herbs one Day for Amuzement,' she wrote in April 1778, before vividly describing their discoveries:

> in a Glass Retort over a lamp & we observed all the Bubbles to be hexagonal. a Thing we could give no account of. Mr Johnson however took occasion from that circumstance to tell me that a Hexagon is that form which contains most Space excepting the Circle, which however not admitting of Coalescence, loses more by being added to another Circle, than it gains by the Superiority of Shape. a Hexagon is therefore on the whole the most capacious form. I have since this was told me, reflected that the Cells of Honeycomb are always hexagonal; & it comes in my Head that Queen Dido when she cut her Bucks hide to build Carthage, set the Slips hexagonally. I'm sure that I have read that She did so.

From chemistry experiments she moved sideways to the Classics via biology and physics. Hester had neither the disciplined intelligence of Elizabeth Carter nor the professional flair of Charlotte Lennox. She would never be celebrated as one of the *Nine Living Muses*. But for almost twenty years she found within herself imagination enough to entertain the restless intellect of one of the great minds of the eighteenth century. When apart, they corresponded frequently, seeking to outdo each other.

'You talk of writing and writing as if you had all the writing to yourself,' Johnson teases her in a letter from Lichfield dated 27 October 1777. 'If our Correspondence were printed I am sure Posterity, for Posterity is always the author's favourite, would say that I am a good writer too.' Johnson suggests that in a man's letter,

> his soul lies naked, his letters are only the mirrour of his breast, whatever passes within him is shown undisguised in its natural process . . .
> Is not my soul laid open in these veracious pages? do not you see me reduced to my first principles? This is the pleasure of corresponding

with a friend, where doubt and distrust have no place, and everything is said as it is thought.

In his published *Life of Pope* Johnson writes that letters are not always easy to decode, nor are they always a true indicator of the writer's character. Pope's letters suggest that he was a happy-natured man, constant and tender with his friends. Yet in print he could be vicious, humiliating his fellow writers with an intent to destroy their reputations. When we write to our friends, we know too well their prejudices and partialities and so we frame our epistles in such a way as to please them, 'if not by favouring them, by forbearing to oppose them'. Beware, then, of reading letters too literally; they are often 'a calm and deliberate performance in the cool of leisure, in the stillness of solitude, and surely no man sits down to depreciate by design his own character'. They are not always a true reflection of events, or of the correspondent.

Yet from Johnson's letters to Hester and her children and especially to her eldest daughter Hester Maria (also known as 'Queeney') another side of his character does emerge, almost by accident. With the Thrale family, he writes often about the small details of daily life, practical and light-hearted. 'Well, but seriously, I think I shall be glad to see you in your own hair,' he tells Hester on 10 November 1777, after discovering that she has decided no longer to wear a wig. 'But do not take too much time in combing, and twisting, and papering, and unpapering, and curling, and frizzing, and powdering, and getting out the powder, with all the other operations required in the cultivation of a head of hair . . .'

Johnson for a while experienced 'Minds naturally in unison' in his friendship with Hester and Henry Thrale. All three were astute enough to gloss over their essential differences of character, each of them understanding what they could gain from the other. Johnson reminded Hester that her husband 'was a man take him for all in all, you ne'er will look upon his like', adding, 'but you never mind him nor me, till time forces conviction into your steely bosom'. Hester retorted, with equal perspicacity, 'Learn of me to be happy,— *You know* the reasons I have to be otherwise;—yet I don't grumble—do I?' Henry meanwhile knew that he had transformed himself from a rich but socially risible brewer's son into the genial host around whose table sat some of the best minds in London.

At Streatham Park, he created a library, giving Johnson £100 to spend on any books he wanted to add to the shelves (with volumes costing anything from two shillings to two guineas). He then commissioned Sir Joshua Reynolds to paint fourteen portraits of all his friends, enough to fill a gallery. The 'Streatham Worthies', as they came to be known, included a colourful double portrait of Hester with her eldest daughter Queeney. Hester sits majestically on a stiff couch, her bright-eyed, quizzical daughter by her side. The portrait of Johnson shows the writer in greatcoat, waistcoat and a curly wig, his left eyebrow raised quizzically, while his left hand clutches one of the large buttons on his waistcoat. He's a striking presence, larger than life. Reynolds transfigured the man whom Hester and Henry sat up with night after night, wearily waiting for him to be willing at last to leave the comfort of the drawing room for the empty darkness of his bedchamber. They knew different; they had glimpsed Johnson's 'naked soul'.

In early 1766, perhaps through overwork on his edition of the plays of Shakespeare, Johnson descended into a period of mental anguish so severe that he was unable to leave the house, not even for his regular dinners with the Thrales. One day they called on him at his rooms in Johnson's Court, concerned they had seen nothing of him for several weeks. They found him sitting curled up on the stairs calling on God to save him from the demons that were threatening to take over his mind.

'I felt excessively affected with grief,' Hester later recalled. Her husband was so shocked that he 'involuntarily lifted up one hand to shut Johnson's mouth, from provocation at hearing a man so wildly proclaim what he could at last persuade no one to believe; and what, if true, would have been so very unfit to reveal'.

With some difficulty, Henry Thrale persuaded Johnson to move down the stairs and helped him out of the front door into his carriage. He then ordered his coachman to take them straight to Streatham Park where Johnson remained for several months, luxuriating in the unaccustomed comfort of a well-furnished house, an amply stocked larder, and the peaceful, balmy air of the estate. The Thrales became to him as family, an arrangement that eased his mind from care and gave Hester the burden of entertaining a not-always-easy house-guest.

Hester, who was born on 16 January 1741, had married young, and not happily. Her snobbish mother claimed descent from Katherine Beraine, cousin to Elizabeth I, and assumed the airs of an aristocrat, while her feckless father,

John Salusbury, squandered what little money he inherited in gallivanting about the Continent on his Grand Tour. He attempted to recover his fortunes by sailing to Nova Scotia in 1749 as an official under Lord Cornwallis, the governor, but he returned four years later even more penniless than before. 'You know I am but a bad manager,' he wrote to his long-suffering wife, 'besides that I have been Cheated, downright Cheated of forty pounds . . .'

Salusbury had been brought up as a 'gentleman' and with no training in business and no aptitude for trade he was unfitted to take advantage of the commercial opportunities presented by life in the New World. His only child, Hester, thought of herself as genteel, yet as an adult she inherited not enough financial means to maintain that gentility. She needed to marry well to preserve her social status, yet she had been indulged as a child and educated to think for herself. This was not the best training for an adult life of neces-sary compromises, yet Hester rose above her difficult situation, never complaining that her marriage was of convenience rather than passion, but instead looking for compensations.

Hester was not particularly attractive, and shorter than average; a 'brown Woman', she said of herself, rather than fair, with chestnut hair and eyes that were light grey in colour. 'Strength' and not 'Delicacy', she remarked, was her 'original Characteristick', with large hands, her 'Salusbury fists' as she called them, and a long, sharp nose. 'By keeping genteel Company however, and looking much at Paintings, learning to Dance almost inces-santly, and chusing Foreign Models, not English Misses as patterns of Imitation; some Grace has been acquired,' she wrote when in middle age.

No portraits of her as a young woman have survived, although it is now thought that as a sixteen-year-old she sat as a model for Hogarth when he painted *The Lady's Last Stake*. The 'Lady' of the title hesitates between losing her honour to the gambling rake with whom she is closeted and having to repay the money she has lost to him at picquet. She certainly does have the look of Hester, the bright, controlling eyes and distinctive nose, but she is also a coquet, posing suggestively beside the fire as her vanquisher in the scarlet uniform of a cavalry officer begs for an answer. It's a strange subject for a genteel young lady in need of a rich husband to provide her missing dowry.

'Mrs Thrale seems to have a sweetness of Disposition that equals All her other excellencies . . . But I *fear* to say all I think at present of Mrs Thrale,— lest some *flaws* should appear by & by, that may make me think differently . . .' wrote the novelist Frances Burney shortly after her first meeting with

139

the Thrales. Her description is deliciously nuanced, as if she felt duty-bound to admire Hester but was unsure whether she could ever love her as a friend:

> She has *Talents* to create admiration,—*Good humour* to excite Love, *Understanding* to give Entertainment,—& a *Heart*, which like my dear Father's, seems already fitted for another World! My own knowledge of her, indeed, is very little for such a Character—but all I have *heard*, & all I *see*, so well agree, that I *won't* prepare myself for a future disappointment.

Burney's wariness of that apparent 'sweetness of Disposition' was intuitively correct. Hester had learnt to play her role in polite society, first as a dutiful daughter of difficult parents and then as the wife of the rich but not well-born Henry Thrale.

She was introduced to Henry by her uncle, Sir Thomas Salusbury, while staying at his country estate in Offley, Hertfordshire. She was just twenty, briskly intelligent and full of the self-confidence of an only child who had been brought up to think of herself as advantaged and well-born. Her parents, though, had never been able to afford a London residence, and Hester was brought up far from the capital at Bach-y-Graig, close to St Asaph in north Wales. They only travelled up to Hertfordshire because from there it was easier to rent a house in London for the Season, and to launch Hester's campaign to find a husband. Henry, in contrast, was a worldly, sophisticated man of thirty-four, who after his education at Oxford University had travelled on the Continent and lived the life of a gentleman about town while waiting to inherit his father's brewing business. He was, as Hester's mother well knew, one of the most eligible bachelors in London, but also a man with a reputation.

'My Mother soon said *this* was the Man for me to *marry*,' reflected Hester when she looked back on her early life. 'The only man She had ever said so of.' Her uncle agreed, telling Hester that Henry 'was a *real Sportsman*, and such sort of Stuff'. Hester thought otherwise:

> but I soon saw clearly that they were both mad for the Match, which I concluded my Father would never endure to hear of, both on account of [Thrale's] mean birth, and of his being *their* Friend first, before *he* saw *him*; which was alone sufficient to make him take a Dislike to anybody.

There is a surprising *froideur* in the way Hester writes about her father's childish resentments and about the man who would become her husband of seventeen years. 'My Friend Dr Collier [her tutor] from whom I concealed nothing, seemed likewise rather to dislike the Business, & I apprehended nothing but Mischief could come of their unlucky Partiality.' But what of her own 'partiality'?

In June 1777 she attempted to write a description of her husband in her journal, 'not because I am in good or ill Humour with him or he with me, for we are not capricious People, but have I believe the same Opinion of each other at all Places and Times'. She tells us, explicitly, chillingly so:

> Mr Thrale's Person is manly, his Countenance agreeable, his Eyes steady and of the deepest Blue; his Look neither soft nor severe, neither sprightly nor gloomy, but thoughtful and Intelligent: his Address is neither caressive nor repulsive, but unaffectedly civil and decorous; and his Manner more completely free from every kind of Trick or Particularity than I ever saw any person's—he is a Man wholly as I think out of the Power of Mimickry.

Hester learnt not to expect too much from Henry, and to be grateful for what she perceived to be his good (or at least not too offensive) qualities. She appreciated his 'Sobriety' and that the 'Decency of his Conversation being wholly free from all Oaths Ribaldry and Profaneness make him a Man exceedingly comfortable to live with, while the easiness of his Temper and slowness to take offence add greatly to his Value as a domestic Man'. But she concluded, 'Yet I think his Servants do not much love him, and I am not sure that his Children feel much Affection for him . . .'

Hester was shrewd. She learnt to live with what she could not avoid.

Her marriage to Henry Thrale was precipitated by extreme emotions – not her own, but rather those of her unruly parents and their relatives. As she had so cleverly predicted, her father was furious when he discovered that his wife and his brother, Sir Thomas, had been matchmaking without his approval. Meanwhile Sir Thomas was himself courting a wealthy widow and threatening to marry her. This was a damaging blow to Hester's marriage prospects because Sir Thomas had previously willed his Offley estate to her. If he did marry the widow, and she should by chance give birth to a son, then Hester would be disinherited. She could hope for nothing from her impecunious father. Who, now, would be prepared to marry the dowry-less Hester?

One afternoon in mid-December 1762 Hester had a terrible argument with her father, who accused her of carrying on a clandestine affair with Henry. She was doubly hurt and enraged because she had only encouraged Henry's visits to please her uncle and her mother. John Salusbury's anger was not just fuelled by his own guilt that he could not provide properly for his daughter. He was uneasy. He knew that gossip linked Henry Thrale's name with a number of society ladies and that Henry was nicknamed the 'Southwark Macaroni' because of his philandering habits. He was concerned his daughter's virtue would be thrown away on such a man, and he refused to sanction his wife's choice of husband for Hester.

The row, which continued until three in the morning, was so intense that Hester fell into a faint. Her fate was being decided by others; what else could she do? Next morning her father set off early from their rented house in Soho for Offley Park to talk sense into his brother. But before he had even gone as far as the Tyburn Gate, he 'dropped down dead – of an Apoplexy'. Hester and her mother were left destitute (or rather without the means to sustain the life of genteel indolence to which they had grown accustomed).

To his credit, Henry continued to visit Hester and her mother in Soho in spite of their changed fortunes. 'Our Courtship,' says Hester, '(if such it might be called), was always carried on under the Eye of my Mother, whose Project it originally was: & this so completely, that except for *one* five minutes only by mere Accident, I never had a Tête a Tête with my Husband in my whole Life till quite the Evening of the Wedding Day.' As well as never having been alone with Henry before her marriage to him, she had never been apart from her mother for longer than twelve hours.

The marriage settlement, which was required to calculate how much Sir Thomas was prepared to contribute to Hester Thrale's dowry and how this would then be entailed to safeguard her future if Henry Thrale should die before her, took several months to be agreed. Meanwhile Hester made a last-ditch attempt to assert a degree of self-reliance by publishing her first poem, 'Imagination's Search after Happiness', in the *St James's Chronicle* on 10 September 1763. (She would not publish anything more until 1786, after Henry's death.) A month later, on 11 October, she was married to Henry in St Anne's Church in Soho, without fuss or ceremony, attended only by her mother and uncle.

From the church, Henry whisked Hester away to Streatham Park. 'A little squeezed miserable Place,' she later recalled, 'with a wretched Court before it, & all those noble Elm Trees out upon the Common. Such Furniture too! I can but laugh when it crosses my Recollection.' In fact, Streatham Park was a considerable, if unfashionable, estate of about 100 acres, with a simple three-storey house, set beyond a sweeping drive. But it was too far out of town, and too plain for Hester's hopes of a grand life to be satisfied.

From the beginning Hester's role in the marriage was made clear to her by Henry. He left early each morning, taking his coach back to the brewery in Borough. (The journey, about eight miles, would have taken just over an hour.) Hester was left twiddling her thumbs in a large but inelegant house far from the city. She was not expected to make her own mark on her new home; on the contrary, Henry took charge of all the renovations. He even controlled the kitchen, choosing all the menus. Although Hester thought of herself as the Mistress of Streatham she was never truly in charge of it.

'I never offer to cross my Master's Fancy . . . unless on some truly serious Occasion,' she later wrote in her diary, 'nor do I think any Occasion serious enough to excuse Contradiction unless Virtue, Life, or Fortune are concerned. Was I to die tomorrow I could swear, I never oppos'd his Inclination three Times in the fifteen Years we have been married.'

With blazing self-disclosure, she explained what she meant:

Was I to propose a Journey Mr Thrale would refuse to let me take; or desire a Tree to be cut down, or planted, & he should—as he most undoubtedly would, give me a coarse Reply and abrupt Negative, it would make *me* miserable: to have one's own un Importance presented suddenly to one's Sight, and one's own Qualities insolently undervalued by those who do not even *pretend* to possess them.—is sufficiently mortifying.

Hester's life was circumscribed by her lack of independent means, which gave her no leverage with her husband, since she was always intensely aware that she had brought relatively little to the marriage except her wit. Her uncle Sir Thomas had married a few weeks after his niece, and an heir was produced, destroying Hester's hopes that she might inherit Offley Park.

Within a year of marriage, she became pregnant for the first time, setting her off on a fourteen-year cycle of almost continual pregnancy, during which she gave birth to twelve children; she also suffered a couple of late-term miscarriages. Of these twelve infants, only four survived into adulthood and they were all daughters; a blow to Henry who wanted a son to inherit his fortune and the family business.

A lesser spirit would have been crushed by this almost unimaginable physical and emotional ordeal. Hester, though, was always oddly matter-of-fact about it, as if she taught herself detachment as a means of self-preservation. After the death of her baby son Ralph, in July 1775, aged just twenty months, she told Johnson she would 'be thankful to God and chearful among my Friends again till new Vexations arise . . . I will not be peevish any more, for it torments nobody but myself.'

Ralph was the fifth of her children to die. Five months later, she lost another, Frances Anna, who was only seven months old. Frances was always a weakling babe, and a heavy head cold, probably caught from her wet-nurse, turned into a fatal bout of influenza. The wet-nurse, too, died shortly afterwards.

As the tragedies of these short lives mounted up, Hester's fears for her remaining children intensified. 'I must endeavour not to provoke Gods Judgments on my Family . . . if I be bereaved of my Children, I be bereaved,' she wrote in 'The Children's Book', a special diary she had begun as a record of her children's 'progress'. But such was her misfortune the record soon turned into a memorial to those who had died. Hester, though, never lingered on what might have been. Her character sought solace by constantly moving on to the next thing, busying her mind as a distraction.

Hester had an admirable, if sometimes heartless, resilience. For many of the years in which she entertained Johnson, she was nauseous and heavy-laden with pregnancy, while watching over those babies who had survived only to see them withering away in front of her: 'This is to be sure one of the great Evils Life has in it, and one had no business to prepare for a Sorrow so uncommon.' Yet she took upon herself the arduous task of keeping Johnson in spirits. Rooms were set aside for his use at the brewhouse in Southwark and in Streatham, where Henry constructed a summer house in the grounds for Johnson to use during the warmer months. (Many years later her daughter Cecilia moved it to her home in Knockholt, in Kent, from where it was transferred to the grounds of Kenwood House in north London, surviving until 1991 when it was destroyed by arsonists.) Henry arranged for the construction of a small 'furnace' or laboratory so that Johnson could conduct

144

his chemistry experiments, 'drawing essences', 'colouring liquors' and blowing those hexagonal bubbles which had reminded Hester of Queen Dido's Carthage. The experiments were soon banned by Henry after a series of terrifying explosions, which by some fluke injured none of the children who had gathered round to watch Johnson playing with test tubes and matches.

Henry sent his coach to collect Johnson from town every Monday evening and to deliver him back to his rooms on Saturdays so that Johnson could ensure his household of dependants had three good meals over the weekend. Since the death of his wife, Tetty, Johnson had gathered round him a group of penniless people who relied on his charity, among them Anna Williams, the blind poet. Also living with him was Robert Levet, an unqualified doctor to the poor on whose death Johnson wrote the most moving of elegies: 'Officious, innocent, sincere, Of ev'ry friendless name the friend . . .' Levet took no payment for his medical visits but was often paid in kind, with a drink. Levet, whom Johnson memorialises as 'Obscurely wise, and coarsely kind', would roll home drunk, too polite and understanding to refuse what had been offered him.

Johnson's household also included Mrs Desmoulins, who was so kind to Tetty in her illness (and to Johnson, too). She had been widowed and left with a young daughter and no money to support her. Later they were joined by Poll Carmichael, whom Johnson had discovered lying exhausted in the street and carried home to care for until she was recovered and able to support herself without resorting once more to prostitution. Most of these dependants stayed with Johnson until death, moving when he did from his capacious house in Gough Square (because he could no longer afford it) to rooms in Staple Inn, then Gray's Inn, and the Inner Temple, followed by Johnson's Court (named after an earlier Thomas Johnson, from the reign of Elizabeth I), and later to Bolt Court, which he rented for £40 a year from his printer Edmund Allen (who once bailed out Charlotte Lennox).

Johnson used his friendship with the Thrales, and after 1766 his weekly retreats to Streatham, as an escape from the constant bickering and bad temper within this ill-assorted household: 'Williams hates every body,' Johnson once complained to Hester. 'Levet hates Desmoulins and does not love Williams. Desmoulins hates them both. Poll loves none of them.' Most of Johnson's friends could not understand why he not only allowed such people to live with him but also provided for them. His biographer Sir John Hawkins declared that Levet especially was 'an unfit companion for a learned man'. Levet had no medical training, yet Johnson would defer to his knowledge. 'Such was Johnson's predilection for him, and fanciful estimation of his moderate abilities,' Boswell concluded in his *Life*, 'that I have heard him say he should not be satisfied, though attended by all the College of Physicians, unless he had Mr Levet with him.'

When the Thrales questioned him about life at Bolt Court, Henry (not Hester) was particularly intrigued about who organised the kitchen. Johnson replied, 'Why sir, I am afraid there is none [to manage it]; a general anarchy prevails in my kitchen.'

To which answer Henry persisted in asking, 'But how do you get your dinners drest?'

Johnson told him, 'Why Desmoulins has the chief management of the kitchen; but our roasting is not magnificent, for we have no jack.' The jack was the mechanism by which the roasting spit was turned over on the range.

Henry Thrale, who loved his food, was horrified. 'No jack? Why, how do you manage without?'

'Small joints, I believe, they manage with a string,' Johnson told him, 'and larger are done at the tavern.' Taverns had large ovens for use by the local community, at a price. 'I have some thoughts of buying a jack,' mused Johnson, 'because I think a jack is some credit to a house.'

'Well, but you'll have a spit, too?'

'No sir, no; that would be superfluous; for we shall never use it; and if a jack is seen, a spit will be presumed.'

Life at Streatham Park was an oasis, far removed from all this domestic business and ill-tempered bickering. If anyone else criticised his house-guests, though, Johnson 'would instantly set about softening the one and justifying the other, and finished commonly by telling me that I knew not how to make allowances for situations I never experienced'. Johnson would encourage Poll to be rude to the notoriously irritable Anna Williams (who, with good reason, was a crosspatch, having lost her sight after braving two bungled attempts to remove cataracts). 'At her again, Poll!' he was supposed to have told her. 'Never flinch, Poll.' Yet when Anna Williams died on 6 September 1783, Johnson wrote that he had 'lost a companion, to whom I have had recourse for domestick amusement for thirty years, and whose variety of knowledge never was exhausted'.

His household was as family to Johnson and he defended them as a parent or sibling would have done. He was always keenly aware of the divide between the privileged and those whose lives had been made difficult by circumstance (hence his loyalty to the difficult Charlotte Lennox). He flourished in the comfortable surroundings of the Thrale household but he never forgot that such luxuries were evanescent and not shared by all. He never stayed away for longer than a few days, returning to tend his tiny garden behind Bolt Court (in which he proudly grew grapes, strawberries and a fig tree), and to supply his 'family' with housekeeping money.

At Streatham, though, under the benevolent rule of Henry, administered by Hester, if Johnson desired peaches for breakfast, he was indulged with not just one but seven or eight from the hothouse at a single sitting. At dinner his favourite meats were served. 'He loves a good Dinner dearly,' Hester noted, 'eats it voraciously . . . a Leg of Pork boyl'd till it drops from the bone almost, a Veal Pye with Plumbs & Sugar, & the outside Cut of a Buttock of Beef are his favourite Dainties, though he loves made Dishes, Soups &c: sauces his Plumb Pudden with melted Butter, & pours Sauce enough into every Plate to drown all Taste of the Victuals.'

Johnson's table manners appalled many of his friends, who watched in amazement as he greedily tucked in until his appetite was satisfied without saying a word to anyone. Henry Thrale, too, was shocked by Johnson's neglect of his appearance, his personal carelessness. He (not Hester) ensured that Johnson's clothes were taken away to be washed, his shoe buckles polished and a new wig bought to replace the greasy tatters of his old one, singed around the edges where Johnson had leant too close towards the candle while struggling to read.

With the Thrales, Johnson discovered both luxury and the ability to relax, to throw off the burden of his upbringing. In the words of Fanny Burney, who like Johnson was semi-adopted by the Thrales and spent several weeks at a time at Streatham Park in 1778 and 1779, 'Dr Johnson has more *fun*, & comical humour, & Laughable & nonsense about him, than almost any body I ever saw.' Boswell was only rarely invited to Streatham Park, and he was unaware of this teasing, nonsensical, jokey Johnson. This Johnson only appears in the pages of Burney's diaries (published by her nieces after her death in 1840), and in Hester's *Thraliana*.

Both women left a vivid private record of the word games and silly rhyme-making competitions with which the company at Streatham whiled away the long, dark wintry nights until Johnson was prepared to retire to bed. They thought of colours and fashion fabrics to characterise their friends (and sometimes enemies, too). Sophy Streatfeild, with whom it was rumoured

Henry Thrale was having an affair, was brilliantly put down by Hester by being described as 'a pea Green Satten' (or satin). In this game, Burney was called 'a lilac Tabby' and Hester 'a Gold Colour'd Watered Tabby' (or heavy taffeta gown). Johnson, 'who helped this Folly forward was to be a Marone', or chestnut.

Their 'next Nonsense' was to compare all their acquaintances to flowers. Sophy Streatfeild was listed as a 'jessamine' or jasmine, with its often over-poweringly sweet scent, Burney as the 'Ranunculus' or buttercup, and Hester as 'a sprig of Myrtle—which the more it is *crushed*, the more it discloses its *Sweetness*'.

With her novelist's eye, Burney delighted in the delicate precision with which Johnson calibrated his language. They talked of colours and the 'fantastic names' given to them:

> & why the palest lilac should be called a *soupire étouffer*—& when Dr Johnson came in, Mrs Thrale applied to him,—'Why, Madam,' said he, with wonderful readiness,—'it is called a *stifled sigh*, because it is *checked in its progress*, & only half a Colour.'

That 'stifled sigh', the *soupire étouffer*, could describe the life led by Hester while she was married to Henry Thrale, a life half-lived, and unfulfilled. Not that she would have dared to acknowledge this to herself until she was left a widow, aged just forty, after Henry's traumatic death from apoplexy on 4 April 1781.

'I cannot help seeing the Danger in which Mr Thrale's Life daily stands,' Hester wrote earlier that year, before adding, strangely yet with brutal clarity: 'Tho' surely, surely, I cannot be charged with wishing his Death, whose happiness has been my constant Care for 17 years together . . .' She continued:

> In great Things have I ever failed to assist him? In little things have I ever even *tryed* to thwart him? nobody ever could say more perfectly after Queen Catherine than I can,
>
> > 'I have been to you a true & humble Wife,
> > In all Things to your Will conformable.'

never did I cross, control or fret him for a Moment that I can accuse myself. never had I a desire beyond his Will—or a Will—except about *my Trees*—beyond his actual desire.

Hester had once thwarted Henry by insisting that the fruit trees her mother had planted at Streatham should not be cut down. Even in 1790 she recalled the quarrel, noting when she visited the estate that 'My poor dear Mother's Trees, that *She said* would one Day be the ornaments of this Place, now turn out truly so.' But she rarely disputed with him, or contravened his wishes, preferring a life of even-tempered, stable, unconflicted domestic relations:

> never for an Instant, tho' I talk of Flirtation—thought the Person of any Man comparable to his own . . . never repeated a Proposal he disapproved, or made Objections to a Thing that he proposed. & *this*—which is known only to Heaven & to myself—this odd confession I mean—*that* Heaven is witness to the Truth of; & yet Mr Johnson thinks—I see he does—that I wish my Husbands death, only because I say he will die.

Hester shocked Johnson, and perhaps herself too, by her willingness to admit that her husband's illness would most probably prove to be fatal.

In June 1779 Henry had suffered a severe stroke, brought on most probably by worries about his business. He had almost lost the brewery once before in the early 1770s after attempting a foolish experiment to brew beer more cheaply without using either malt or hops. The beer failed and the brewery lost almost a year's worth of business. Then in 1778, when the stock market was superficially buoyant, Henry was tempted to begin speculating on the future price of beer. He overbrewed that year in response to the boom, but then had to sell off the excess beer at a lower price, when the boom burst, doubling his losses.

At first he appeared to have made a good recovery from the stroke, but he was left with an odd side effect, extreme gluttony, and the household thereafter lived on a knife-edge, watching helplessly as their husband, father and friend began behaving more and more erratically. Henry ignored all the advice given him by his doctors, eating and drinking to excess as if succumbing to the dance of death. In this crisis, Hester showed herself efficiently capable, preparing herself for the worst by thinking about who might best act as executors of the business and estate, 'if Mr Thrale should leave me as 'tis very likely'.

One evening in early April 1781, in the house they were renting in Grosvenor Square so that Hester could satisfy her desire for a home in the most sought-after part of the West End, Henry suffered another apoplectic fit after gorging himself on dinner. Hester, appalled by the vision of her husband, grossly overweight and strangely blank-eyed, lying on the floor and refusing to get up, could not at this point face the reality of what had happened to him. She retired to bed, abandoning her husband as he lay close to death. Johnson, though, rallied to Henry's need and sat through the night watching over his mute, insensible friend. It was Johnson who felt 'the last flutter of his pulse' and looked for the last time 'upon the face that for fifteen years had never been turned upon me but with respect or benignity'.

Hester 'ventured in once, & saw them cutting his Clothes off to bleed him', but she was too shocked to remain and was not with her husband when he died at four o'clock the following morning. The next day, 5 April, she set off early for Streatham, and from there continued on to Brighton, leaving behind Johnson, as if she were trying to escape from him and her own contorted feelings, part grief and part relief. 'There I had Time to collect my scattered Thoughts,' she confided in the private pages of her diary, 'to revise my past Life, & resolve upon a new one.'

At first, Henry's death drew Hester and Johnson closer together. Johnson was joint executor of Henry's will, along with Hester and three male representatives, taking responsibility for the brewery and the children. 'If an Angel from Heaven had told me 20 Years ago, that the Man I knew by the Name of *Dictionary Johnson* should one Day become Partner with me in a great Trade, & that we should jointly or separately sign Notes Draughts &c for 3 or 4 Thousand Pounds of a Morning, how unlikely it would have seemed ever to happen!' Hester declared. Soon, however, the altered dynamic between them created such confusions that the friendship began to falter.

Johnson could not understand why Hester looked upon the brewery as a dreadful burden and why she could not wait to escape from Southwark and all its unhappy memories. He had not suspected that she also did not like Streatham Park. He was appalled when, within three months, she had rushed through the sale of the brewery for £135,000 (about £8 million in today's money): 'I have by this Bargain purchased Peace & a stable Fortune,' she confided in her diary, adding, 'Restoration to my original Rank in Life, and a Situation undisturbed by Commercial Jargon; unpolluted by Commercial Frauds; undisgraced by Commercial Connections.' Now, she hoped, she could at last free herself from the ignominy of being nothing but a brewer's wife.

There was a coldness about Hester, behind all the spirited repartee and lively sense of fun. No sooner had Henry died than Hester made clear to all who

150

knew her that for the last twenty years she had been living a life that had not been of her own choosing. Her behaviour appeared to suggest that she regarded her friendship with Johnson as part of that burden.

By 1781, he was seventy-two, wheezy, and at the end of his writing career. His talent for intellectual argument was becoming more of a vice than a virtue, as his dislike of being worsted in argument 'even when he had taken the wrong side' became more pronounced, often tipping over into rudeness. In November 1781 he wrote to Hester from Lichfield, 'Do not neglect me, or relinquish me,' as if aware that she was thinking of breaking free from all that had gone before.

Johnson had himself more or less abandoned his visits to Streatham, finding its atmosphere too much changed without the presence of 'the Master'. He was far too astute not to have noticed the change in Hester's relationship with him. On 25 April 1782 he told her, 'Do not let Mr Piozzi nor any body else put me quite out of your head, and do not think that any body will love you like, Your &c . . .' Piozzi was an Italian tenor whom Hester first met in February 1778 at a musical party in the home of Dr Burney.

Their first encounter was far from auspicious. Fanny Burney's younger sister Charlotte, also a diarist, wrote a humorous account of the evening – which was a disaster. Johnson said nothing, as was often the case. He was notorious for rarely initiating a discussion but only responding once a subject had been raised. Hester, meanwhile, was so bored by the company, and so frustrated by Johnson's refusal to play the game of politeness, that she decided to liven things up. As Piozzi stood up to sing, Hester discreetly stepped up behind him and in full view of the rest of the company began to mimic and ridicule Piozzi's every gesture, shocking Charlotte and everyone else in the room with her reckless rudeness. Just a year later, though, Hester had 'picked up' Piozzi (as she confessed in the *Thraliana*) while staying in Brighton, and had asked him to teach singing to her eldest daughter, Queeney.

Johnson's sly comment about Piozzi begins to look weirdly prescient, rather than fiercely possessive. By September 1782 Hester was writing in her *Thraliana* that the 'little dear discerning Creature Fanny Burney says I'm in love with Piozzi'. Hester neither confirmed nor denied Burney's assertion but instead discussed in great detail the dilemma that would be posed if she decided to marry again:

I am the Guardian of five Daughters by Mr Thrale [she was shortly to lose another one, Henrietta, who died on 25 April 1783, aged four], and must not disgrace *their* Name & Family . . . I married the first Time to please my Mother, I must marry the second Time to please my Daughters—I have always sacrificed my own Choice to that of others, so I must sacrifice it again:—but why?'

She added, as if in answer to that question:

Oh because I am a Woman of superior Understanding, & must not for the World degrade my self from my Situation in Life, but if I *have* superior Understanding, let me at least make use of it for once; & rise to the rank of a human Being conscious of its own power to discern Good from Ill—the person who has uniformly acted by the Will of others, has hardly that Dignity to boast.

Suppose she did decide to marry Piozzi? What would be the harm?

My Marriage may assist *my* Health, but I suppose it will not injure *theirs* [her daughters]: will his Company or Companions corrupt their Morals; God forbid, if I did not believe him one of the best of our Fellow Beings I would reject him instantly. Can it injure their Fortunes? And could he impoverish (if he would) five Women to whom their Father left £20,000 each . . . ?

Then she asked:

To what then am I Guardian? To their Pride and Prejudice?

Her choice of wording is intriguing – the fate of five (shortly to be just four) unmarried daughters was at stake, but Hester believed it was her future that was in jeopardy, dictated by the pride of family and the prejudice of society. Hester was writing long before Jane Austen, but it's intriguing to think she may have influenced Austen via Burney, who used the phrase in her 1782 novel, *Cecilia*, to describe the plight of her orphaned heroine, torn between her fortune and the pride and prejudice of her guardians. Burney would not have read the *Thraliana*, but perhaps she had discussed with Hester the difficulties of 'pride' and 'prejudice' when choosing a husband. Hester had done her best (without success) to find Burney a husband among the guests who came to Streatham Park. (Burney was too reluctant to lose her independence, or too poor to attract the kind of men who knew Henry Thrale.)

*

Hester appalled everyone when she married Gabriel Piozzi on 23 July 1784 in the Catholic chapel at the French Embassy in London – and especially her closest friend Johnson. A forty-three-year-old widow, she married for pleasure, not duty, and put her own happiness above that of her unmarried daughters. Her husband, Piozzi, was Italian, a singer and a Roman Catholic, loyal to the Pope and not the British monarch. In June 1780 there had been violent riots as Parliament tried to pass a bill that would allow Catholics to work for the government and attend university. Henry Thrale, who had been an MP since his election in 1765 as the Member for Southwark on a liberal–conservative agenda (drafted with the help of Johnson), supported the bill and in retaliation his brewery was attacked by the marauding crowds looking for Catholics and their supporters.

At the time the Thrales were staying in Bath and missed the drama in the capital, where from the evening of Sunday 4 June until the morning of Friday 9 June the rioters looted and firebombed houses that had been daubed with a telltale white-painted cross because they were thought to belong to Catholics. Dr Burney, whose house was in St Martin's Street, just behind Leicester Fields, had to shout out 'No Popery' to prevent his house being attacked because his neighbours on either side happened to be Catholic. When the violence spread beyond the capital to Bath, the Catholic chapel in the spa town was torched in the early hours of Friday morning. The Thrales fled the city, but dared not return to London and spent the next fortnight touring the south coast until the hostilities had subsided.

Hester Thrale would have had no illusions that her marriage to Piozzi just four years later would result in ostracism at best and possibly personal danger. She did not, however, anticipate that her own celebrity as Johnson's close friend would arouse such intense interest in her future marriage plans. Scurrilous speculations about the brewer's widow and the great lexicographer had begun appearing in the newspapers soon after Henry Thrale's death. The *Morning Post*, on 15 October 1782, announced that a marriage treaty had been brokered between Johnson and Hester, and three days later described the ceremony in vivid detail. In the following months, despite all the evidence to the contrary, the story kept reappearing in print, growing ever more detailed along the way. So frequent were the stories, which were written with emphatic verve, even Johnson's so-called friends began to believe that a marriage was imminent. They never paused to ponder the huge gulf in age (from seventy-two to forty-one), or that, by marriage to Hester, Johnson would also be taking on responsibility for her daughters, then aged from five to eighteen.

He had always taken a keen interest in the development of the Thrale children. With Queeney, in particular, the eldest child whom he had known almost from birth, and with whom he shared his birthday celebrations (she was born on 17 September, the day before his own birthday), he wrote letters that were exactly suited to a bright child's character. 'My sweet, dear, pretty, little Miss,' he wrote to her on 29 July 1771, informing her that she was six years, ten months and twelve days old. 'Please to tell little Mama, that I am glad to hear that she is well, and that I am going to Lichfield . . . Tell dear Grandmama that I am very sorry for her pain. Tell Papa that I wish him joy of his new Girl [their seventh child], and tell Harry [Queeney's younger brother, just four years old] that you have got my heart, and will keep it . . .' He knew how to endear himself to the regal Queeney whose nickname was no accident.

The following year, when he was again staying in Lichfield, he addressed Queeney as his 'Dear Sweeting' and asked her to look after her younger sisters by giving them a good example, 'for all the little girls will try to be like you'. He was glad to hear 'of the improvement and prosperity of my hen' (Queeney had adopted a pet hen, encouraged by Johnson), and told her that his stepdaughter Lucy's 'fine black cat' had just died.

He taught Queeney French, Latin, geography and chemistry and bought her a tall cabinet, with a small box on top filled with tiny drawers, some with keys, which he suggested she should fill with 'curiosities' – shells and fossils and other geological and scientific specimens. 'The great pleasure of life is the influx of novelty,' he told 'My dear Love' on 9 April 1780, 'and probably for that reason only our earliest years are commonly our happiest, for though they are past under restraint, and often in a very unpleasing course of involuntary labour, yet while every hour produces something new, there is no deep impression of discontent . . .'

Johnson, unusually for a man with such a powerful intelligence, never lost touch with his childhood, still delighting, as an ungainly man in his fifties and sixties, in rolling down hills, jumping over stiles and running races for the sheer joy of it. 'The truth is,' Hester once wrote, 'Mr Johnson was often good-humouredly willing to join in childish amusements, and hated to be left out of any innocent merriment that was going forward.'

The *Thraliana* is full of anecdotes about Johnson's relationships with the

Thrale children, and the constant stream of advice he gave Hester about their upbringing, not always welcome. 'Old people I have often heard him observe,' she wrote in 1777, 'were very unfit to manage Children; for being most uncommonly idle themselves they filled up their Time as he said by tormenting the young Folks with Prohibitions not meant to be obeyed & Questions not intended to be answered.' Waspishly, though, she added, 'He was in his Turn extremely indulgent to Children, not because he lov'd them, for he loved them not, but because he feared extremely to disoblige them.'

She was not amused to be told by him, 'You teach your daughters the diameters of the planets, and wonder when you have done that they do not delight in your company. No science can be communicated by mortal creatures without attention from the scholar; no attention can be obtained from children without the infliction of pain, and pain is never remembered without resentment.' Girls were less displeasing to him than boys, said Hester, because they were less likely to grow up into scoundrels: 'As their temptations were fewer (he said), their virtue in this life, and happiness in the next, were less improbable; and he loved (he said) to see a knot of little misses dearly.'

Hester, with her keen-eyed and dispassionate gift for observation, had noticed Johnson's affection for young women such as herself, for the teenage Charlotte Lennox and much later for the young novelist Frances Burney. She suggests that he enjoyed their company because they looked up to him, didn't disagree with him, sought his approval. She almost resented his friendship with Queeney, as if it meant he no longer sought such uncomplicated conversation with her. 'You are frisking and skipping about Bath,' he wrote to Queeney just before her sixteenth birthday in September 1780, 'and every body talks of pretty Miss Thrale, and proud Miss Thrale, and Miss Thrale in this place, and Miss Thrale in that, but I am all for my own dear Miss Thrale in the Borough.'

Two months later the family moved on to Brighton, without him, and he wrote again to Queeney:

You, dear Madam, I suppose wander philosophically by the seaside, and survey the vast expanse of the world of waters, comparing as your predecessors in contemplation have done its ebb and flow, its turbulence and tranquillity to the vicissitudes of human life. You, my Love, are now in the time of flood, your powers are hourly encreasing, do not lose the time. When you are alone read diligently, they who do not read can have

155

nothing to think, and little to say. When you can get proper company talk freely and cheerfully, it is often by talking that we come to know the value of what we have read, to separate it with distinctness, and fix it in the memory. Never delight yourself with the dignity of silence or the superiority of inattention. To be silent or to be negligent are so easy, neither can give any claim to praise, and there is no human being so mean or useless, but his approbation and benevolence is to be desired.

Queeney had a reputation for stubborn resistance, for being 'captious', and Johnson was concerned that such behaviour would harden into discontent and friendlessness. A year later, he wrote another letter to her on the same theme, almost as if he was giving her a *Rambler* essay in miniature, written specially for her:

before you mingle in the crowd of life I wish you to exterminate captiousness from your mind, as a very powerful and active cause of discontent, of such discontent as is very often without reason, and almost always without remedy. Captiousness is commonly the resentment of negative injuries, or offences of omission, of which the ill intention cannot be proved, and should therefore very rarely be supposed. As the provocations of captiousness can seldom be declared, they operate in sullen silence, and undermine those friendships which could perhaps have withstood the battery of an open quarrel. Captiousness is a slow poison which destroys confidence and kindness by imperceptible corrosion. The captious man often determines wrong though he always determines against himself, and after years passed in gloom and malevolence, often discovers at last that he was never injured. The rule to be observed is, never to impute to design those negligences or omissions which can be imputed to forgetfulness, nor ever to resent as deliberate and malignant enmity, such offences as may be the effect of accidental levity or hasty petulance.

This, my lovely Dear, is a very grave and long lesson, but do not think it tedious. I have told you not many things more worthy of your attention and memory.

Johnson's relationships with the Thrale children were perhaps as important to his well-being as his friendship with Hester and Henry. 'I have a mind to look on Queeney as my own dear Girl,' he told Hester in a letter of November 1781.

To which Hester replied, with a touch of asperity, 'What honour you do my Queeney! Taking her for your own indeed, and writing her such sweet letters.'

Hester was at first devoted to Queeney, her firstborn, the only child whom she breastfed rather than farming out to a wet-nurse. Her first entry in 'The Children's Book', which she began on 17 September 1766 on Queeney's second birthday, reads:

> This is to serve as a Memorandum of her [Queeney's] Corporeal & Mental Powers at the Age of two Years . . . She can walk & run alone up & down all smooth Places tho' pretty steep, & tho' the Backstring is still kept on it is no longer of Use . . . & is strong enough to carry a Hound/puppy two Months old across the Lawn at Streatham . . . She can speak most Words & speak them plain enough too, but is no great Talker . . . She can tell all her Letters great & small & spell little Words as D,o,g, Dog, C,a,t, Cat . . . She knows her nine Figures & the simplest Combinations of 'em as 3,4, 34; 6,8, 68; but none beyond a hundred: She knows all the heathen Deities by their Attributes . . .

Six months later, she recorded that Queeney 'knows the Compass as perfectly as any Mariner upon the Seas; is mistress of the Solar System . . . The Comets she knows at Sight when represented upon Paper, & all the chief Constellations on the Celestial Globe.' Queeney, at two and a half, could reel off the capital cities of all the countries in Europe, recite the Nicene Creed and the Decalogue, and tell the story of the Fall of Man.

By the time Queeney was four, however, Hester was recording not only her accomplishments but also her severe temperament: 'Her Temper is not so good; reserved to all, insolent where She is free, & sullen to those who teach or dress or do anything towards her. Never in a Passion, but obstinate to that uncommon Degree that no Punishment except severe Smart can prevail on her to beg Pardon if She has offended.' Perhaps sullen silence was the only way Queeney could resist her mother's impulse to model her into the perfect child.

Hester was never sentimental about her children, once writing of Susannah, then aged two, that she was 'small, ugly & lean as ever; her Colour is like that of an ill-painted Wall grown dirty'. Her detachment would have been a defence against the fear attached to those first few years when life was so fragile.

The first of her children to die was her second daughter Frances, born on 27 September and dead less than a fortnight later on 6 October 1765. The next, Anna, died at almost one year old in 1770. Penelope died ten hours after she was born on 15 September 1772, and Lucy Elizabeth (named after Johnson's stepdaughter Lucy Porter and his wife Tetty) died the following year, on 22 November, aged just four. Ralph died in July 1775, aged twenty months, and five months later Frances also died, at seven months.

The most terrifying, though, of all these infant deaths, was that of Harry, who fell ill and died within a few hours on Saturday 23 March 1776, shortly after celebrating his ninth birthday. Named after his father, he was the first son to live beyond infancy, and was doubly precious to the Thrales, both Hester and Henry, in their desire for an heir. 'He is happy, healthy wise & good,' reported his mother on his birthday with great relief. A month later, having spent the first part of the morning 'in perfect health', Harry suddenly at about ten o'clock fell ill, wriggling and writhing, as if in pain, and 'crying as if he had been whipt instead of ill'. Hester sent for the doctor and in the meantime gave him a large glass of 'emetic wine' in the hope that this would force him to be sick and relieve the pressure. It made no difference. On the contrary, Harry was weakening by the minute.

Hester was already frantic with worry about Queeney, who had been ill for some days with a high fever and was still not improving. In a panic, with no doctor yet arrived, she sent another servant out from the brewery, 'with orders not to come back without *some* Physician . . . whichever he could find'. Meanwhile she rushed between Queeney's bedchamber and Harry's room, trying every remedy she knew to bring out Harry's fever, first plunging him into a tub of hot water 'up to his middle' and then lying him in a warm bed.

When Dr Jebb eventually arrived, he gave Harry hot wine, a dose of usquebaugh (whisky) and some Daffy's Elixir (a laxative), all in such rapid succession that Hester became even more concerned, 'tho' I had no Notion of Death having seen him so perfectly well at 9 o'clock'. She put mustard poultices on Harry's feet, hoping this would bring down his temperature, while the doctor administered broth to make him vomit, and wine enemas.

As a last resort Harry was given five grains of ipecacuanha, the dried bark of a South American plant, but when this had no effect Dr Jebb rushed away to find another doctor. Harry 'all this while spoke well & brisk; sate upright to talk with the Doctor; said he had no Pain now but his breath was short'. By three o'clock, he was dead.

Hester recorded the moment in 'The Children's Book': 'Soon a universal Shriek called us all together to Harry's Bedside, where he struggled a Moment—thrusting his Finger down his Throat to excite Vomiting, & then—turning to Nurse said very distinctly—don't Scream so—I *know* I must die.'

Both Harry and Queeney were perhaps suffering from meningitis but Queeney being much older was strong enough to resist the infection. Henry Thrale never recovered from the shock. Hester wrote, 'So ends my Pride, my hopes, my possession of present, & expectation of future Delight.' She did give birth to two more children, Cecilia (who lived until she was eighty) and Henrietta, who died aged four in April 1783. But she took surprisingly little interest in them. When she married Piozzi in July 1784, she abandoned the four girls to have survived. Johnson was so shocked he told Queeney, 'What I think of your Mother's conduct I cannot express. You have not left your Mother, but your Mother has left you.'

Hester waited until the very last minute before telling Johnson of her decision to remarry, as if scared he might try to warn her that hope rarely triumphs over experience. He knew nothing until he received a copy of the formal letter she sent to all the trustees of the Thrale estate advising them of her intentions, as if he were no more than a distant business acquaintance. She did enclose a short note of explanation, because 'our Friendship demands somewhat more':

> it requires that I should beg your pardon for concealing from you a Connection which you must have heard of by many People, but I suppose never believed. Indeed, my dear Sir, it was concealed only to spare us both needless pain: I could not have borne to reject the Counsel it would have killed me to take . . . the dread of your disapprobation has given me many an anxious moment, & tho' perhaps the most Independent Woman in the World—I feel as if I was acting without a parent's Consent—till you write kindly to your faithful Servant.

But those words 'a parent's Consent' appalled him. Hester could not have given Johnson a more hurtful rebuff, rewriting the past seventeen years of their friendship.

He replied on 2 July with a stinging rebuke, written in haste, without thinking of the impact his words might have:

Madam

If I interpret your letter right, you are ignominiously married: if it is yet undone, let us once talk together. If you have abandoned your children and your religion, God forgive your wickedness; if you have forfeited your fame and your country, may your folly do no further mischief. If the last act is yet to do, I who have loved you, esteemed you, reverenced you, and served you, I who long thought you the first of Human kind entreat that, before your fate is irrevocable, I may once more see you. I was, I once was, Madam, most truly yours, Sam: Johnson

He added, mournfully, 'I will come down if you permit it.'

Hester was incensed. What right had he to preach to her, who had for so long put up with his late nights, uncouth manners and overbearing conversation? She fired off an equally unguarded response:

Sir,

I have this morning received from you so rough a letter in reply to one which was both tenderly and respectfully written, that I am forced to desire the conclusion of a correspondence which I can bear to continue no longer. The birth of my second husband is not meaner than that of my first; his sentiments are not meaner; his profession is not meaner, and his superiority in what he professes acknowledged by all mankind. It is want of fortune then that is ignominious; the character of the man I have chosen has no other claim to such an epithet. The religion to which he has been always a zealous adherent will, I hope, teach him to forgive insults he has not deserved; mine will, I hope, enable me to bear them at once with dignity and patience. To hear that I have forfeited my fame is indeed the greatest insult I ever yet received. My fame is as unsullied as snow, or I should think it unworthy of him who must henceforth protect it.

Fatally, Johnson waited four days before sending a reply. The damage had been done and there was little he could say to repair the hurt. 'What you have done,' he tried to mollify Hester, 'however I may lament it, I have no pretence to resent, as it has not been injurious to me; I therefore breathe out one sigh more of tenderness, perhaps useless, but at least sincere.'

It was not enough for Hester, who was no longer content to tailor herself to suit the demands of others. She did not care to repair their friendship before leaving for Italy with her new husband, and five months later Johnson was dead.

Johnson told Boswell, 'Sir, she has done everything wrong since Thrale's bridle was off her neck!' Hester, though, outdid Johnson's shocking betrayal of their friendship (without of course knowing that he had been so rude about her to Boswell) when in 1786 she published her *Anecdotes of the Late Dr Samuel Johnson, during the last twenty years of his life*, the first such book to be published by an intimate of Johnson after his death. She made no effort to suppress her true feelings about him and the problems she encountered in dealing with his fretful and sometimes domineering personality, especially once her husband fell ill: 'when there was nobody to restrain his dislikes, it was extremely difficult to find any body with whom he could converse, without living always on the verge of a quarrel, or of something too like a quarrel to be pleasing.' She added, most insultingly, that to escape from him she had 'to plead inability of purse to remain longer in London or its vicinage' and she had retired to Bath, where she knew 'Mr Johnson would not follow me, and where I could for that reason command some little portion of time for my own use'.

Hester's embittered revelations in the *Anecdotes* are discomfiting to read. She complains of Johnson's habit of not rising until noon, at which time she had to make breakfast for him – did Hester actually make the tea and butter the toast? She suggests that her initial veneration for Johnson's 'virtue', his gift for conversation, was worn thin by the 'perpetual confinement' of being stuck with his company. She complains, 'In Johnson's intellect mine was swallowed up.'

Hester shocks her readers by not withholding. Worst of all, she draws attention unfavourably to Johnson's infirmities, saying that he was 'a sad Man to carry to a publick Place, for every body knew him, & he drew all Eyes upon one; & by his odd Gestures & perhaps loud Voice get People to stare at one in a very disagreeable Manner'.

In the 1940s, the scholar who edited *Thraliana* made some startling connections. Katharine C. Balderston was unusual in that she had studied Hester's private papers with great thoroughness. When she came across a strange, unexplained item in the details of the sale of the Thrale library (which took place in Manchester after Hester's death in 1823) – 'Johnson's padlock, committed to my care in 1768' – she recalled that in the margins of *Thraliana* there is a puzzling annotation, 'the Fetters & Padlocks will tell Posterity the truth'. Could the 'padlock' and the 'Fetters' be linked? she wondered.

Balderston also knew of two letters between Hester and Johnson which mention the use of keys and locks. They were both staying in the same house, Streatham Park, so why did they feel the need to write to each other? And why in French rather than English?

It was May 1773 and Johnson had been unwell, suffering from an eye infection that had prevented him from reading and working on his *Lives of the Poets*. Hester's mother was dying from cancer, two of her daughters had been seriously ill with tonsillitis and anaemia, and she herself was in the early stages of yet another pregnancy, her ninth in nine years. She tried to dissuade Johnson from coming to Streatham because she knew she would not have time or energy to indulge him, but she then changed her mind and sent the coach to fetch him from Johnson's Court, where he then had rooms.

Johnson arrived to find the household in chaos. Henry had retreated to the brewery in Southwark (which he always did in the face of domestic tribulation) and Hester was exhausted with worry about her children and concern for her mother. Johnson, feeling abandoned and alone in his room, wrote to her in French, complaining that he had been cut to the quick by Hester's neglect:

> Il faut agir tout a fait en Maîtresse, afin que vôtre jugement et vôtre vigilance viennent a secours de ma faiblesse . . . Tournez, Madame tres honorèe, vos pensèes de ca côte la. Il n'y a pour vous rien de difficile; vous pourrez inventer une regime pratiquable sans bruît, et efficace sans peril . . . Je souhaite, ma patronne, que vôtre autoritè me soit toujours sensible, et que vous me tiennez dans l'esclavage que vous sçavez si bien rendre heureuse . . .

In English translation his letter reads:

> You must act wholly as Mistress, if your judgment and your vigilance are to come to the rescue of my weakness . . . Most honoured madam, turn your thoughts to that subject. There is for you nothing difficult

in it; you can devise a regime practicable without fuss, and efficacious without danger . . . I hope, my lady, that your authority over me will always make itself felt, and that you will keep me in that bondage which you know so well how to make into a happiness . . .

Earlier in the letter, he had asked her to spare him the necessity of confining himself by '*tourner le clef dans la porte, deux fois par jour*'. All he is asking of her, he says, is 'the turning of a key in the door, twice every day'. What was Johnson suggesting? Perhaps he used French because he was not clear himself what he wanted to express, the nuance, the precise meaning, and he feared that in English what he wrote would sound too blunt, too clumsy, too open to misinterpretation.

Hester replied, but in English, briskly urging her house-guest to:

shake off these uneasy Weights, heavier to the Mind by far than Fetters to the body. Let not your fancy dwell thus upon Confinement and Severity . . . yet if you find this irksome and dangerous Idea fasten upon your fancy, leave me to struggle with the loss of one Friend, and let me not put to hazard what I esteem beyond Kingdoms, and value beyond the possession of them.

If we go on together your Confinement shall be as strict as possible except when Company comes in . . .

She ended, 'I will detain you no longer, so farewell and be good; and do not quarrel with your Governess for not using the Rod enough.'

No witnesses were present as these letters were written and received. Their survival, perhaps deliberate, but just as possibly accidental, secreted away and forgotten about because they were of no real significance. The written evidence is not always truthful. There is often an indecipherable subtext, and it is tempting sometimes to read too much into what was originally not intended to be taken literally.

Johnson was often melancholic, capable of deep despair and twisted imaginings. As Gerard Manley Hopkins was later to write:

O the mind, mind has mountains; cliffs of fall
Frightful, sheer, no-man-fathomed.

The mind has a will of its own, and sometimes takes you into frightful regions of the greatest darkness. Letters are often, but are not always, carefully formed epistles of intent. Sometimes they are written *in extremis*, without conscious thought or expectation. There's a danger in stripping them apart, word by word, image by image. Would Johnson and Hester really have carried on a strange physical relationship under the same roof as her husband Henry Thrale?

The existence of these letters does suggest, none the less, that there was something not stated at the heart of Hester's relationship with Johnson. She was a highly intelligent, ambitious woman, married to a man whom she respected but could not love, trapped in a never-ending cycle of pregnancy and frustrated by a lack of recognition of her own literary talents. In Johnson she had found an instructive companion and a friend with whom she could flex her lively mind. But, after so many years of friendship, he, too, had begun to make unreasonable demands on her attention and her emotions, relying too much on Hester's company as a solace for his own difficulties. It was too convenient for him to ignore the compromises she lived under as a woman and the wife of Henry Thrale.

Thrale had provided Hester with all the comforts that money could bring, but in return she was required to support him in his business, entertain on his behalf when he was campaigning to be elected to Parliament, and provide him with an heir. She was not encouraged to develop her literary aspirations. Meanwhile, she knew to her cost that her husband had continued his 'macaroni' lifestyle, indulging in affairs with other women that were not always hidden from her, or from the gossips. With Henry's death, she was at last free to act upon her own wishes, and to accept the kind of uncomplicated adoration which Piozzi offered her, although to do so meant abandoning her daughters.

For months she prevaricated, almost collapsing with nervous exhaustion. But in June 1784 she retreated to Bath to make arrangements for her marriage to Piozzi, beyond the glare of London opinion. Her three elder daughters, Queeney aged nineteen, 'ugly and lean' Susannah aged fourteen, and Sophia, almost thirteen, refused to accept Piozzi as a possible stepfather. To prevent a scandal, Hester insisted they should all travel together to Salisbury, where their paths would simply diverge, Hester travelling on to Bath while Queeney and her sisters turned east for Brighton where they could stay in the house on West Street bought years ago by their father. Her youngest surviving child, seven-year-old Cecilia, was simply left behind with 'a woman' at Streatham.

Hester wrote to Queeney:

Pray for me my dearest Tit, I am really half out of my Mind—Now I shall lose all the pleasure of *Hope* in *Possession* [Piozzi had followed her to Bath]. Well! Hope is a sweet soft Passion; mild & nourishing like Milk, but like Milk too, when *long kept* it turns sour on the Stomack, and is the hardest of all things to *bring up again*. Elegant Metaphors indeed! but this is a very exact one . . .

This must have been a strange letter for Queeney to receive. She had not just been left behind in charge of her sisters; her own marriage prospects were seriously jeopardised by the scandal of her mother's behaviour.

In his penultimate letter to Queeney, dated 12 August 1784, Johnson told her how much he loved her, and loved her father 'and I loved your Mother as long as I could'. And then he added two maxims: the first, 'Let it be your care to please God, that awful and just God before whom you must at last appear,' and the second:

In matters of human judgement, and prudential consideration, consider the publick voice of general opinion as always worthy of great attention; remember that such practices can very seldom be right, which all the world has concluded to be wrong.

Johnson, though, had forgotten that when he married Tetty he scorned the world, and their relatives. Tetty put her second husband before her children, so that she never saw her sons again and when she joined Johnson in London she left her daughter Lucy to face up to the scandalmongers of Lichfield and the burden of running the bookshop. Lucy was nineteen when her mother remarried; just like Queeney. Was Johnson's concern for Hester Thrale's daughters prompted by a belated recognition of the effect Tetty's decision to marry him must have had on her children?

Johnson could be accused of double standards in his unwillingness to bless Hester's future life with Piozzi. Also of wilful blindness in failing to remember just how much he owed Hester (and Henry, too) – for almost twenty years she had offered him a comfortable home, which he visited almost every week. He had an open invitation to join them as a family, a constant supply of friendship and entertainment, a buffer against his endemic loneliness. Yet Hester's behaviour towards her daughters is still difficult to understand. While the newly-weds swanned off to Italy on honeymoon, Queeney, herself at an age to marry and travel through Europe, was stuck in London with no access to her inheritance, which was left in a trust fund until she reached twenty-one. Without money or a home (Streatham Park had been rented out) she and her sisters were obliged to live with a chaperone.

Hester wrote joyous, romantic letters from her travels. 'You are very generous,' she told Queeney on 25 July, 'in saying it does not teize but comfort you to hear of my Happiness. If I loved him before we lived so continually together, how certainly have his Manners and Conduct towards me since his return rivetted my Regard!' Was Queeney really not 'teized' to read such stuff? 'In a word I *am* very happy, and never spent six or seven Months so deliciously in my Life before,' Hester wrote from Milan, before moving on to Cremona, Mantua, Verona and Padua. She and Piozzi travelled by barge along the canal from Brenta to Venice, Hester admiring the Palladian villas while listening to her husband as he played music by Guglielmi and Rauzzini on his new fortepiano.

Queeney kept her own counsel, writing polite but businesslike letters in response. Why, Hester asked her daughter, are you treating me 'so coldly and so queerly'? In July 1787 she complained to Queeney that she had not been looking after her sisters properly. Queeney had made other arrangements for Cecilia's schooling without consulting her mother:

> And I must add, that to bathe a lean growing Girl of large Expectations, whom *you* say is unhealthy—in the Sea, without more & nearer Medical Advice than the Isle of Wight would afford—seems somewhat a rash Step when taken by a young and single Lady who cannot pretend to the smallest Degree of Legal Power over the Child's Person.

Queeney's response was to refuse to have anything to do with her mother for the next six years.

'I have seen and judged characters all my life instinctively: but hers passes all my calculations and combinations. I truly cannot comprehend its materials,' declared Fanny Burney about Hester Thrale. Burney prided herself on her acute eye for character, her ability to sketch a person in just a few words, but with Hester she was stumped. She could not do justice to such a complex personality in a single phrase.

*

The friendship that developed between Hester and Johnson from their first meeting in 1765 was never an alliance of equals, but rather crossed the generations, as so many of his close relationships did. There was a twenty-one-year age gap between Johnson and his wife Tetty, and thirty-two between him and Hester. She was the wife of a very wealthy man and the mistress of a large country estate and an establishment in town; he lived in a condition of not-so-genteel poverty. She was the mother of children; he cared for a household of dependants but not his immediate family. She enjoyed the luxury of never having to take up a profession; he struggled for years to earn money not by writing what he wanted but as a scholarly drudge, churning out parliamentary sketches and laboriously compiling first a catalogue of books, the *Harleian Miscellany*, and then the *Dictionary*.

'Madam,' he wrote to her at the beginning of 1773:

> The inequalities of human life have always employed the meditation of deep thinkers, and I cannot forbear to reflect on the difference between your condition and my own. You live upon mock turtle, and stewed rumps of beef; I dined yesterday upon crumpets. You sit with parish officers, caressing and caressed, the idol of the table, and the wonder of the day [Hester was fulfilling her duties as the wife of a politician]. I pine in the solitude of sickness, not bad enough to be pitied, and not well enough to be endured. You sleep away the night, and laugh or scold away the day. I cough and grumble, and grumble and cough. Last night was very tedious, and this day makes no promises of much ease . . .

Perhaps because Hester herself was so emotionally unavailable – until she met Piozzi – Johnson became with her quite sentimental, confessing to her even his darkest and most fearsome thoughts, knowing that she would receive all this without flinching or indeed making much comment. In return, though, she withheld a part of herself, just as she had learnt to do with her husband.

Hester aspired to literary fame, and as soon as she had freed herself from the life she had been born into, by dashing off to Italy with her new husband, she launched herself as a writer. In 1786 she published her first book, her *Anecdotes* of Johnson, swiftly followed by an edition of their letters in 1788. The following year she published *Observations and Reflections Made in the Course of a Journey through France, Italy and Germany*, modelled on Johnson's account of the trip he made to the Western Isles of Scotland with Boswell in 1773.

Her books divided the critics, just as in person she aroused both love and disapproval. Horace Walpole deplored the way that Hester, now Mrs Piozzi, insisted on writing naturally, not wishing the language in her books to appear artificial: 'Her friends plead that she piques herself on writing as she talks: methinks, then, she should talk as she would write.' The *Morning Post* insinuated that 'the literary crudities of this lady afford a lamentable proof of what *vanity* will do when it is associated with wealth'.

Undeterred, Hester continued to publish. *British Synonymy*, from 1794, was a new kind of dictionary, collecting definitions of words with similar meanings, designed for those who, like Piozzi, spoke English as a second language. Subtitled 'An Attempt at Regulating the Choice of Words in Familiar Conversation. Inscribed, with Sentiments of Gratitude and Respect, to such of her Foreign Friends as have made English Literature their peculiar Study', it provided an idiosyncratic, but very imaginative, guide to the meaning of words like 'fascination' and the difference between 'eagerness', 'earnestness', 'vehemence', 'avidity' and 'ardour'. Not popular at the time, it could now be a useful book for students of English as an additional language who are struggling to find the right word among a selection with similar but not quite correct meanings.

Finally, she produced *Retrospection* in 1801 as a millennial, and highly ambitious, retrospective of the last 1,800 years of civilisation. Hester attempted to summarise Roman, medieval and modern history, spiced with her own chit-chat about various historical personalities and their respective relevance to the present day. The reviewers were sniffy. Hester missed out dates, provided no authorities for her facts and opinions, and wrote with the same lack of coherence as in her family journals. 'To the learned, it must appear as a series of dreams by an old lady . . . Far less is it fit for the perusal of youth, of either sex; since the numerous errors, and the air of sufficiency with which they are written, might leave impressions difficult to be eradicated by the genuine pages of history,' condemned the *Critical Review*.

If Johnson had still been alive Hester would have had the benefit of his advice and editorial interventions, as so many others did. As we shall discover in the next chapter, both Sir Joshua Reynolds and his sister Frances drew on Johnson's advice for encouragement and practical help when publishing their works on art, taste and beauty, Johnson correcting proofs and suggesting editorial changes. Hester, though, published nothing through all her years of friendship with Johnson. These were her years of pregnancy and child-rearing, when she would have had time or energy for little else but her children and protecting her own health, but it is still surprising that Hester was not encouraged by Johnson to write for publication.

'You have every right to distinction and should therefore be distinguished,' he told her in a letter from June 1775. Yet he never suggested that Hester had talents worthy of public acclaim. He advised her instead to support her husband by finding out about the brewing business, and to write letters and family notebooks which would be for her private use only. He asks her in a letter, for instance, to give him an account of the high-society regatta she has just been invited to attend: 'When you are in this scene of splendour and gaiety, do not let one of your fits of negligence steal upon you. *Hoc age*, is the great rule whether you are serious or merry, whether you are stating the expenses of your family, learning science, or duty from a folio, or floating on the Thames in a fancied dress . . .'

Hester does not disappoint Johnson, and she does not fail us either, recreating the scene vividly with her talent for word-painting:

> So yestermorning a flag flying some conspicuous steeple in Westminster gave notice of the approaching festival, and at noon the managers determined to hold it on that day. In about two hours the wind rose very high, and the river was exceedingly rough; but the lot was cast, and the ladies went on with their dresses. It had been agreed that all should wear white; but the ornaments were left to our own choice. I was afraid of not being fine enough; so I trimmed my white lutestring [a lustrous silk fabric] with silver gauze, and wore black ribbons inter-mixed . . .
>
> The water was rough, even seriously so; the time glided away in deliberation of what was to be done; and we resolved at last to run to the house of a gentleman in the Temple . . . and look at the race from his windows . . . Of the race, however, scarce anything could be seen, for clouds of dust that intercepted one's sight; and we have no balconies to see shows from, as are provided in countries where proces-sions make much of the means of entertainment; so we discomposed our head-dresses against each other, by struggling for places in an open

window, and then begged pardon with curtsies, which exposed our trains to be trod on, and made us still more out of humour. It was however a real pleasure to look at the crowd of spectators. Every shop was shut; every street deserted; and the tops of all such houses as had any catch of the river swarmed with people like bees settling on a branch. Here is no exaggeration, upon my honour; even the lamp-irons in Westminster bridge were converted into seats, while every lighter lying in the Thames bore men up to the top-mast head. This was the true wonder of the day . . .

But even in this account of a fun day out, Hester slips in an odd reference to her marriage when at the end of her account she reveals that her dress of 'white lutestring' was not of her own choosing but had been decided on by her husband: 'You will be told that I was too fine, and 'tis partly true, but the other extreme would have been worse, and Mr Thrale chose my dress himself,' she told Johnson.

Johnson was jealous of her busy social life: 'When you read my letters, I suppose you are very proud to think how much you excel in the correspondence; but you must remember that your materials are better. You have a family, and friends, and hopes, and fears, and wishes, and aversions, and all the ingredients that are necessary to the composition of a letter.' He was reflecting on the contrast with his own, what he considered solitary, life. But at the same time he was confining Hester to the role in which he preferred to see her: supporting and nurturing her household of husband, children, and for much of the time Johnson too. Any writing she did should be as a private, domestic pursuit; never for public consumption.

Her *Anecdotes*, the published account of their friendship, were written after they had fallen out so badly, and Hester was no longer living in England. They are a curious blend of self-justification and honest insight. *Thraliana*, written as a private journal and never intended for publication, provides insights into the 'domestick privacies' and 'invisible circumstances' of Johnson's life with the Thrales, and also into the puzzling personality of the woman who wrote them. She was clever, sharp-eyed and blessed with a keen wit, but in the end she abandoned Johnson as an elderly, sick man, just as she so casually shrugged off all responsibility for the children on whom she had at first lavished such care and attention.

Hester, though, brought out aspects of Johnson's personality – his love of life, his energy, his engaging charm – which were not so evident until his comfortable years as almost part of the family at Streatham Park. Her stifled sigh as the mistress of the house, who night after night kept herself awake until the early hours while Johnson put off the ending of the day, talking till dawn, allowed him ease of mind and a good night's sleep.

7

'Renny Dear'

In January 1759, Johnson wrote to a friend, 'Miss is much employed in Miniatures.' Johnson's 'Miss' is Frances Reynolds, his 'Renny dear', sister to the artist Sir Joshua, and like her brother a gifted portraitist. Johnson sat for her on several occasions, telling her on 16 June 1780, 'I am very willing to wait on you at all times, and will sit for the picture, and, if it be necessary, will sit again, for whenever I sit, I shall be always with you.' But Frances was keenly aware that Johnson also had reservations about women indulging in portraiture. He once announced while she was in the room, 'Public practice of any art, and staring in men's faces, is very indelicate in a female.'

Frances herself was always conflicted about the proper place of the woman artist. 'I never thought it a suitable profession for my sex, and very far from meritorious to give up so much time as the attainment of that Art required for amusement only.' A clergyman's daughter of deep religious convictions, she worried that she was indulging herself by devoting so much of her time to something she enjoyed but which had no practical purpose. She also understood that to succeed as an artist requires diligence and a compulsion that verges on obsession. Her brother Joshua often wrote about the twenty-four-hour dedication required of the true artist, constantly practising and refining his techniques. He advised a young protégé James Barry (who later portrayed Johnson as an old man in his great mural for the Royal Society of Arts): 'Whoever is resolved to excel in painting, or indeed in any other art, must bring all his mind to bear on that one object, from the moment he rises till he goes to bed.'

Such single-minded, all-consuming dedication is difficult for women, most of whom have obligations to fulfil that have nothing to do with their art. Frances confided in her private, unpublished commonplace book, 'It is unnatural in a woman to quit the private domestic path for a public one . . . It is this consideration that has made painting, which every person thought I pursued only for amusement, a torment as it clashed with the honourable province of family duties.'

Only a half-dozen or so surviving full-scale portraits have definitely been attributed to Frances. But these character studies suggest she had an unusual talent. Her studies, especially of Hannah More and Johnson, focus on the interior, the domestic, the private lives of her sitters, and precisely because of this simplicity and lack of sophistication convey a great depth of feeling, of direct communication between the sitter and the receptive gaze. The Johnson portraits thought to be by her are very different in style from those by other artists, especially a grim-looking depiction of him as an old and very ill man. It's daunting in its realism, nothing touched up to disguise the fact that when she painted him he was close to death.

Frances was born on Saturday 10 May 1729 'just before 10 in the morning', the last but one child of Theophila Reynolds and the Revd Samuel Reynolds, a clergyman schoolmaster in the village of Plympton in Devon. Theophila experienced eleven births but only five of her children survived into adulthood, three girls and two boys. One daughter, named Theophila after her mother, died when she was just a toddler after falling out of a window. Frances's brother Joshua was three when the accident happened. In a diary that he wrote up many years later, he stated baldly, 'Tuesday morning, about 7 o'clock, Offy fell out of the window, and died between 6 and 7 at night.' Theophila had not been forgotten. Frances, who was six years younger than Joshua, was not yet born when the tragedy occurred, but she was not quite the baby of the family. This was Martyn, who died when he was just nine, in the same year that their eldest brother Humphrey was drowned, aged twenty-eight, lost at sea on his way home from India, where he had been serving as a naval lieutenant.

The surviving Reynolds children – Robert (born in 1714), Mary (known as 'Molly', 1716), Elizabeth (1721), Joshua (1723) and Frances – were all talented and industrious, as if making up for those who had been lost. Mary later published a book celebrating country life, A *Devonshire Dialogue*, and Elizabeth was an amateur artist and biblical scholar, whose four-volume commentary on the teachings of the Old Testament prophet Ezekiel was published in 1781–5. Paper and pencils were expensive luxuries, but the schoolhouse had large rooms and long passageways between them; there was plenty of wall space for the children to experiment with drawing on the lime-washed walls using sticks of charcoal. In this, Frances showed more natural, intuitive skill than her brother Joshua. In her book *The Obstacle Race*, a study of woman artists through the ages, Germaine Greer claims that as a boy Joshua was jealous of his little sister's technical facility. Yet in reality Frances had far more reason to be envious of her brother since as soon as he was old enough he was sent off to London as an apprentice in the studio of Thomas Hudson, an established professional artist.

Hudson in 1740 was a busy, if not very imaginative, painter. He was criticised for turning his art into 'a manufactory', wasting no time on establishing character or experimenting with new approaches and poses: 'A few formal attitudes served as models for all his subjects.' Horace Walpole once said of Hudson, with priggish sarcasm, that he satisfied 'the country gentlemen . . . with his honest similitudes, and with the fair tied wigs, blue velvet coats, and white sattin waistcoats, which he bestowed liberally on his customers'. But Joshua did learn some valuable lessons from Hudson on how to make a good living as a painter. When at last he had funds enough to set up his own studio he had a keen sense of how to market his business, always having on display works in progress of his most famous clients, employing a team of assistants to colour in the backgrounds, which speeded up production, and, most importantly, building up a large circle of friends among the rich and influential.

The middle decades of the eighteenth century were the perfect time to set up a business in such a luxury trade as portraiture. The emerging middle-class families were anxious to enhance their social stature and to decorate their newly built houses by buying into permanence through the ingenious art of pasting oil pigments on to canvas. Joshua himself admitted that his skill at draughtsmanship was less than genius, but he made up for this by his willingness to work very hard, his highly tuned commercial sense, knowing almost before it appeared what was fashionable and in demand – and by his honest gift for friendship.

By the end of 1744, after just four years in the capital, Joshua was already socialising with the group of writers, artists and publishers who frequented Old Slaughter's Coffee House in St Martin's Lane, behind Charing Cross and the Strand. Over tiny cups of bitter chocolate or sweet coffee he met the artists William Hogarth and Allan Ramsay, the novelist Henry Fielding, and Martin Folkes, a scientist and friend of Isaac Newton. 'I understand that Joshua by his master's means is introduced into a club composed of the most famous men in their profession,' his father remarked proudly to a friend. Joshua was making enough money to rent rooms in the heart of Covent Garden, the perfect setting for an artist in need of an income, poised between the commercial interests of the City and the artistic life of the capital, much of which was carried on in the bustling lanes that surrounded the two great patent theatres of Drury Lane and Covent Garden and the Opera House on the Haymarket. (Since 1737, the Licensing Act had strictly limited the number of theatres in the capital as the government attempted to control public performances of plays and entertainments. Only Drury Lane and Covent Garden could stage plays which first had to be approved by the Lord Chamberlain.)

But in 1745 Samuel Reynolds died, leaving his wife and daughters with nowhere to live (the schoolhouse came with the job) and no money to live on. Joshua, conscious of his family obligations, returned to Plympton to sort things out. His mother eventually decided to live with her elder daughter Mary, who by then was married to a local lawyer John Palmer, but Joshua took on the responsibility of caring for his unmarried sisters, Frances and Elizabeth, setting up home with them in Plymouth, then a thriving naval city. From these years survives a portrait of Frances, aged seventeen. It's not a 'society' portrait of a recognised beauty but an affectionate brotherly depiction of a diffident, rather plain-looking country girl. Yet she fascinates, looking out with such unselfconscious directness, not at us, her audience, but to what lies ahead.

Little is known about Frances in these years – no letters survive, no diaries – but as soon as she was old enough she took a job as a milliner. Millinery, with its hat-making, petticoats and lace frills, was one of the few 'creative' professions open to working women at that time. But as places which made and sold the most intimate of female garments and where women were often in a state of undress, there lingered about them the whiff of the brothel.

In the late 1770s Fanny Burney wrote a comedy, *The Witlings*, which opens with a scene in a milliner's shop, where the heroine Cecilia is choosing her bridal trousseau. Burney wanted to illustrate the contrast between Cecilia's life of leisured ease and the tedious toil of working women, but her unusual choice of setting, commercial and 'vulgar', may well have been one of the reasons why the play was never performed in public, suppressed by Burney after criticism from her father and a family friend (also male). They feared the audience might be shocked, and titillated, by the ambivalence surrounding millinery.

A few years later Mary Wollstonecraft commented that fine ladies are taught 'to look down with contempt on the vulgar employments of life', such as the milliners and mantua-makers. (The mantua was the loose black robe worn by 'ladies' to cover up their finery when in church, to be more demure, or as a disguise at the masquerade.) In fact, suggested Wollstonecraft in her *Vindication of the Rights of Woman*, milliners are 'reckoned the next class' above prostitutes, because they helped women to dress up and attract men. At the front of the shop would be displayed embroidered tippets and lace-trimmed shawls, saucy caps and velvet ribbons. Who knows what went on at the back?

A more obvious choice of employment for Frances would have been to become a governess. Frances, though, was not prepared to suffer the humiliation of being treated as no more than a live-in servant. At least as a milliner she could continue to live with her sister and have some free hours each day in which to paint. Working in the shop, making hats and undergarments, also gave her the opportunity to study the anatomy of fashion, the superficial surface of portraiture, which in some ways made up for the fact that as a woman she would never be allowed to study the science of what was underneath.

An early self-portrait shows Frances with her sister Mary. Once again, the viewer is struck by the power of Frances's gaze, her definition of character. The picture also has a surprising informality. The two sisters are at ease, simply dressed, their hair unpowdered, as if caught unawares. As Frances plays the lute, Mary appears to be dancing around her, full of life and family affection. (A version of this portrait shows two sisters behind Frances, but recent cleaning has revealed that the third figure was added later.)

Joshua, meanwhile, was soon receiving commissions from the naval officers based at Plymouth Docks, charging £3.10s a portrait (or about £300). Blessed with an amiable, optimistic disposition, he made friends wherever he went, always eager to listen and be entertained. 'He was so easy, so uniformly cheerful, so willing to please and be pleased,' wrote his friend, the Shakespeare scholar and editor Edmond Malone, 'so fond of the company of literary men, so well read in mankind, so curious an observer of character, and so replete with various knowledge and entertaining anecdotes, that not to have loved as well as admired him would have shown great want of taste and sensibility.' In 1749 he was invited by Commodore Augustus Keppel to travel with him to Lisbon and the Mediterranean; a truly life-changing opportunity for Joshua to visit Italy and study the works of the ancient masters.

The extraordinary clarity and whiteness of the light in the countries of southern Europe was itself a revelation, but Joshua was also confounded by the works he saw in the galleries of Paris, Rome and Venice. He felt himself not capable of understanding the true mastery of Titian and Michelangelo. When he first saw Raphael's frescoes in the Vatican, he knew the inadequacies of his talent and education: 'My not relishing them as I was conscious I ought to have done, was one of the most humiliating circumstances that ever happened to me.'

Joshua had until then thought of himself as an accomplished painter. Now for the first time he was seeing truly great works of art and he realised the crudity of his own techniques and the lack of inspiration available to him in England. 'All the indigested notions of painting which I had brought with me from England, where the art was in the lowest state it had ever been in (it could not indeed be lower),' he later wrote, 'were to be totally done away and eradicated from my mind.'

Travel for Joshua really was an education, showing him paintings of a style and grandeur he had never seen before and which he could only study by personally visiting the buildings which they decorated. He resolved to stay on in Italy until he had learnt all that he needed, spending his days in the Vatican, jotting down notes about the paintings and making sketches. Moving on to Venice he had the opportunity to study Veronese's epic *The Marriage of Cana* and the paintings of Tintoretto and Titian. He never forgot these paintings, many years later writing down his impressions, especially of his great favourite, Titian: 'By a few strokes he knew how to mark the general image and character of whatever object he attempted; and produced, by this alone, a truer representation than his master Giovanni Bellini, or any of his predecessors, who finished every hair.'

A surviving sketchbook from these travels shows Joshua patiently sketching the same leg on several occasions, struck by its accuracy of form. Another charcoal sketch shows an old man, bearded, sitting in a room, perhaps a copy of Ghirlandaio's portrait of St Jerome in his study. Other rough sketches are of young women, nude, as if drawn from life while visiting a brothel.

While her brother was educating himself on the Continent, Frances was stuck in Plymouth, laboriously stitching lace on to cuffs and working ribbons round a straw bonnet. 'As the mind must have some pursuit,' she wrote later, 'and I unhappily having none that is so satisfactory, or that appears to me so praiseworthy as painting, having been thrown out of the path nature had in a peculiar manner fitted me for, and as it is natural to endeavour to excel in something, I confess I can't help pleasing myself with the hopes that I might arrive at a tolerable degree of perfection in these little pictures . . .' She began painting miniatures in the privacy of her bedroom as a discipline, perfecting her draughtsmanship as best she could. Miniatures, too, could be accomplished in secrecy and hidden away from unappreciative eyes. Joshua could not resist teasing his younger sister by telling her that her oil paintings made other people laugh and him cry. He thought he was making fun; she experienced it rather differently.

When Joshua eventually returned to England in October 1752, he spent a few months in Devon with his family before leaving again for London, taking Frances with him. She was to be his housekeeper while he concentrated on establishing himself as a 'society' painter, building on the confidence he had acquired from studying the Italian masters *in situ*. Frances was expected not just to keep house but also to act as chaperone when female clients were sitting for her brother, and also as his hostess, entertaining his friends. Joshua never appeared to have intended to marry, although there were rumours of liaisons with a number of women, especially the artist Angelica Kauffmann. He relied instead first on Frances and then on his nieces to organise his household and manage his domestic affairs. For Frances the arrangement should also have been beneficial, allowing her to leave behind the drudgery of millinery and to live among the 'arts and sciences' of the capital, as she had dreamt. But the siblings were temperamentally too different, and Frances soon discovered she had swapped one kind of drudgery for another.

'The poor lady is always miserable, always fretful,' Hester Thrale noted about Frances in her *Thraliana*. Hester was one of the few people never to have been taken in by Joshua's charm, and with acidic perspicuity she added that Reynolds 'certainly does not love her [Frances] as one should expect a man to love a sister he has so much Reason to be proud of'. Hester, herself surrounded by men who did not fully appreciate her ambitions, suggested that Joshua was infuriated by Frances (the only person with whom he displayed such ill temper) because, 'she paints too well, or has learned too much Latin, and is a better Scholar than her Brother'.

Frances was neither a satisfactory housekeeper, nor an obliging hostess. Her heart lay elsewhere. She tried to reassure her brother that her intention to paint 'does not proceed from a cast of mind inconsistent with the delicacy of the female character whose true excellence consists in not endeavouring to excel out of the private domestic sphere'. But she also admitted that she 'envy'd the female competitors in the exhibition' at the Royal Academy. Her brother was not just an exhibitor at the Academy; for many years he was the President.

There were women who earned a living as professional artists in these middle years of the century. Angelica Kauffmann, for instance, was admired as a portraitist, and she retained both her virtue and her independence. She was heralded by Richard Samuel in his portrait of the *Nine Living Muses*, depicted at her easel, her palette in hand. Kauffmann, though, did not have a powerful brother to offend, nor the complex personality of Frances, who worried away at her pretensions to artistic talent. Were such public performances unbecoming in a woman, and deleterious to her spiritual well-being?

Frances first met Johnson through her brother Joshua sometime in 1756. The two men had been introduced at a dinner given by the spinster daughters of Admiral Cotterell, and had both impressed each other by their remarks 'so much above the common-place style of conversation'. Joshua brought Johnson home with him afterwards for supper, keen also to have the author of the *Dictionary* sit for him. Johnson thought highly of Joshua, telling Boswell that he was 'the most invulnerable man he knew; whom, if he should quarrel with him, he should find the most difficulty how to abuse'. (Boswell dedicated his *Life* to Reynolds, as the 'intimate and beloved friend of that great man'.) With Frances, Johnson was equally impressed, telling Hester Thrale, 'I never knew but one mind which would bear a microscopical examination, and that is dear Miss Reynolds's, and hers is very near to purity itself.' He admired Frances's spiritual rigour, her purity of heart, and he became 'her truest friend and most faithful counsellor'.

In July 1771 Johnson wrote to her from Ashbourne (near Lichfield) promising that he would be back in town within ten days or a fortnight when he 'will drink tea with Dear Miss Renny' ('Renny' was Johnson's affectionate name for her). A few years later, after the death of the Thrales' young son Harry, he suggested that Frances should visit Harry's grieving mother: 'A visit from you will be well taken, and I think your intimacy is such, that you may very properly pay it in a morning. I am sure it will be thought seasonable and kind, and wish you not to omit it.'

Frances knew Johnson as a friend and confidant. She told him off for writing such short letters to her; he replied, teasingly, 'Dear Madam, You are as naughty as can be. I am willing enough to write to you when I have anything to say . . .' Her portraits of him show him without reserve.

She never signed her works, as if in denial that she had ever had the audacity to paint them, and there is no consensus as to which portraits are definitely by her. The most likely to be of her creation is a copy of her brother's 1775 portrait of Johnson reading, his eyes close to the page, devouring the text. Joshua in his portrait shows Johnson curling over the pages of the book he is reading in his eagerness to absorb the words and ideas. His huge, muscular hands are clutching on to the volume in an obvious reference to his desire to devour knowledge. Frances's Johnson is more reserved, and if anything more intense. She takes our gaze away from the pages of the book to Johnson's deep-set eyes, his furrowed brow, the intensity of his thought. Her Johnson is pre-eminently a thinker.

Her portrait of Johnson in old age (now owned by Haverford College, Pennsylvania) gives us Johnson without artifice. His face sags, his eyes have lost their intensity. He looks weary, grey with fatigue and illness. The portrait has usually been attributed to Joshua, but it is much more characteristic of Frances's naturalistic style and her open brushwork. Johnson, we know from his correspondence, did sit for her on a number of occasions in late 1779 and 1780, and also in 1783, by which time she was no longer living with her brother. In August 1783 he told Hester Thrale, 'I sat to Mrs Reynolds yesterday for my picture, perhaps the tenth time, and I sat near three hours, with the patience of *Mortal born to bear*. At last she declared it quite finished and seems to think it fine.' He, though, was appalled by the finished portrait, bewailing that Frances had made him look like a 'grimly ghost'.

He does, indeed, appear ghost-like in this portrait, and close to death. Frances does not fudge but depicts Johnson as she knows him, in all the ghastliness of old age, not how she thinks he might wish to appear. If she had tried to make a career as a portraitist, it is doubtful she would have succeeded. Her temperament was too honest, too direct ever to appeal to those who could afford to pay for their picture to be painted.

Joshua, in contrast, knew exactly how to best please his prospective clients. He never forgot the cryptic advice he had been given as a young man, which he copied and kept by him: 'A man in some measure must be the Trumpet of his Fame.' To be successful he needed to be his own PR person and marketing manager. He must ensure that his sitters feel comfortable in his studio, and to do this he must create the illusion that he is himself a gentleman of leisure, not grubbing out a living as an artist. But with this sleight of hand, Frances was never comfortable, because it implied a negation of their upbringing as a plain and simple Christian family in a small West Country village. Joshua also committed what for Frances was a mortal sin by working on Sundays to maximise his potential earnings (many years later she asked Johnson to recommend in his will that Joshua should stop doing this, to save his soul). His career was more essential to him than his faith.

Frances, though, was too clear-sighted not to admit deep down that when she castigated Joshua for his desperate desire to appear wealthy and well-born she was not being entirely fair.' She knew that she needed Joshua to be successful so that she herself could share in his profits and live semi-independently as an unmarried woman. Yet in living under his patronage and conforming to his social pretensions she felt that she was presenting a false image of herself to the world. More confusing still was the frustration of being obliged to present this image of herself as a fine lady when this prevented her from becoming what she most wanted to be: a working artist like her brother.

No wonder she was fretful and indecisive, never able to make up her mind about anything, torn between pleasing her brother, her patron, and satisfying her own wishes. She disliked the 'shewy' life indulged in by her brother, and refused to ride in the grand carriage which he bought from a former Lord Mayor of London to complement his new and very prestigious house in green and leafy Leicester Fields. She felt uncomfortable in these new grandiose surroundings, their house much larger than anyone else's, with extra studios for Joshua's team of painting assistants and a gallery to show off his latest commissions.

Joshua's business had now become, like Hudson's, a mini-'manufactory', so that he often worked on five different portraits in a day, with his assistants adding backgrounds and fussing over details. He was far too busy painting to be seen careering around town in his smart new coach, with its brand new coat of arms. This was Frances's job, he told her, advertising the Reynoldses' coat of arms, the Company of Reynolds. But she was far too shy and retiring and was 'quite ashamed to be seen' out and about in a carriage fit for a lady. As her friend the writer Ellis Cornelia Knight once said of her, 'She was an amiable woman, very simple in her manner, but possessed of much information and talent, for which I do not think every one did her justice, on account of the singular *naiveté* which was her characteristic quality, or defect, for it often gave her the appearance of want of knowledge.'

Frances could not associate the Joshua of No. 47 Leicester Fields with the brother she once knew in their cottage back in Plympton. Joshua was by then earning at least £6,000 a year (or about half a million pounds). He, in turn, could not understand his sister's unwillingness to share in his gathering celebrity, commissioned to paint Garrick as Hamlet and Richard III, and responsible for crafting the queen-like image of the actress Sarah Siddons. His portrait of Siddons as the Tragic Muse, dressed in a gown of burnished gold and seated on a throne, is an arresting study not of a mere Drury Lane actress but of a woman of regal stature.

Meanwhile Frances was expected to keep her talent under wraps. Joshua was only too happy to grant his sister a portion of the life he was enjoying, but he would not share with her the one thing she most desired: his knowledge of art history, anatomy and the chemistry of paint. 'He never gave her the slightest instruction,' asserted the Victorian biographer Ellen Clayton who in 1876 compiled an anthology of *English Female Artists*. She included an essay on Frances, suggesting that her talent was of sufficient distinction to bring her recognition even several decades after her death.

In her commonplace book, only one volume of which has survived, Frances copied out passages from Seneca, Aristotle, Plato, Archimedes. Her selection of quotations could be read as an indication of her pent-up ambition, her claustrophobic life, her inability to fulfil the talent she believed it was her Christian duty to cultivate. 'Seneca says that had I been debarred from the study of physiologica it would not have been worth coming in to the world,' reads one page. On the next, Frances has copied out a passage which vividly describes the impact on the personality of being confined 'useless' in a gilded cage, not free to 'observe', to take note of the natural world which surrounds us:

He that neglects this study seems to live like a spider in a palace who taking notice only of those objects that obtrude themselves upon her senses lives ignorant of all the other rooms of the house save that wherein she lurks and discerning nothing either of the architecture of the stately building or of the proportion of the parts of it in relation to each other and to the entire structure makes it her whole business by entrapping flies to continue an useless life or exercise herself to spin cobwebs which tho' consisting of very subtle threads are unserviceable for any other than her own trifling ones.

Spiders, webs, trapped flies. The imagery is potent and perhaps reflects what Frances was beginning to feel about her life in London.

On another page is pasted a cutting from a newspaper, advertising language classes in Greek, Latin, French and English, 'taught by a graduate of the University of Paris . . . at half a guinea per month . . . or one shilling per night'. Gentlemen, or ladies, could be taught privately, 'either at home or away'. Was Frances thinking of learning French? Was she planning to make her escape?

Frances's dilemma was that, unlike her brother, she could not please if this meant compromising her principles. Hester Thrale noted that Frances 'seems resolved – nobly enough – not to keep her Post by Flattery if She cannot keep it by Kindness'. Frances's unwillingness, or rather inability, to bend to circumstance, to put on a carapace of wit and good humour, was something that her brother simply could not understand, or tolerate.

When Fanny Burney met Frances in the 1770s she was struck by her inability to decide on anything: 'Whatever she suggested, or planned, one day, was reversed the next; though resorted to on the third, as if merely to be again rejected on the fourth; and so on, almost endlessly.' Burney had no patience with Renny, declaring sharply but probably astutely that she 'made throughout life the great mistake of nourishing a singularity which was her bane, as if it had been her greatest blessing . . . it was that of living in an habitual perplexity of mind, and irresolution of conduct, which to herself was restlessly tormenting, and to all around her was teasingly wearisome.' A virtue had been turned by her situation and a succession of personal setbacks into a vice.

Even Johnson was at times frustrated by Frances's habit of over-apologising, over-compensating, never being sure enough of herself to make a clear and clean decision. 'My dearest Dear,' he writes to her on 28 June 1774, 'I have no suspicion of your being to blame, with respect to me, nor do I want so much apology for what you cannot help.' But this irresolution, this 'singularity', was Frances's 'defensive Eloquence', the only way she could assert her 'own Performance' by refusing to conform to what was expected of her.

To his friends, Joshua was always the genial host, beaming with the benevolent good humour he created in his self-portraits. Boswell dedicated his *Life of Samuel Johnson* to Reynolds because Joshua's home had so often been the venue for the conversations from which Boswell's version of Johnson was leached. His house in Leicester Fields became 'a common centre of union for the great, the accomplished, the learned, and the ingenious'. Dinner with Joshua and Frances was always entertaining because of the mix of company, from the sociable musician Dr Burney to the politician Edmund Burke. The food, though, was often 'execrable'. 'A table, prepared for seven or eight, was often compelled to contain fifteen or sixteen.' Guests would be invited at the last minute or asked to stay on after sitting for Joshua. 'When this pressing difficulty was got over, a deficiency of knives and forks, plates and glasses succeeded.' Edmond Malone recalled, 'There seemed to be a general, though tacit, agreement among the guests, that *mind* should predominate over *body*; that the honours of the turtle and the haunch should give place to the feast of wit, and that for a redundant flow of wine the flow of soul should be substituted.'

Frances enjoyed the meeting of minds, but Joshua soon tired of his sister's patent deficiencies as a housekeeper, her inability to bargain with the fishmonger, run the kitchen, rule the servants. He became to her 'a gloomy tyrant', unwilling to allow her to do anything more than run errands for him. Eventually, after almost fifteen years of mutually increasing antipathy, she arranged to visit a friend who had married a Frenchman and was living in Paris, leaving Joshua and London for several months.

The timing of her departure, coincidentally, or perhaps deliberately, was not long after Joshua had been elected as the first President of the Royal Academy in 1768 and had simultaneously been knighted for his services to art. The recognition of Joshua's talent may have heightened the sibling rivalry, and also his desire to sort out his household arrangements to make them more congenial. But another reason for Frances's decision to leave not just London but England for a while might be found in her commonplace book.

A mysterious 'Mr P.', sometimes also known as 'Mr B.', is at first mentioned frequently. He is obviously a close friend, but then her references to him change their tone. Reading between the lines, Frances gradually and almost imperceptibly had fallen in love with Mr P. But when she declared her love she was abruptly and coolly rejected.

Frances confesses, ruefully, in her commonplace book:

> How dangerous . . . to commence a Friendship with a man of Sense, for from the kind, the generous Friend our Hearts we strive not to defend. Meanwhile the god of Love prepares his pointed Dart his subtle snares by thy approaches buys his power and gains upon you every Hour.

Was Mr P., as has been suggested, really Mr J., and was Frances another contender to be Johnson's 'second wife'? Her nieces teased her that this was Johnson's intention after he had gone on a summer trip with Joshua and Frances in 1762, visiting their Reynolds relatives in Devon. Johnson could certainly have been that 'man of Sense'. But it seems unlikely. The friends never fell out; and Johnson remained steadfast until death.

Frances did not stay long in Paris, returning after just a few months. She suffered deeply from her disappointment and humiliation, but she was far too honest with herself not to admit that much of her pain came from her own hurt pride:

> Yet Reason often whispers me
> Was chiefly Shame my Heart regained
> The waked remorse, the roused up pride
> Then gave my Breast unusual pain . . .

Bruised, she decided that the single state was unnatural:

> Else why to man were social passions given
> Joys unimparted lose their power to please
> And life's best comforts sink to tasteless ease . . .

Yet she never married, and her last years were peripatetic, moving house to find cheaper rooms while her brother continued his life of luxury in Leicester Fields. She died in 1807.

*

Frances's honesty and wit were shared by Charlotte Lennox, whom Frances knew through her brother and Johnson. They were friends in need, rather than temperament. When, in 1775, Lennox was seeking subscriptions for her latest playscript, *Old City Manners*, she applied to Frances for help, knowing that she and her brother were at the heart of London life. Frances, though, felt unequal to the task of touting round her friends for money to support Lennox, and she complained to Johnson that Lennox was asking too much of her. Johnson tried to help Frances out with her friend, by writing Lennox a letter in which he told her, 'You complain of Miss Reynolds who probably knows not three people whom She can properly solicit.' By expecting too much from your friends, he added, 'you discourage them, for they finding themselves unequal to your expectation, will rather do nothing and be quiet, than do their utmost, and yet not please'. Frances was forgiven by Lennox, and for some months they shared rooms in Somerset House and also in Queen Square, Westminster; two women struggling to support themselves without a regular source of income.

Frances, though, had made the most of her stay in Paris, visiting the Louvre to study paintings by the great masters that Joshua had told her about but she had never seen. She also displayed an uncharacteristic verve and entrepreneurial talent by buying up paintings at auction that she hoped to sell on her return, providing herself with a small annuity on which she could begin to live independently. She had in mind as customers her friends Henry and Hester Thrale who needed paintings to fill the new extension to Streatham Park. But she neglected to ask them in advance what they would like, and her collection of paintings, although of exquisite taste, were too expensive and too singular for the Thrales. Her plans for independence began to unravel.

Sir Joshua meanwhile had invited his favourite niece, the startlingly beautiful Theophila (or 'Offie') Palmer, to take over Frances's housekeeping duties while she was away. The arrangement proved so congenial that he was unwilling to allow his sister to take up the reins at Leicester Fields on her return. Frances was obliged to retire to Devon, taking comfort in the familiarity of her childhood scenes. She wrote in her commonplace book:

> Far from this cruel man removed
> which once too tenderly I loved
> Here fate has kindly driven
> My shattered bark at length to rest . . .

Whether she was referring here to her 'cruel' brother, or the lover who had disappointed her, she did not make clear. 'Mr B.' was perhaps the more likely target since with Joshua her relations had always been difficult, and could never be described as 'tender'. But that brother and sister had fallen out soon became the talk about town.

Like Johnson, Frances had become addicted to London and she soon discovered she could no longer be contented with life among her sisters and their families in Devon. 'My faculties are all becalmed in the dead region of Torrington,' she confided in her notebook. 'I want some incentive of emulation to awake my slumbering faculties.' For a while she moved to rooms in Windsor, close enough to London but not too close to draw comments from within her brother's circle. Even so, Hester Thrale remarked on the estrangement between the siblings in her *Thraliana*: 'Why should he [Sir Joshua] refuse his Purse and even his Civilities to a Sister so amiable & so accomplished as Miss Reynolds – I cannot find it out.'

Sir Joshua not only had his huge house and gallery in Leicester Fields; he had also built for himself a grandiose house on the top of Richmond Hill (now called Wick House), commissioning William Chambers to design it. The views from the back of the house, overlooking the Thames and Petersham Meadow, were so spectacular that Reynolds was tempted to paint his only landscape, *A View from Richmond Hill*. Yet he rarely stayed in the house, preferring to return to Leicester Fields so that he could wake early and start work in his studio.

Frances suggested that she should move into Wick House, where she could live within her brother's patronage but rarely in his company. Joshua sent her a cold and ironical reply:

Dear Sister

I am very much obliged to you for your kind and generous offer in regard to the house at Richmond, not only in giving me leave to use it occasionally but even as long as I live, provided I will give it to you, but as I have no such thought at present I can only thank you for your kindness. Tho I am much older than you I hope I am not yet arrived to dotage as you seem to think I am, voluntarily to put myself in the situation of receiving the favour of living in my own house instead of conferring the favour of letting you live in it.

I am your most affectionate Brother . . .

Frances's reply was frosty, but she asked Johnson to look it over before she sent it, since she didn't want to make her relations with her brother any worse. Johnson suggested she should tone it down to make it seem more conciliatory. His version read:

> Dear Brother,
> I know that complainers are never welcome yet you must allow me to complain of your unkindness, because it lies heavy at my heart and because I am not conscious that I ever deserved it. I have not perhaps been always careful enough to please but you can charge me, and I can charge myself with no offence which a Brother may not forgive.
>
> If you ask me what I suffer from you, I can answer that I suffer too much in the loss of your notice; but to that is added the neglect of the world which is the consequence of yours.
>
> If you ask what will satisfy me, I shall be satisfied with such a degree of attention when I visit you, as may set me above the contempt of your servants, with your calling now and then at my lodgings and with your inviting me from time to time with such parties as I may properly appear in. This is not much for a sister who has at least done you no harm, and this I hope you will promise by your answer to this letter; for a refusal will give me more pain than you can desire or intend to inflict . . .

'Take your choice,' Johnson told Frances, 'and if you like mine, alter any thing that you think not ladylike . . .' Frances could not bring herself to send Johnson's version because she knew it not to be honest. She also reckoned that Joshua, knowing his sister, would never believe that she had written it. She sent him her original letter.

In a way, Frances was relieved. The truth had finally been said. The siblings did not like each other, and in her view Joshua was mean, parsimonious and ungodly. But she paid a huge price for her self-disclosure, ending up with nowhere to live and no income. At first she stayed with her friends John Hoole and his wife (Hoole was a member of their dining circle, a scholar who had translated Ariosto). They lived in the Adelphi, the fashionable complex built by the Adam brothers where the actor David Garrick and his wife also had rooms. Frances paid for her stay in kind by painting Hoole – a rare, formal portrait which was used as the frontispiece for Hoole's best-selling translation of Ariosto's *Orlando Furioso* (published in 1783). Hoole is depicted as the earnest scholar, wearing heavy-rimmed spectacles, and drawn in profile, his gaze, unusually, averted from the viewer towards some object far away and beyond.

In the next few years, Frances moved constantly, burdened always with her 'luggage of pictures', bought in France. She kept them with her, so precious had they become she was unable to contemplate the thought of selling them, even though she needed the money. Johnson wrote to her at Dover Street, Piccadilly: 'You are not to think that I neglect you, for your nieces will tell you how rarely they have seen me' (those nieces who were living with her brother in great pomp in Leicester Fields). 'And yet you must resolve to talk things over without anger.' He did not cricitise his friend Frances for the breakdown of relations, nor did he blame Joshua. He chose the more difficult option of steering a middle course between brother and sister, successfully keeping both of them as friends, empathising with Frances but also understanding why Joshua was so irritated by her.

'Dearest Madam,' he began a letter to Frances on Tuesday 19 October 1779:

You will do me a great favour if you will buy for me the prints of Mr Burke, Mr Dyer, and Dr Goldsmith, as you know a good impression.

If any of your own pictures be engraved, buy them for me. I am filling a little room with prints . . .

Johnson was by now living in such comfort and ease at Bolt Court that he was thinking of hanging prints upon his walls. These would have been large mezzotints, printed on fine parchment. He asked Frances to buy prints of portraits by Joshua, but tactfully also requested prints by herself. Two days later he wrote again to his 'Dear Madam': 'I want no company but yours, nor wish for any other . . .' He even suggested he should sit for her again, encouraging her to keep on painting.

Frances agreed to paint Johnson again, but by then she had taken up writing – just like her brother. Since 1768, Joshua in his capacity as President of the Royal Academy had given annual lectures to the students, which were later published as the *Discourses* (a project in which he was greatly assisted by Johnson as editor). Frances decided she wanted to make her own contribution to these debates on the 'principles of taste' and the 'ideas of beauty'. By 1781 she had written enough of her *An Enquiry Concerning the Principles of Taste, and of the Origin of Our Ideas of Beauty, etc.* to show the manuscript to Johnson and to the leading patron of women writers at the time, Elizabeth Montagu. She told Montagu, 'I wished to leave behind me a respectable memorial of my existence, which I then flattered myself this would be.'

Johnson's initial reaction was muted, choosing his words very carefully. 'There is in these pages such force of comprehension,' he told her, 'such nicety of observation, as Locke and Pascal might be proud of.' But then he added his killer blow: 'However, it cannot be published in its present state.' And he pulled no punches in telling her why: 'Many of your notions seem not to be very clear in your own mind; many are not sufficiently developed and expanded for the common reader: it wants everywhere to be made smoother and plainer.' As a wise editor, he ended with some encouragement, but advisedly: 'You may by revisal and correction make it a very elegant and a very curious work.'

Frances, singular and unbending as ever, did very little revision and a year later Johnson wrote to her again: 'Dearest Madam, Your work is full of very penetrating meditation, and very forcible sentiments. I read it with a full perception of the sublime, with wonder and terror, but I cannot think of any profit from it; it seems not born to be popular.' Knowing the market, he told her, 'If a Bookseller would buy it at all, as it must be published without a name, he would give nothing for it worth your acceptance.'

The *Enquiry* is curiously original. Frances devises a diagrammatic understanding of the progressive stages, or degrees, of 'human excellence'. 'In the exact centre of my circle of humanity,' she writes, 'I have placed nature, or the springs of the intellectual powers,' rising through Common Sense towards Beauty and Truth and culminating in 'the pinnacle, or ultimate point, *sublimity*'. Few, very few, will attain Sublimity, but it is the goal to which we all should aspire.

Beauty and Truth she defines as 'that beauty which is demonstrable truth, and that truth which is demonstrable beauty' – but she fails to elucidate her meaning, only giving herself forty-nine short pages to get to grips with the philosophical questions that lie behind artistic expression. 'Though all truth resolves into one truth, one beauty, one good,' writes Frances in another muddled sentence, 'as all colours resolve into one light; though the scientifical intellectual colours, classes, or leading principles of science, the *physical*, the *moral*, the *metaphysical*, &c, &c, resolve into intellectual light, beauty, or good; it is, I imagine, the moral truth, that is the characteristic truth of beauty, for were we to analyse the pleasing emotions we feel at the sight of beauty, we should, I imagine, find them composed of our most refined moral affections . . .'

Framed by Frances's religious beliefs, the *Enquiry* is less an essay on art appreciation than an attempt by Frances to equate her artistic endeavours with the life of the spirit. But her ambition was greater than her ability. She argues, for instance, that 'the beauty of each sex is seen only through the medium of the virtues belonging to each'. But this she can only explain by asserting, 'The softness and mildness of the feminine expression would be displeasing in a man. The robust and determined expression of the rigid virtues, justice, fortitude, &c would be displeasing in a woman.'

Frances appears to be saying that the sexual difference is not just about gender, but also involves personal qualities. 'It is cultivation,' she argues, 'that gives birth to beauty as well as to virtue, by calling forth the visible object to correspond with the invisible intellectual object.' Without such 'cultivation', through the exercise of the intellect, beauty and virtue are not possible to attain. But did she really believe this? That virtue was impossible to attain without education?

Regardless of the consequences of what she writes, Frances plunges on: 'The negro-race seems to be the farthest removed from the line of true cultivation of any of the human species; their defect of form and complexion being, I imagine, as strong an obstacle to their acquiring true taste (the produce of mental cultivation) as any natural defect they may have in their intellectual faculties.'

It's a shock to read these sentiments from the gentle, pure, religious woman who emerges from her letters, and many of Frances's readers in 1785 would not have agreed. Her friend Hannah More was an active anti-slavery campaigner, writing pamphlets in support of those who argued that the slave trade must be abolished. Elizabeth Carter, too, wrote to a friend in June 1788, at the height of the debates about slavery:

> I am sure you have too gentle & humane a disposition not to be inter-
> ested for the poor Negroes, & therefore you will rejoice with me that
> Mr Pitt has in so decided a manner declared himself in their favour.
> The putting an end to this dreadful cruelty & oppression will do Honour
> to our Age, to our Country & our Religion. There is something very
> noble in not suffering any little particular commercial Interest to
> outweigh the Importance of a measure founded on the eternal &

universal Laws of Justice & Mercy. Wherever a Regard to what is right in itself is made the leading principle of Action, the Event must be happy to nations, as well as to Individuals.

Johnson, too, in his pamphlet about the American fight for independence, *Taxation No Tyranny*, asked, provocatively, 'How is it that we hear the loudest *yelps* for liberty among the drivers of negroes?'

Frances's brother had a black footman for a number of years in the 1770s, who may well have sat for his portrait of *A Young Black*. Johnson also had a black servant, Frank Barber, who arrived in Gough Square from Jamaica where he had been a slave, born on a sugar plantation, and later brought to England by his owner. Barber was given to Johnson as a young boy, not long after Tetty Johnson's death, to help in the house and to give him a familial responsibility that would take his mind off his loss. Barber lived with Johnson until his death, whereupon he became Johnson's sole heir, much to the chagrin of some of his employer's friends who believed it unseemly for a black man to inherit the life savings and surviving trinkets of the dictionary-maker. But Johnson always treated Frank with the same respect he gave the other members of his disparate household.

When Frances wrote of the differences between racial groups, she was not necessarily explaining her actual experience of the black people she met in London. But her naivety and her lack of intellectual rigour troubled Johnson. He told her if she must publish, then she should do so anonymously: 'You would then see the opinion of the publick without hazard, if nobody knows but I.' Knowing too well her stubborn character, he added, 'If any body else is in the secret, you shall not have my consent to venture.'

He was unwilling, though, to disappoint her, and he did negotiate with his friend, the printer Edmund Allen, for 250 copies of Frances's *An Enquiry Concerning the Principles of Taste, and of the Origin of Our Ideas of Beauty, etc.* to be printed (with the changes he had suggested). On 12 April 1784, just months before his death, he wrote to Frances, 'You must send me the copy to show the printer. If you will come to tea this afternoon we will talk about it together.' By the end of the month he told her, 'Mr Allen has looked over the papers and thinks one hundred copies will come to five pounds.' Johnson, though, was still hoping that he could persuade Frances to make the changes he had recommended, and which he knew were necessary.

In the end, Johnson died before the *Enquiry* was printed. But in the following July Frances went ahead and arranged for the 250 copies to be privately printed, just as she had written it, no changes made, and with a dedication to Elizabeth Montagu. A few days later, she confessed to Mrs Montagu that she had ignored Johnson's advice, 'from an opinion I had conceived of Dr Johnsons being strongly prejudiced against women's literary productions'. Now, though, she was regretting her obstinacy – and her misguided view that Johnson was not being supportive enough – and was forced to admit, 'I deceived myself . . . he judged justly of the work, and his opinion exactly corresponded with yours!' Montagu had also warned her that the *Enquiry* was too slight, and too 'ingenious', to gain the applause of 'the present set of Readers'.

Yet Frances could paint. Those few portraits to have survived have a subdued yet mesmerising intensity. Her painting of Hannah More, for instance, completed in 1780, is unusual in showing More in her professional capacity as a writer, seated at a desk, poised in thought, and yet also in achieving an informal, intimate quality. Hannah is dressed in a simple rust-red gown with a plain white chemise underneath. She has no ruffles, no bows, no jewellery of any kind, except in her hair, which is drawn back off her face and braided over her shoulder. She is not dressed for 'society' but is at work, earning her living. If we are in any doubt as to her career, a shelf of books is shown behind her left shoulder. Frances asserts Hannah More's stature as a successful playwright, but she also conveys More's warmth of character. The portrait has a real presence, commanding our attention.

In her portrait of Elizabeth Montagu, Frances achieved a power, a rigour that is not always comfortable. In Sir Joshua's portrait, the wealthy and influential Montagu is seated on an elegant chair as if in a Grecian temple. Her elaborately ruffled silk dress signifies her social stature; her demure, thoughtful expression gives away little real character. In Frances's small oval portrait, Montagu has the same pose, in profile, her eyes downcast, her expression thoughtful, but the similarity goes no further. Frances's Montagu is a thin-lipped, slightly severe woman, somewhat sad, by no means the poised and successful society lady painted by her brother and by other male artists such as Allan Ramsay.

Frances also once portrayed Johnson's house-guest, the peevish Anna Williams. This, too, is a discomfiting picture. Frances does not flinch from suggesting Williams's blindness, and the difficulties of her disability, by showing her staring blankly into the distance, her pallid face drawn tight with frustration. The painting now hangs in Dr Johnson's House in Gough Square, and has been studied by artists interested in the portrayal of disability. Frances does not dissemble; she shows Williams as a blind and irritable old woman. She does not try to attract our sympathy. She portrays Williams as truthfully as she can, and thereby honours her.

We shall never know for sure which portraits of Johnson are by her. But Frances also left us a portrait of Johnson in words, which is incontrovertibly her own. She never published her 'Recollections', but they were preserved by her family and eventually included by the Victorian scholar, George Birkbeck Hill, in his collection of *Johnsonian Miscellanies*. Frances writes about her memories of Johnson in the same randomly assorted style as Hester Thrale uses in her *Anecdotes*, but Frances gives us insights into those parts of Johnson's life and character on which no one else reflected any light.

Hester Thrale, setting herself up as a literary biographer, begins the *Anecdotes* (which were published by her in 1786) with an aphorism worthy of Johnson himself, 'Too much intelligence is often as pernicious to Biography as too little.' Frances begins her 'Recollections' by using her observational powers as an artist to convey what she understood to be Johnson's most essential quality – his compassion, his charity, his humanity:

> The first time I was in company with Dr Johnson I remember the impression I felt in his favour, on his saying that as he return'd to his lodgings about one or two o'clock in the morning, he often saw poor children asleep on thresholds and stalls, and that he used to put pennies into their hands to buy them a breakfast.

Johnson's habit of emptying his pockets to the poor and needy was unusual among his contemporaries, and Frances loved him for it.

Her 'Recollections' of Johnson have an authority derived from this sureness of observation. Frances, for instance, suggests that Johnson's constant movements of hands, arms and legs are of a psychological, rather than neurological, nature. Many of Johnson's friends have left us descriptions of these extraordinary gestures or 'anticks', but Frances adds to her description layer on layer, like an artist applying paint, first giving us one detail to reflect on, and then adding another to deepen our understanding. Her account surpasses even Frances Burney's diary entry in its accuracy, its analysis.

Burney was famous in her time as a novelist who created vivid character studies in just a few words; after her death she was admired as a diarist who brought to life the people she had known. Burney tells us of Johnson's 'almost perpetual convulsive motions, either of his Hands, lips, Feet, knees, & sometimes of all together'. She adds:

> the sight of them can never excite ridicule, or, indeed, any other than melancholy reflections upon the imperfections of Human Nature; for this man, who is the acknowledged Head of Literature in this kingdom, & who has the most extensive knowledge, the clearest understanding, & the greatest abilities of any Living Author,—has a Face the most ugly, a Person the most awkward, & manners the most singular, that ever were, or ever can be seen.

Burney was almost two generations younger than Johnson and was a little overawed by his stature as the 'Head of Literature'. Renny, in contrast, knew him more than twenty years earlier, when he was still burdened with grief for his recently deceased wife and struggling with debt before he was granted the royal pension. She was not subdued by his reputation, and the Johnson she tries to convey is the man who was her most loyal friend. She records his difficulties, not to belittle him or show his strangeness, but to portray his full meaning as a person, to prove his greatness of soul.

She recalls how obsessively he would have to go through a routine of strange movements every time he entered a building from the street, or a room of people. He could not stop himself from doing them, even when escorting the blind Anna Williams, and holding on to her arm to prevent her bumping into anything. Williams would find herself being spun around, whirling and twirling as if in a dance. Even then, Johnson could not stop himself moving, explains Frances, swinging his feet and stretching his arms, to the danger of everyone else in the room:

> Sometimes he would make the back part of his heels to touch, sometimes the extremity of his toes, as if endeavouring to form a triangle, or some geometrical figure, and as for his gestures with his hands, they were equally as strange; sometimes he would hold them up with some of his fingers bent, as if he had been seized with the cramp, and sometimes at his Breast in motion like those of a jockey on full speed; and often would he lift them up as high as he could stretch over his head, for some minutes.

She gives us a precise image – 'like those of a jockey on full speed' – of Johnson holding his arms to his chest in tension, as if in a race.

Burney tells us that Johnson 'has a strange method of frequently twirling his Fingers, & twisting his Hands', which Sir Joshua depicted in his 1769 portrait, where the extraordinary feeling expressed in the movement of the hands reflects Johnson's pained expression. But only Renny of all Johnson's biographers seeks to explain the cause of these obsessive actions:

> Sometimes he would with great earnestness place his feet in a particular position, sometimes making his heels to touch, sometimes his toes, as if he was endeavouring to form a triangle, at least the two sides of one, and after having finish'd he would beat his sides, or the skirts of his coat, repeatedly with his hands, as if for joy that he had done his duty; and what was very extraordinary, after he had quitted the place, particularly at the entrance of a door, he would return to the same spot, evidently, I thought, from a scruple of conscience, and perform it all over again.

Renny's suggestion that Johnson's obsessive movements were caused from a 'scruple of conscience' is an intriguing psychological insight: as far as we know his nervous afflictions did not trouble him until his teenage years, when 'conscience' kicks in with merciless intent. She adds proof that the cause was 'in the mind':

> Many people have supposed that they [his extraordinary gestures of hands and feet and sometimes both at the same time] were the natural effects of a nervous disorder, but had that been the case he could not have sat still when he chose, which he did, and so still indeed when sitting for his picture, as often to have been complimented with being a pattern for sitters . . . I remember a lady told him he sat like Patience on a monument smiling at grief, which made him laugh heartily at the ridiculous coincidence of the idea with his irksome situation; for irksome it doubtless was to him, restraining himself as he did, even from his common and most habitual motion of seesawing, the more difficult for him to effect because the most habitual.

She had spent hours alone with Johnson while painting his portrait and had observed that he was able to remain still for long periods. This, too, is a tribute to Renny's friendship with Johnson, her quality of personality: he was always sufficiently at ease in her company not to feel compelled to twitch restlessly.

Only in Frances's 'Recollections' do we also discover that Johnson was discomfited by the strange, unsympathetic impression he made on those who did not know him. One day she was walking with him in Twickenham Meadows from her brother's house at the top of Richmond Hill. A whole crowd of 'men, women and children gathered round him, laughing'. Later when he sat down on a pile of logs by the riverside and began reading from a book in Latin (Grotius's *De Veritate Religionis*), the concentration required led him to see-saw 'at such a violent rate as to excite the curiosity of some people at a distance to come and see what was the matter with him'. He looked up and saw them looking at him, which 'put him in a passion', Renny recalled.

She was reminded of another occasion when his 'oddity' provoked a reaction:

> Once, in the street, he was annoyed by 'an impudent fellow', who stopped, and not only stared at but mocked him – his uncouth gestures and queer ways – so ludicrously that the Doctor could not refuse to recognise the burlesque. Obliged to resent the offence, he stepped up to the aggressor: 'Ah!' said he, 'you are a very weak fellow, and I will convince you of it.' Giving the man a blow which knocked him from the footpath into the gutter, flat on his back, he calmly resumed his walk.

Johnson, according to Renny, had the rough manners of a provincial man; and, like his uncle, the hefty physique of a boxer.

Boswell in the *Life* tells us of Johnson as a middle-aged man (and beyond) swimming in a deep pond outside Oxford, rolling down a hill, riding through Scotland. But Renny shows how Johnson, even at fifty-two, wanted to prove his physical strength in front of others. On another occasion, while he was on a visit to Devonshire with Joshua and Frances in 1762, he took on the ladies in a race:

> . . . at a gentleman's seat in Devonshire, as he and some company were sitting in a saloon, before which was a spacious lawn, it was remarked as a very proper place for running a Race. A young lady present boasted that she could outrun any person; on which Dr Johnson rose up and said, 'Madam, you cannot outrun me;' and, going out on the Lawn,

they started. The lady at first had the advantage; but Dr Johnson happening to have slippers on much too small for his feet, kick'd them off up into the air, and ran a great length without them, leaving the lady far behind him, and, having won the victory, he returned, leading Her by the hand, with looks of high exultation and delight.

Hester Thrale was chagrined to admit that Renny had a friendship with Johnson quite different from her own. She wrote in the *Thraliana*, 'Strange Connections there are in this odd World! his with me is mere *Interest* tho';— he loves Miss Reynolds better.' Johnson told Frances that he would rather sit with her than 'sit upon a throne'. He wrote her some flippant verses, inspired by the many afternoons they sat drinking tea together:

> I therefore pray thee, Renny dear,
> That thou wilt give to me.
> With cream and sugar soften'd well,
> Another dish of tea.
>
> Nor fear that I, my gentle maid,
> Shall long detain the cup,
> When once unto the bottom I
> Have drunk the liquor up.
>
> Yet hear, alas! this mournful truth,
> Nor hear it with a frown,
> Thou canst not make the tea so fast
> As I can gulp it down.

Johnson, insisted Frances, 'set a higher value upon female friendship than, perhaps, most men'. In return, Renny's 'singularity' allowed Johnson to unburden himself, confessing his fears about his mental state. She was not disturbed by Johnson's 'terrifying melancholy, which he was sometimes apprehensive bordered on insanity'.

Just as she did not shrink from painting Johnson as he really appeared to her in his old age, Frances did not hold back from writing about his fears for his sanity. 'That Dr Johnson's mind was preserved from insanity by his Devotional aspirations may surely be reasonably supposed,' she wrote in the 'Recollections'. 'No man could have a firmer reliance on the efficacy of Prayer, and he would often with a solemn earnestness beg of his intimate friends to pray for him.' She was not seeking to imply by this that Johnson was more religious than others, or more saintly. She merely related what she believed to be significant about his character: he used prayer as a form of protection, against his own demons and those he believed to haunt the world beyond our understanding.

In her 'Recollections' Frances Reynolds shows us the difficulties of her friend as well as his virtues. She had watched him struggling 'almost incessantly with some mental evil', and had witnessed the often uncomfortable singularity of his behaviour. She gives us a portrait of Johnson with all his 'lights and shades', noting that he 'had a most sincere and tender regard for Mrs Thrale', but that this did not stop him on occasion from speaking so very roughly to her 'that every person present was surprised how she could bear it so placidly'. Renny, as a portraitist, does not disguise what she has observed; she discloses.

8

The Taming of a Female Wit

'I have got the headache today by raking out so late with that gay libertine Johnson,' confessed Hannah More in 1776. She had not long arrived in London from the West Country but was already at the heart of the capital's literary and artistic circles, dining with Frances Reynolds and her brother, Sir Joshua, and taking tea with Elizabeth Montagu. A playwright whose debut on the West End stage was such a success it secured her financial independence, More arrived just in time to be included in Richard Samuel's 1778 portrait of the *Nine Living Muses*, portrayed as Melpomene, the Muse of the dramatic arts. She found it difficult, though, to sustain her career in the theatre without compromising her respectability, and a few years later More retreated from London, as if scared of the consequences of her success. Why did she feel the need to do this? Was this something to do with her own character, or the reflection of the difficulties faced by women who attempted to outdo their male rivals?

As a young woman, Hannah was not afraid to flash her wit, especially when seated next to Johnson at one of the chaotic dinner parties in Leicester Fields given by Joshua Reynolds and his sister Frances. 'They were both in remarkably high spirits; it was certainly her lucky night! The old genius was extremely jocular, and the young one [i.e. Hannah] very pleasant,' her sister Sarah recalled. 'You would have imagined we had been at some comedy had you heard our peals of laughter. They, indeed, tried which could "pepper the highest", and it is not clear to me that the lexicographer was really the highest seasoner.'

Hannah first met Johnson at the home of Sir Joshua, where she was amazed to find 'Abyssinia's Johnson! Dictionary Johnson! Rambler's, Idler's and Irene's Johnson!' standing in the middle of the drawing room with Sir Joshua's pet macaw sitting on his hand, as if he were having a conversation with the bird. Born on 2 February 1745, Hannah was young enough to be Johnson's daughter but she matched up to the 'Female Buffs' and 'Lady Hussars' he had conjured up in one of his *Idler* essays from 1758. In No. 5, Johnson teasingly advocates that women should be encouraged to join the army, echoing John Fayram's bombastic portrait of Elizabeth Carter with breastplate and shield. After all, 'Strength is of less importance since fire-arms have been used; blows of the hand are now seldom exchanged; and what is there to be done in the charge or the retreat beyond the powers of the sprightly maiden?'

In times of crisis (Britain was at war with France over its colonial posses-sions in Canada and India), Johnson suggests, women's talents should be fully utilised alongside men. 'The prejudices and pride of man have long presumed the sword and the spindle made for different hands, and denied the other sex, to partake the grandeur of military glory,' he argues. 'It were to be wished that some man, whose experience and authority might enforce regard, would propose that our encampments for the present year should comprise an equal number of men and women, who should march and fight in mingled bodies.'

Johnson welcomed at first Hannah's sprightly company; her uncomfortable observations on the behaviour of men and women when in society. She was another young woman whose refreshingly bright personality enlivened his last years. Hannah, though, often annoyed him by her anxiety to please. 'He never opens his mouth but one learns something; one is sure either of hearing a new idea,' she gushed, 'or an old one expressed in an original manner.' When the sometimes waspish, always snobbish Hester Thrale ranked all those within her circle of acquaintance from one to twenty she put Hannah at the top for 'worth of heart' and 'useful knowledge' but rated her 'Person, Mien & Manner' at zero. She did not care for Hannah's earnestness, her lack of sophistication.

Hannah grew up in a small four-roomed cottage attached to the school-house in the village of Fishponds, just a few miles from Bristol. Her parents were not wealthy or privileged. Jacob More had expected to inherit a considerable fortune but the will was contested by a litigious relative and

201

he lost out. He took up teaching, becoming the master of a charity school, and devoting his life to good works inspired by his deep religious convictions. Without sons, he ensured instead that his five daughters were all given an excellent grounding in the Classics, and the tenets of the Christian faith. Hannah was his star pupil – until he discovered that she was beginning to outclass him.

Unlike Nicholas Carter, who took great pride in his daughter Elizabeth's intellectual accomplishments, Jacob More had 'a strong dislike of female pedantry'. He feared for the future of his daughters if they failed to find husbands. What man would be willing to take a wife who was superior to him in wit and learning? Jacob stopped all his lessons in Latin and geometry, encouraging his girls to devote their energies instead to the 'domestic arts'. But it was already too late – not one of the More girls married.

Hannah of all the sisters was the most talented; an incessant scribbler of verses, rhymes, moral stories and plays. As a teenager, she declared she wanted to 'go to London and see the booksellers and bishops'. Her sisters, too, were not content to sit around stitching samplers and painting watercolours while waiting for husbands to arrive. In the spring of 1758, her eldest sister Mary left home aged twenty to set up her own school in Bristol; but not, like her father's, a charitable mission for the poor and underprivileged. On the contrary, Mary aimed much higher, taking on the rent of a house in the most select part of town, just behind the cathedral, close to College Green. Bristol was second only to London as a commercial city, a busy port with boats travelling to and from the West Indies via America laden with cargoes of sugar and slaves. Mary, assisted by her sister Betty (and later Sarah, Hannah and Patty), intended her school to attract the daughters of these newly affluent merchants.

The school's advertisement in the *Bristol Journal* declared that the 'Young Ladies' would be taught 'French, Reading, Writing, Arithmetic, and Needlework'. Dancing lessons would also be available to those willing to pay extra. The curriculum was thorough, but also very 'safe', designed to prepare girls for useful lives as wives and daughters. These girls (there was also a small number of boy pupils) were to leave school, having learnt how 'to be wise without vanity, happy without witnesses, and content without panegyrics; the exercise of which will not bring celebrity, but improve usefulness', as Hannah would later write in her *Strictures on the Modern System of Female*

Education (published in 1799). An 'exact mind' was the ultimate goal, not necessarily Elizabeth Carter's desire for an equal mind. Carter had been writing as the publishing revolution of the 1720s and 1730s encouraged the opening up of ideas and possibilities for women writers with books and magazines flooding on to the market. That women should achieve equal status with their male counterparts did not sound so far-fetched. It would not always be so.

The More sisters proved to be much more adept at managing a school than Johnson and his wife Tetty twenty years before them, or Mary Wollstonecraft and her sisters thirty years later. They were better equipped to teach than the Johnsons (benefiting from their father's knowledge and his experience of running a school) and more astute commercially than the Wollstonecrafts. Their curriculum was carefully designed to appeal to the aspirational merchants, who wanted their daughters to be taught the finer arts, but not to threaten them with too much ambition. In just four years the school roll had risen to sixty pupils, providing a financial independence for the More sisters. Johnson was hugely impressed when he heard about the school; he knew to his cost how difficult it was to make money from education. 'I love you all five,' he declared. 'I never was at Bristol—I will come on purpose to see you— what! five women live happily together!'

Hannah, nine years younger than her eldest sister Mary, at first attended the school as a pupil and was soon reading Racine, Voltaire and Metastasio in French and Italian. (Metastasio's plays were very popular in mid-century, Mozart using a libretto by him for his opera *Clemenza di Tito*.) By this time the sisters had moved their school to larger premises in Park Street, including the addition of a hall in which the girls could stage dramatic entertainments. As soon as she was old enough Hannah was roped in to teach. She also began writing plays for the girls to perform at the end of term. Here, she first experienced the thrill of hearing an audience applaud words that she had written.

The Search After Happiness, first performed at the school in 1762 and later published by Sarah Farley, the Quaker printer in Bristol, had a conventional theme – how to be happy. The setting, too, came straight out of theatrical tradition: a pastoral idyll full of shepherdesses and girls in ringlets and frilly dresses carrying milking pans. Four young ladies 'of distinction' set off in search of happiness, rather like Johnson's Rasselas. On their travels they happen upon the shepherdess Urania who teaches the young women lessons on life. The speeches are very moral and improving, as you might expect of

a play for the entertainment of 'young ladies', until suddenly you are startled
by Cleora's confession:

> I long'd to burst those female bonds, which held
> My sex in awe . . .

Such lines must have resonated powerfully with the fifteen-year-olds in the
audience. Cleora goes on:

> The thirst of Fame my bosom robb'd of rest,
> And envious Spleen became its constant guest.

Is this how Hannah felt, poised between restless ambition and female modesty?
Laurinda, in contrast, is shown to have too little ambition:

> From ignorance my chief misfortunes flow,
> I never wish'd to learn, or car'd to know . . .
> And busy trifles fill'd the tedious day . . .
> I lived extempore, as fancy fir'd,
> As chance directed, or caprice inspir'd;
> Too indolent to think, too weak to chuse . . .

Without purpose or activity, she has formed no thoughts or ideas of
her own:

> I took my colouring from the world around . . .
> Till nothing of my genuine self remain'd;
> My pliant soul from chance receiv'd its bent;
> And neither good perform'd, nor evil meant;
> From right to wrong, from vice to virtue thrown,
> No character possessing of its own.

Education for women is vital, declares Hannah. It encourages the development of personality, the fulfilment of talent. But then, suddenly, she switches
voices, as if aware she has said too much. Her four female adventurers, and
their audience, are warned:

> Taste, elegance and talents may be ours,
> But learning suits not our less vigorous powers.
> Learning but roughens, polished Taste refines,
> For woman shines but in her proper sphere.

'Science,' we are told, firmly, 'for *female* minds was never made.' Not every-thing is suitable for a woman.

In *The Search After Happiness*, Hannah reveals the conflicting impulses that would shape the course of her life. She was clever, witty, far-seeing and in thrall to the dramatic arts. Like Cleora, she thirsted for fame and longed to break free from the narrow world in which she had grown up, constrained by lack of money (with not enough even to buy the quires of paper she needed to satisfy her urge to write) and the constant struggle not to be downtrodden by circumstance. But she was also a very devout Christian and suspicious of the superficiality of the very things she so admired. Throughout her life she was beset with crippling illnesses, fevers, headaches, exhaustion.

By the 1760s, women of her modest upbringing did have many more opportunities to experiment with independence and a degree of autonomy. The More sisters, through the success of their school, became economically and personally self-sufficient; the task of educating young women, and giving them a much broader curriculum, provided them with a living *and* a purpose in life. Hannah, though, wanted more. She had read that women were being acknowledged as authors in the *Gentleman's Magazine*, and had enough confidence in her own ability to believe she was good enough to join them. If she knew about the difficulties faced by women writers who dared to make public their work, and especially female playwrights, she ignored the warn-ings. She would later read reports of Charlotte Lennox's play *The Sister* being booed off the stage at Covent Garden in February 1769 by a rent-a-mob crowd organised by a rival male playwright. But this did nothing to deflate her dream of going to London and of seeing her plays on stage in the West End.

But then, just as she was poised to break away, she received an unexpected proposal of marriage – and from an extremely eligible man. Her admirer, William Turner, was twenty years older than her but he was wealthy with an attractive estate at Belmont, not far from Bristol. Hannah taught his nieces and in the summer of 1766 was invited to spend a few days with them in the comfort of their uncle's country house. Turner was a confirmed bach-elor, but Hannah's energy, wit and understanding captivated him and he asked her to marry him.

It is easy to imagine why he would have chosen Hannah of all the More sisters. From her surviving portraits, she emanates an unusual calmness and an open, unfussy charm, as if she is someone who would have been very easy to live with. When her friend Frances Reynolds portrayed her in 1780, she shows her to be a professional woman, holding her quill and with a sheaf of papers at her desk. Hannah looks up at us as if poised in thought in the very act of composing her next scene. She appears thoughtful, preoccupied, but also very accessible, and not at all proud. She told her sisters afterwards, as if to explain why the portrait is so flattering, that Johnson had interrupted one of her sittings with Reynolds, saying 'good things to me by way of making me look well'.

Turner was not just rich; he was also known to be kindly, benevolent and respectably devout. How could Hannah refuse him? A date was fixed for the wedding, and Hannah prepared herself for her new role as lady of the manor. At least she could do good works while still having time (and a room of her own) to continue writing. What she didn't anticipate was Turner's chronic indecisiveness. For no apparent reason, apart from a bachelor's resistance to change, he proved incapable of acting upon the engagement and, for six long years, he kept Hannah hanging on, post-poning the date of the wedding – again and again and again. Whenever Hannah threatened to break off from him, tired of waiting for Turner to make up his mind, he begged her to reconsider. Yet still he could not bring himself to the altar.

Hannah was free neither to disentangle herself nor to pursue her desire to go to London. Meanwhile, the local gossips relished the story, speculating on what had gone wrong between Hannah and her fiancé to delay the marriage. Her parents did nothing to save her reputation, unwilling to assert themselves against a man so much wealthier and more socially powerful. After all, if the wedding did take place, Hannah would be elevated into a life of great comfort and stature, which could in turn be very helpful to her dowry-less sisters.

At last the situation was resolved through the mediation of a concerned family friend, the Revd James Stonhouse, who persuaded Turner that since he was obviously not intending to marry Hannah he should release her from their betrothal. Stonhouse also ensured that Hannah was recompensed for the humiliation, arranging for Turner to pay her an annuity of £200. Hannah was not at all happy to accept the money, almost as if she had been paid off. But what else could she do? Her reputation had been tainted, but not Turner's (who never married). She had waited six years for him to make up his mind, which she could have spent pursuing her ambition to publish and be famous.

Her annuity of £200 (the annual wage of a lady-in-waiting at Court) gave Hannah enough to live as a modest gentlewoman, without needing a husband. But the scandal of her abandoned engagement never quite left her. Even thirty years after the affair, the *Anti-Jacobin* newspaper (which frequently attacked Hannah because of her religious views) repeated the claims of an unauthorised biography of 'Miss More' that 'she purchased an annuity of £200 *at a very easy rate*', as if she imperilled her virtue to get hold of Turner's money.

Hannah did not allow the experience to embitter her or hold her back. On the contrary, as soon as she was free to leave Plympton, she set off for London with her sister Sarah, taking with her the manuscript of her latest play, *The Inflexible Captive*. She was so full of self-belief that she imagined if she hung around outside the stage door in Drury Lane waiting for David Garrick to appear, she would bump into him, charm him, and persuade him to read the manuscript of her play, which she just happened to have with her. If he read it, Garrick would surely accept it for his next production, she believed.

Hannah had no doubts about her talent, which is probably why she annoyed Johnson. Her contradictions were not about self-belief, but arose from her sense of moral purpose. Should she devote her talent to causes that had nothing to do with her Christian faith?

The plot of *The Inflexible Captive*, inspired by one of Metastasio's most popular opera libretti, was carefully calculated by Hannah to catch Garrick's interest. Set in the Roman empire, its historical setting was very appealing to audiences just as the period had been when Johnson wrote *Irene*. She and Sarah installed themselves in lodgings in Henrietta Street, as close to Drury Lane as possible. But Hannah was not prepared for the noise, the expense and the difficulties of life in the capital in freezing midwinter (she and Sarah arrived at the end of January 1774). To her dismay, Garrick was ill (the beginnings of the kidney disease that would kill him five years later) and was not able to act in any of his planned performances at Drury Lane. She did not see him on stage, let alone meet him by chance. Hannah retired to bed with a fever, and after just two months the sisters retreated home to Devon, their mission not accomplished.

Disappointment, though, only served to spur Hannah on. She had seen how different life in the capital could be, and understood very quickly that it was not as easy to make connections and meet the right people as in the small communities of the West Country. No one would recognise her name from an insignificant play that had only been staged at a girls' school and printed in Bristol. To impress Garrick, she must first publish another play, this time sold through a London printer, and to meet him she would need an introduction from someone who knew him.

In March 1774, she commissioned Thomas Cadell, prestigiously based in the Strand and who also published Johnson, to print copies of *The Inflexible Captive* with 'By Miss HANNAH MORE' in large capital letters on the title page. She wrote a dedication addressed to the Honourable Mrs Boscawen, widow of an admiral and herself a formidable patron and literary hostess to whose salon Hannah hoped to be invited. Like Charlotte Lennox, Hannah was not averse to name-dropping to ensure she was noticed.

In her play a father and his daughter tussle for emotional power. Attilia, the heroine, declares she will 'subdue the *woman* in my soul' because:

> A Roman virgin should be something *more*—
> Shou'd dare above her sex's narrow limits.

Attilia's father Regulus, the ruler of Rome, threatened by the Carthaginians, volunteers to be taken into capitivity to save Rome, even though he knows he will probably be killed. Attilia steels herself not to weep as she watches her father being escorted out of Rome under armed guard. She reaches beyond the 'narrow limits' of her gender. But then Hannah confuses us by insisting that Attilia's bravery is only in response to her father's will. She is not acting from her own volition. In her own life, Hannah displayed remarkable daring and sureness of purpose, counterpoised with periods of withdrawal and retreat.

She and Sarah arrived back in London in early May, bringing with them their younger sister Martha (also called 'Patty') for moral support. This time they found rooms as close as possible to Garrick's residence in the Adelphi, the new development designed by the Adam brothers on the banks of the Thames, just below the Strand. Garrick would have no chance of eluding Hannah and her sisters on this visit. Just in case, Hannah carried with her a letter of introduction from her friend Mrs Gwatkin, wife of a Bristol merchant and soap manufacturer, whose daughters Hannah had taught at the More sisters' school. The letter was addressed to Frances Reynolds, known to Mrs Gwatkin through her West Country connections. (Mrs Gwatkin's son Robert later married Frances's niece, the much-favoured Theophila.)

Frances was by then no longer living permanently with her brother Sir Joshua, but she was still very much a friend of Johnson and other members of the Literary Club. Hannah hoped through her to meet not just Garrick but Johnson too, as well as the bluestocking women such as Elizabeth Carter, Hester Thrale and especially Frances Boscawen and Elizabeth Montagu, both keen patrons of female writers.

On Monday 16 May, Hannah with her sisters bought tickets to see Garrick in one of his most famous Shakespearean roles, Lear. 'I felt myself annihilated before Him,' she wrote afterwards to Mary and Betty in Bristol, '& every Faculty of my Soul was swallowed up in Attention . . . I thought I should have been suffocated with Grief.' Garrick was accustomed to arousing such extravagant praise. At about the same time, Frances Burney admitted to her diary that she 'idolised' Garrick.

Hannah wrote also to her father's friend and her saviour, John Stonhouse, full of excitement about Garrick's performance. Stonhouse knew Garrick and forwarded the letter to him, casually mentioning that the writer just happened to be the author of a tragic drama, the manuscript of which he should have received a few weeks earlier.

Something in Hannah's letter caught Garrick's interest. She had so accurately and perceptively described his performance – those fleeting changes of mood, of expression, which betray the inner turmoil, the true humanity of Shakespeare's tragic heroes. He was intrigued by this young woman from Devon who wrote with the eye of a true critic, insightful but also rigorous. A week later, on Thursday 26 May, Hannah received a letter from the Great Roscius himself, advising her that his coach would call for her the next day to bring her and her sisters to the Adelphi for tea in the Garricks' apartment.

The tea party was a success and before long Hannah was a regular visitor at the Adelphi, treated almost like a daughter by the Garricks who had no children themselves but loved the company of young people. The actor-manager in charge of the Drury Lane Theatre wrote to Stonhouse with advice for Hannah on how she should set about writing her next play. She had a gift for writing quickly? Then she must learn to:

> . . . *correct* slowly . . . were I worthy to direct her she should first chuse a happy subject and well adapted to her genius—then she should take some time carefully to distribute her fable into Acts—*Character* & *circumstances*, alias *Situations*; should be well attended to . . . a Play without them is mere Dialogue . . . I could wish to see her *outlines*, before she writes one verse, and when the road is made a true Dramatic Turn Pike, I would have her seat herself upon Pegasus and gallop away as fast as she pleases—if she writes without Plan I will not insure her success.

Garrick was not well at this time, and was struggling to keep up his performances, but he perceived in Hannah a rare talent and in spite of his illness he took the trouble to give her a masterclass in writing. He had tact, too, and unusual sensitivity to the fragile confidence of novice writers, sending his advice via her old friend rather than giving it to her straight. His lesson was elementary, but crucial: Hannah had great strengths as a writer but she needed to learn how to create dramatic pace. Garrick was willing to teach her.

It was unlucky for Hannah that she arrived in London just as Garrick was planning his retirement from the stage and from the management of Drury Lane. But she was just in time to witness his series of farewell performances, sitting at his invitation in the best seats in the house, right next to the stage, where she could observe every gesture, every facial expression.

On Saturday 27 April 1776 Garrick played Hamlet for the last time. His performances in this role were so celebrated that a party of French enthusiasts, including Madame Necker, wife of the finance minister and mother of Madame de Staël, travelled from Paris to see him. Hannah gives us that rare thing: an insight into how Garrick worked upon his audience. 'In every part he [Garrick] filled the whole soul of the spectator, and transcended the most finished idea of the poet,' she enthused. 'The requisites of Hamlet are not only various, but opposed. In him they are all united, and as it were concentrated . . .' She then explains:

To the most eloquent expression of the eye, to the handwriting of the passions on his features, to a sensibility which tears to pieces the hearts of his auditors, to powers so unparalleled, he adds a judgment of the most exquisite accuracy, the fruit of long experience and close observation, by which he preserves every gradation and transition of the passions, keeping all under the control of a just dependence and natural consistency.

Garrick was delighted to have such a responsive and descriptive critic, and one who was young enough to be moulded by him. He hoped that through Hannah something of his power as an actor would be preserved for posterity to read about. This, he knew, was the only way his evanescent genius could live on. Hannah fully repaid his generosity, and her letters (preserved after her death and published in 1834) are one of our best sources for understanding what made his performances so popular (a complement to the letters of the Burney sisters who write about Garrick at the height of his powers in the late 1760s). She writes:

So naturally, indeed, do the ideas of the poet seem to mix with his own, that he seemed himself to be engaged in a succession of affecting situations, not giving utterances to a speech, but to the instantaneous expression of his feelings, delivered in the most affecting tones of voice, and with gestures that belong only to nature. It was a fiction as delightful as fancy, and as touching as truth.

The Garricks invited Hannah to move into rooms in the Adelphi so that she would have a desk to write at, and the opportunity to talk to David at length about the process of stagecraft. 'It is not possible for anything on earth to be more agreeable to my taste than my present manner of living,' she told her family in Devon. 'I am so much at my ease; have a great many hours at my own disposal, to read my own books, and see my own friends; and, whenever I please, may join the most polished and delightful society in the world! Our breakfasts are little literary societies; there is generally company at meals, as they think it saves time, by avoiding the necessity of seeing people at other seasons.' Garrick, she continued, 'sets the highest value upon his *time* of anybody I ever knew. From dinner to tea we laugh, chat, and talk nonsense; the rest of his time is generally devoted to study.'

Hannah had acquired a full-time tutor in the dramatic arts, and not just any old instructor but the most famous actor in Europe. In *The Search After Happiness* she had demonstrated an ability to write effective blank verse, but there is little drama and not enough stage action. From Garrick, she learnt how to get her characters on to the stage, and off again, how to advance the plot without burdening the audience with too much detail, and how to move an audience to tears, or to laughter, in just a few words. When Hannah began work on her new play, a tragedy called *Percy*, she created a moving story with real dramatic tension and clever plotting.

In return, she enlivened Garrick's retirement from the stage and gave him new purpose. When she left London briefly to visit her family and to find a place where she could write quickly, without the constant disruptions and temptations of city life, Garrick missed his pupil, telling her, 'We have wanted You at some of our private hours—Where's our Nine? We want our Nine! Silent was Every Muse—I can Say no more, but in plain English we love & esteem You—Yours my dear Miss More most affectionately.' Garrick loved to give his friends nicknames and for Hannah he chose 'Nine' after the Nine Muses.

Long before her big success on the London stage, he recognised Hannah's potential as a playwright, with talent enough to outdo her male rivals. Hannah did not disappoint him, and in a couple of years she was included by Richard Samuel in his group portrait of the *Nine Living Muses*. She stands behind Elizabeth Montagu, holding a silver chalice, her face raised heavenwards. Samuel, either intentionally or by accident, had captured the essence of More's character: her earnestness and capacity for rapture.

Percy, which was first performed at Covent Garden on 10 December 1777, was an immediate hit. A tragedy set in Northumberland during the Crusades, it tells the story of Elwina who is forced into marriage to the evil Douglas by her obdurate father, though she loves his most bitter rival, Percy. Meanwhile, Douglas constantly suspects his new wife of betraying him with Percy in a plot device reminiscent of *The Winter's Tale* and also *Othello*, with a crucial role played by an errant scarf.

Tragedies were very popular in the second half of the eighteenth century but with the exception of Shakespeare, Marlowe and Otway very few of them have stood the test of changing taste. More's drama, though, still works to great effect. She simplified her plot, boiling it down to the tormented relations of Elwina, Percy and Douglas. 'She lives to be my curse,' mutters Douglas, his jealousy giving him constant nightmares. Ravaged by emotional pain, he vows that Elwina, too, will suffer 'the sharp, keen tooth of gnawing Grief' on learning that her lover Percy is dead, killed by her husband. Percy, forewarned of Douglas's intent, flees for his life, but takes one last look at Elwina: 'One last, short glimpse of day,/ And then a long, dark night.'

Garrick guided More through every stage of the drama's development. On 20 August 1776 he warned her that the third act was too weak: 'I am not satisfy'd with it, it is the Weakest of the four, & raises such Expectation from the Circumstances, that a great deal more must be done, to content your Spectators & Readers.' (Play texts were usually published to coincide with the first performance, often making considerable sums of money for the authors, even if the staging itself was less successful.) By December 1776 More had rewritten the third act, which was 'much improved', said Garrick, but now the fourth act 'will not stand Muster—that must be changed greatly but how, I cannot yet Say'. Garrick told her that in these last scenes the pace of the drama must not falter; the fifth act must 'tear the heart to pieces, or woe betide you! I shall not pass over any scenes or parts of scenes that are merely written to make up a certain number of lines. Such doings, Madame Nine, will neither do for you nor for me.'

Garrick was a tough critic, but Hannah was an extremely gifted pupil and the extra hours she spent on polishing the text of *Percy* really paid off. The drama races along with breathless speed and in extremely taut, economical verse, as the love triangle between Elwina, Douglas and Percy unravels to bloody effect.

By 1 September 1777 the script was finished. Garrick, though, did not wish to see such a promising play in which he had invested so much time being turned into a success by his former rival, Sheridan, who had succeeded him as the manager at Drury Lane. Instead he sent it straight to Thomas Harris at Covent Garden, promising that he would write the Prologue and Epilogue himself. 'He thinks of nothing, talks of nothing, writes of nothing but *Percy*,' Hannah told her family with undisguised pride.

Harris not only accepted the play but announced the First Night for 10 December, just a few weeks away. All through November Hannah was kept busy revising the text as the read-throughs and rehearsals in the Green Room revealed where the action needed to move on more quickly to heighten the dramatic tension. When Frances Burney wrote her first play, a comedy, a couple of years later, she never saw it performed, in part because she was reluctant to become so closely involved in its production. The Green Room, she was firmly told by her father, was no place for a genteel woman. Perhaps Burney agreed, or found it too painful to watch actors recreating characters that until then had stayed safely private within her imagination. Hannah had no such shyness or reservation. Even though she had to deal with Harris, and not her friend and mentor Garrick, she was involved at every stage of the production until the First Night, which she attended, sitting in Harris's private box.

'I come the friend and champion of my sex,' announces the actress Mrs Bulkley in the Prologue, written for Hannah by Garrick, which greatly enhanced *Percy*'s cachet as a new play. 'We can as well as men do any thing.' Garrick not only gives the speech to an actress when it was more usual for a male actor to introduce the play, he also makes it clear that he welcomes and applauds Hannah's talent as a dramatist.

> Nay, better too, perhaps – for now and then
> These times produce much bungling among men . . .
> The men, who grant not much, allow us charms—
> Are eyes, shapes, dimples, then, our only arms? . . .
> A brave man will protect, not hurt a woman;
> Let us wish modestly to share with men,
> If not the force, the feather of the pen.

Hannah was here daring above her sex's 'narrow limits', says Garrick.

Hannah was delighted by the reaction of the audience. 'One tear is worth a thousand hands, and I had the satisfaction to see even the men shed them in abundance,' she told her sisters, adding:

The critics (as is usual) met at the Bedford [a coffee house in Covent Garden frequented by newspapermen] last night, to fix the character of the play. If I were a heroine of romance, and was writing to my confidante, I should tell you all the fine things that were said; but as I am a real living Christian woman, I do not think it would have been so modest. I will only say, as Garrick does, that I have had so much flattery, that I might, if I would, choke myself in my own pap.

A couple of nights later, though, Hannah was less comfortable with being in the playhouse and watching her own play. 'It is very odd, but it does not amuse me.' She had become self-conscious about her success. Having achieved her ambition to hear the applause of an audience in a London theatre, she was no longer so sure it was what she really wanted.

On the ninth night, she again attended the performance and discovered a 'brilliant', if intimidating, audience. 'Lady North [wife of the Tory Prime Minister] did me the honour to take a stage-box. I trembled when the speech against the wickedness of going to war was spoken, as I was afraid my lord was in the house, and that speech, though not written with any particular design, is so bold, and always so warmly received, that it frightens me, and I really feel uneasy till it is well over.' Lord North was in charge of the war against the American colonies. Hannah was beginning to experience the discomfort of being in the public eye.

The run of performances continued for an exceptional twenty-one nights from December right through into January. Hannah made £600 from the box office and another £150 from the publication of the text (or about £47,000 in today's money). 'Our Tragedy,' Garrick told a friend, 'has succeeded beyond our warmest expectations. It was receiv'd with the most cordial applause, & there was not a dry eye in the house, so I have done my duty.'

Garrick had written the Prologue and Epilogue, and had read the manuscript at every stage, but it was cheeky of him to assume that the play was 'Our Tragedy'. The words, the plotting and the execution all belonged solely to Hannah. Yet she was not always given credit for it, even by other women. Kitty Clive, a close friend of Garrick who had worked with him for more than thirty years as one of his leading actresses, told him, with more than a hint of spite, 'I must needs say I admire you (with the rest of the world) for your goodness to Miss More; the protection you gave her play, I dare say, she was sensible was of the greatest service to her . . . for you dandled it, and fondled it, and then carried it in your arms to the *town* to nurse [it].'

Even her sisters had to be cajoled into making the trip to London to support Hannah in her triumph. 'I think some of you might contrive to make a little jaunt, if it were only for one night, and see the *bantling*. Adieu, and some of you come,' Hannah wrote wistfully from Gerrard Street, where she had rented rooms to be close to the theatre. Finally, on the twelfth night, her sisters did see the play, and were suitably impressed, though they teasingly reminded Hannah that Sheridan's *The School for Scandal* was playing at 'the other house'. The bursts of applause and the shrieks of laughter from that theatre, they told her, were enough to bring the roof down.

Hannah began to understand that fame was not all she hoped for. It was cutting her off from her sisters. She was also required to play the part expected of a successful dramatist. Already, in early 1776, she had complained about the crowds at the Pantheon, London's latest and most fashionable venue for operettas and light entertainments. A few hundred yards to the east of Oxford Street, it had been designed with a huge dome to look like Hagia Sophia in Constantinople and could house up to 1,500 people. 'I find my dislike of what are called public diversions greater than ever, except a play; and when Garrick has left the stage, I could be very well contented to relinquish plays also; and to live in London without ever again setting my foot in a public place.' A few weeks later she admitted, 'What most people come to London *for*, would keep me *from* it.'

With remarkable speed, Hannah had infiltrated the highest echelons of London society through her talent alone, sparked by her determination. But she soon began to wonder whether success was something she truly desired. She was invited to a dinner given by Elizabeth Montagu, 'a name not totally obscure', she told her family with more than a hint of ironic understatement. Montagu had been married to one of the wealthiest men in England, profiting from the discovery of coal on his estates in the North-east. After her husband's death, she used her fortune to promote her own literary endeavours (an edition of Shakespeare and some poetry) and those of her fellow bluestockings. Johnson, Frances and Sir Joshua Reynolds, Elizabeth Carter and Frances Boscawen were also guests at the dinner plus 'some other persons of high rank and less wit . . .' Hannah began to feel uncomfortably aware of her humble background: 'I felt myself a worm, the more a worm for the consequence of which was given me by mixing me with such a society.'

Hannah had no money, and no inclination, to dress herself up à la mode or to have her hair dressed in the latest fashion:

> . . . nothing can be conceived so absurd, extravagant, and fantastical
> as the present mode of dressing the head . . . I have just escaped from

one of the most fashionable disfigurers; and although I charged him to dress me with the greatest simplicity, and to have only a very distant eye upon the fashion, just enough to avoid the pride of singularity, without running into ridiculous excess; yet, in spite of all these sage didactics, I absolutely blush at myself, and turn to the glass with as much caution as a vain beauty just risen from the small-pox.

She was both amused and 'annoyed' by such frivolity: 'Some ladies carry on their heads a large quantity of fruit, and yet they would despise a poor useful member of society, who carried it there for the purpose of selling it for bread.'

In her portrait by Frances Reynolds, Hannah More is very different from her more fashion-conscious contemporaries. She appears as a woman in her study with no thought of what she may look like. 'Hannah More has very good intellects . . . but she has by no means the elegance of Miss Burney,' decided Johnson, who always noticed what the women in his company were wearing in spite of his short-sightedness and his own disorderly appearance. The conversation was recorded by Miss Burney herself, who, like Kitty Clive, suffered twinges of envy when she heard of More's instant success as a playwright. Burney could not resist gossiping to her sisters about More, who had once too often fallen into the trap of trying too hard to please Johnson.

Burney was not a witness to Johnson's comments about More's lack of elegance but she heard of them from Hester Thrale, who was no friend to More. Johnson apparently snapped at More: 'Madam, before you flatter a man so grossly to his Face, you should consider whether or not your flattery is worth his having!' To which Burney unsympathetically added, 'Good God, how the poor Creature must have been confounded! Yet she deserved *some* rebuke for laying it on so thick & clumsily.'

Hester Thrale's version of Johnson's put-down in her *Anecdotes of the Late Samuel Johnson* troubled Boswell because it showed Johnson in such a bad light. 'I have been often in his company,' Boswell insists in the *Life*, 'and never *once* heard him say a severe thing to any one.' He gives his readers an account of the conversation but ensures they will put the blame for Johnson's rudeness firmly on Hannah. According to Boswell, Hannah ignored or did not notice Johnson's increasing irritation and continued to layer on the praise, until 'provoked by this indelicate and *vain* obtrusion of compliment, Johnson exclaimed, "Dearest lady, consider with yourself what your flattery is worth before you bestow it so freely."' Boswell then insults Hannah himself by explaining that she had only just arrived in London 'from an obscure situation in the country' and was therefore too much the country bumpkin to realise just how much she was annoying Johnson.

Boswell had little in common with Hannah, and every reason to tell stories against her. She once snubbed him when he became 'too familiar' with her after dinner one evening when 'much disordered with wine'. Boswell was probably trying to persuade her to tell him stories about Johnson and Garrick when they were young men in the city which he thought she might have heard from Garrick. She told him off so sharply that 'I fancy he will not easily forgive me.'

Burney and Thrale had less excuse for betraying a fellow bluestocking. More, though, had a knack for arousing antipathy. Perhaps it was her mixture of inner confidence but superficial deference. Hannah talked of feeling like a worm when in 'society', but she never doubted her talent. Her religious intensity also made her presence sometimes discomfiting. Hannah was simply too good for her own good.

She thought of herself as an intimate member of Johnson's circle, reporting to her sisters how he called her 'nothing but "child", "little fool", "love", and "dearest"'. Yet she was not really a close friend of Johnson. 'I have claims upon Dr Johnson, but as he never knows me when he meets me, they are stifled in the cradle,' she was forced to admit to herself. She was invited to dinner at Mrs Garrick's on that afternoon in May 1784 when Johnson enjoyed her company along with Elizabeth Carter and Fanny Burney, and afterwards declared that 'three such women are not to be found', before insulting every one of them by suggesting that Charlotte Lennox was superior to them all.

By this time Johnson's infirmities had become such a trouble to him that he was often irritable and overbearing when in company. He slept badly, was troubled with asthma and with dropsy in his legs, and in June 1783 had suffered a stroke in the night which left him without words, although still with the use of his hands. When he woke next morning and found himself speechless he composed verses in Latin to reassure himself that his mind was still working. 'I will be conquered; I will not capitulate,' he told his friends, defiantly.

In the summer of 1784 he made what had become his annual visit to

Lichfield, but his health was so bad he could barely walk. His letters from these months are filled with requests for advice about what medicines he should take, and the realisation that he should tidy up his affairs. On his way back to London in mid-November he was too ill even to go and see the second ascent of a hot-air balloon which took place in Oxford as he was passing through. He sent Frank Barber, who was travelling with him, to see it in his place.

Hannah was rarely in town during Johnson's last months, and she was not among the many visitors who tried, but failed, to see him in the weeks before his death on the evening of 13 December. Two days later his body was taken away to the School of Anatomy set up by William and John Hunter. Here, his physicians dissected his body, particularly intrigued to discover what the brain of such a giant intellect would look like.

Of his surviving letters, there are very few addressed to Hannah More other than short confirmations of appointments made for tea or dinner. Their relationship was uneasy; Johnson never really warming to the earnest More, and perhaps a little suspicious of her steely wit. After those first few whirl-wind years, socialising with the Garricks and their friends and with the bluestockings, Hannah withdrew not just from company but also from the theatre.

She was always torn between her desire for acclaim as a writer, and what she believed to be her Christian duty. 'To what is called learning I have never had any pretension,' she wrote in the preface to an edition of her collected works, published in 1801 when she was only halfway through her busy life:

> Life and manners have been the objects of my unwearied observation . . . I have been contented to pursue myself, and to present to others (to my own sex, chiefly), those truths, which, if obvious and familiar, are yet practical, and of general application; things which, of little show, are yet of some use; and which, if their separate value be not great, yet their aggregate importance is not inconsiderable. I have pursued, not that which demands skill, and insures renown, but 'That which before us lies in daily life'.

She did write one more play for the stage, *The Fatal Falsehood*, but she had only completed four acts before Garrick's death (probably from kidney failure) on 20 January 1779, aged sixty-two. Thomas Harris, anxious to cash in on the success of *Percy*, agreed to stage it, but he insisted on rushing it into production without giving More time to revise it. On the second night, the performance was momentarily stopped when a woman in the audience shouted out, 'That's mine! That's mine!'

That woman turned out to be a rival playwright, Hannah Cowley, once also a protégée of Garrick, who claimed that More had plagiarised her manuscript, having seen it on Garrick's desk and copied down from it what she could. The critics went to town on the affair, loving a catfight, and More was forced to defend herself, which cost her much pain:

> It is with the deepest regret that I find myself compelled to take a step repugnant to my own Feelings, and to the delicacy of my Sex . . . My moral character thus grossly attacked, I am under the necessity of solemnly declaring that I never saw, heard, or read, a single line of Hannah Cowley's tragedy, nor did I ever hear she had written a tragedy, till after the Fatal Falsehood came out at Covent-garden . . .

Cowley retaliated with a letter guaranteed to attack More in her weakest spot: 'I wish Miss More had been still more sensible of the indelicacy of a newspaper altercation between women, and the ideas of ridicule which the world are apt to attach to such unsexual hardiness.' More was stunned into silence. Her play was withdrawn after three nights, and never again performed in public. She never again attempted to have a play produced on the London stage, unwilling to risk another public roasting. But she did not stop writing. On the contrary, she used this experience to resolve the conflict between ambition and virtue that had long beset her, discovering an outlet for her talent with no guilt attached – by writing for a cause.

More had one last fling, writing a long and witty poem on the London *salonnières*. *The Bas Bleu* was never intended for publication. Hannah wrote it, she claimed, solely 'to amuse the amiable Lady to whom it is addressed' – her friend Elizabeth Vesey, widow of an Irish MP and hostess of one of the bluestocking salons. But bits of the poem began appearing in the press, after copies of it had been circulated among her friends, and eventually in 1786 she agreed that Horace Walpole should print the whole poem at his Strawberry Hill press 'lest it should steal into the world in a state of still greater imperfection'.

In *The Bas Bleu* Hannah names all the leading female bluestockings (mindfully keeping her own name out of it) and declares that each should receive the honour that is their due. 'Our intellectual ore must shine,' she writes, 'Not slumber idly in the mine', arguing that women must shine through the glitter of their conversation:

> Let education's moral mint
> The noblest images imprint;
> Let taste her curious touchstone hold,
> To try if standard be the gold;
> But 'tis thy commerce, Conversation,
> Must give it use by circulation;
> The noblest commerce of mankind,
> Whose precious merchandise is MIND!

Conversation, not endless games of whist and quadrille, should prevail:

> 'Tis more than Wit, 'tis moral Beauty,
> 'Tis Pleasure rising out of Duty.

Through a meeting of minds, ideas are sparked off, one after the other:

> No dry discussion to unfold
> The meaning, caught as soon as told:
> But sparks electric only strike
> On souls electrical alike;
> The flash of Intellect expires,
> Unless it meet congenial fires.

More was always in touch with popular ideas, adopting images from the latest enthusiasm to illustrate her theme (Joseph Priestley's *The History and Present State of Electricity* was published in 1767). She also insists that everyone should be welcome at these gatherings for conversation, no matter their sex or social standing:

> Here sober Duchesses are seen,
> Chaste Wits and Critics void of spleen;
> Physicians, fraught with real science,
> And Whigs, and Tories in alliance;
> Poets, fulfilling Christian duties,
> Just Lawyers, reasonable Beauties;

Bishops who preach, and Peers who pay,
And Countesses who seldom play . . .

Elizabeth Carter praised the poem to her friends, and Frances Burney longed to own a copy. Johnson had a rare sighting of it before his death, shown him by Frances Reynolds. He told Hester Thrale that he thought it 'a very great performance'. *The Bas Bleu*, though, was Hannah's last 'frivolous' publication. On Lady Day 1785, or the Feast of the Annunciation of the Virgin Mother, 25 March, Hannah bought a small plot of land in Somerset, two miles outside the nearest town, Wrington. She used the money she had made from *Percy* to build a house which she called Cowslip Green. There she began to spend most of her time, only visiting London to meet with her friends among the bluestockings. In town, she decided, 'there is dress, there is restraint, there is want of leisure, to which I find it difficult to conform for any length of time'.

She was not quite done with London. Every so often she would return, to satisfy 'her appetite for grandeur', and enjoy a 'very comical dinner' with just eight other women guests, where the company agreed, 'that men were by no means so necessary as we had all been foolish enough to fancy'.

Nor had More quite reconciled her unworldly principles with her desire for recognition. In the summer of 1784 she adopted the cause of Ann Yearsley, the wife of a not very successful tenant farmer, who to make ends meet sold milk door to door in Bristol, including to the school run by her sisters. Hannah was astonished to discover that this 'farm labourer' with six children read for pleasure and knew Virgil, Milton and Edward Young. She was also writing her own poetry, which Hannah decided was of real merit. She resolved not just to help Yearsley financially but also to bring out a volume of her poetry, persuading the wealthy patron Elizabeth Montagu to contribute towards the costs, and preparing the poems for the press herself.

The case of Ann Yearsley, also known as 'Lactilla', the Bristol milkmaid, became a literary cause célèbre, ending in a vicious falling-out between the women, conducted in public in the newspapers. Hannah More instructed her own publisher Thomas Cadell to print 1,250 copies of Yearsley's *Poems on Several Occasions* (a vastly over-optimistic print run), but ensured that she and Montagu, not Yearsley, would be the trustees of any profits. Hannah's intentions were good. She did not want Yearsley's impecunious husband to benefit from his wife's talent and industry. But Yearsley misunderstood and accused More of trying to make a profit from her poems. More retaliated by accusing Yearsley of behaving 'more like a Demon than a human Creature', and of spending her profits on 'fine Gauze Bonnets, long lappets, gold Pins, etc.' rather than on her starving children.

At this point, More should have withdrawn, but as if a glutton for punishment she arranged for another collection of Yearsley's works, *Poems on Various Subjects*, to be published in 1787. This time Yearsley was furious with More for making editorial changes without consulting her.

More underestimated Yearsley's spirit, and had judged her according to her own character. When Garrick had suggested she should make changes to her work, she had been only too happy to accept them, acknowledging his superior experience. Ann Yearsley had much less respect for Hannah. She was too smart not to realise that in some ways she was being used by Hannah, who wanted to prove to her bluestocking friends that she, too, could be a patron. Badly scalded by the furore, which filled the gossip columns for weeks, Hannah resolved to give up her 'love of reputation' and to devote herself to good works, without further distraction.

In 1782 More had published a selection of short dramatisations of stories from the Bible. Thomas Cadell, her publisher, deplored the direction in which his star writer was turning. You're 'too good a Christian to be an author', he complained. Yet More was actually in tune with popular sentiment. The Evangelical Revival was sweeping through the Church of England in these years, seeking to wake it up from within. More's *Sacred Dramas* became a standard text, and even seventy years later, in 1858, was still sufficiently popular for George Eliot to mention it (along with Johnson's *Rasselas*) as one of Miss Linnet's favourite books in *Scenes of Clerical Life*.

'I am become a perfect outlaw from all civil society and regular life. I spend almost my whole time in my little garden, "which mocks my scant manuring". From "morn to noon, from noon to dewy eve", I am employed in raising dejected pinks, and reforming disorderly honeysuckles,' Hannah told a friend in June 1787, in a letter that echoes Elizabeth Carter's paean to Deal. But Hannah was less reconciled to her retreat than Carter. She told the Revd John Newton, 'I have always fancied that if I could secure to myself such a quiet retreat as I have now really accomplished, I should be wonderfully good; that I should have leisure to store my mind with such and such maxims of wisdom; that I should be safe from such and such temptations

. . . Now, the misfortune is, I have actually found a great deal of the comfort I expected, but without any of the concomitant virtues. I am certainly happier here than in the agitation of the world, but I do not find that I am one bit better . . .'

She needed a cause – and Newton was just the man to present her with one. A former ship's captain who had witnessed the barbarity of the slave trade, transporting slaves on his ships between Africa and the West Indies, he had since his Christian conversion worked with William Wilberforce in galvanising the movement to abolish the slave trade. More published her blast against slavery, *Slavery: A Poem*, on 8 February 1788:

> While the chill North with thy bright ray is blest,
> Why should fell darkness half the South invest?
> Was it decreed, fair Freedom! at thy birth,
> That thou shou'd'st ne'er irradiate *all* the earth?
> While Britain basks in thy full blaze of light,
> Why lies sad Afric quench'd in total night?

Unlike her friend Frances Reynolds, Hannah interpreted her Christian faith to mean that all men, and women, were equal, if not at birth at least before Christ's judgement:

> Perish the proud philosophy, which sought
> To rob them of the pow'rs of equal thought!
> Does then th'immortal principle within
> Change with the casual colour of a skin?
> No: they have heads to think, and hearts to feel,
> And souls to act, with firm, tho' erring zeal;
> For they have keen affections, kind desires,
> Love strong as death, and active patriot fires . . .
> Strong, but luxuriant virtues boldly shoot
> From the wild vigour of a savage root.

In her poem, she exposes the terrible truths behind this trade in people:

> Whene'er to Afric's shores I turn my eyes,
> Horrors of deepest, deadliest guilt arise;
> I see, by more than Fancy's mirror shown,
> The burning village, and the blazing town:

> See the dire victim torn from social life,
> The shrieking babe, the agonising wife!
> She wretch forlorn! is dragg'd by hostile hands,
> To distant tyrants sold, in distant lands!

How could Christian people live with themselves, knowing that the sugar in their tea was brought to them through such cruelty?

Hannah thought her poem was 'too short, and too much hurried' (she wrote it in barely a fortnight), but its vivid depiction of the suffering, the horror of what was being done to line the pockets and sugar the lives of so many in England had a real impact. An Oxford cleric, Dr Horne, reported:

> My wife has been much disturbed about this business of the slave-trade; till, yesterday morning, she consulted Mrs Onslow, who was a native of one of our West India islands. She came home much comforted, with the hope that matters might not be quite so bad as they had been represented, and in the afternoon put into her tea the usual quantity of sugar. I have not yet ventured to read your poem to her, because, as she knows *you* never say the thing that is not, I am afraid it will be the occasion of withdrawing one lump, and diminishing the other . . .

It would take another twenty years of active campaigning before the slave trade was at last abolished, at least in the British colonies. Hannah More continued to meet with Wilberforce and Newton and to write on behalf of the abolitionists, visiting a slave ship to see for herself how the Africans were transported from their homes to the plantations of the West Indies. But once the movement had gathered momentum she no longer found a role within it. Instead she looked for a cause of her own – and found it much closer to home, in Cowslip Green. She was shocked by the levels of drunkenness, illiteracy and lack of religion among the local people, and with a reformer's zeal she set about her own mini-revival.

In late 1789 she told Elizabeth Carter, who had herself set up a charity school in Deal, of her scheme to bring education to the rural poor:

> My dear Mrs Carter
> It is a pity that you and I should both of us have so much of obstinacy in our disposition as not to speak till we are spoken to . . . While we are sending missionaries to India, our villages are in pagan darkness, and upon many of them scarcely a ray of Christianity has shone . . .

In one particular spot, for instance, there are six large parishes without so much as a resident curate . . . Through the kind assistance of a friend or two, I am endeavouring to fix schools and other little institutions in the most destitute of these places, and as they are from six to ten miles distant, you will judge that it employs a good deal of my time . . .

Hannah and her younger sister Patty rented an old barn in the heart of the village of Cheddar in the Mendip Hills of Somerset and converted it into a schoolroom so that they could set up a Sunday school. To find pupils, they visited every house in the village, 'getting at the characters of all the people, the employment, wages, and number of every family'. At last thirty girls were signed up for weekly lessons in reading, sewing, knitting and spinning – all the skills that More deemed necessary for these children of the labouring classes. She was strangely unenlightened when she considered what her pupils should be learning, insisting, 'The chief end to be proposed in cultivating the understanding of women, is to qualify them for the practical purposes of life . . .' Not, for her pupils, Carter's 'equal mind'.

'Is the author then undervaluing her own sex?' she wrote in 1779 in *Strictures on the Modern System of Female Education*. 'No. It is her zeal for their true *interests* which leads her to oppose their imaginary *rights*. It is her regard for their happiness which makes her endeavour to cure them of a feverish thirst for a fame as unattainable as inappropriate . . . A little Christian humility and sober-mindedness are worth all the empty renown which was ever obtained by the misapplied energies of the sex . . .' Yet Hannah herself had set out in search of the 'fame' and 'renown' she now disowns. What had happened to the Miss More who had once encouraged the heroine of *The Inflexible Captive* to dare beyond the narrow limits of her sex?

Hannah More has often been accused of pious sanctimony, believing herself to be of a different class from the people she was trying to help. She set up opportunities for schooling for those with no access to it, but she was careful to ensure that her pupils were given a syllabus that limited their horizons. Her philanthropic endeavours always had an agenda. Yet her spirit and industry cannot be denied. She and Patty encountered verbal and physical threats, the windows of their school were smashed, and their attempts to preach the gospel were shouted down. The gentleman farmers feared their labourers and tenant farmers would start demanding higher wages if they became infected with ideas about equality before God (they

226

had heard that across the Channel the French were demanding equal rights); the curates in the parishes tried to smear More's reputation by claiming she was a Methodist and preaching against the Church; and the labourers themselves refused to send their children, even though the education was free, 'because they were not sure of my intentions'. They were concerned that she might 'acquire a power over them, and send them beyond the sea'.

A couple of particularly 'poor and ambitious' clergymen brought absurd charges against her, claiming her to be a republican revolutionary. More had to defend herself in an ecclesiastical court against the accusation that she had hired 'two men to assassinate one of these clergymen . . . and to crown the whole, that I was concerned with Charlotte Corday in the murder of Marat!'

Undaunted, she wrote a stirring defence to the Bishop of Bath and Wells:

> I need not inform your lordship why the illiterate, when they become religious, are more liable to enthusiasm than the better-informed. They have also a coarse way of expressing their religious sentiments, which often appears to be enthusiasm, when it is only vulgarity or quaintness. But I am persuaded your lordship will allow that this does not furnish a reason why the poor should be left destitute of religious instruction . . . I do not vindicate enthusiasm; I dread it. But can the possibility that a few should become enthusiasts be justly pleaded as an argument for giving them *all* up to actual vice and barbarism . . .
>
> If the grosser crimes alleged against me be true, I am not only unfit to be allowed to teach poor children to read, but I am unfit to be tolerated in any class of society . . . I am not of a sex to expect preferment, nor of a temper to court favour; nor was I so ignorant of mankind as to look for praise by means so little calculated to obtain it; though, perhaps, I did not reckon on such a degree of obloquy . . .

Hannah had indulged in politics, but no one could possibly accuse her of undermining the state. At the height of the French Revolution, in 1792, she published *Village Politics*, addressed to 'all the Mechanics, Journeymen and Day Labourers in Great Britain'. In this political text, written for the working classes, More debates in everyday language the revolutionary arguments of the French versus British democracy.

Jack Anvil, the blacksmith, takes the part of the British against his republican opponent Tom Hod, a mason. Frances Burney read *Village Politics* while at Court, serving in the Queen's household, and thoroughly approved of its royalist sentiments and colourful writing: 'It makes much noise in London, & is suspected to be by some capital Author.' *Village Politics* could not have been more patriotic, but Hannah had by now learnt some caution and she published anonymously.

She need not have worried. *Village Politics* was a huge success, which persuaded her to come up with a new 'Plan' to encourage 'good morals among the Poor'. Why not publish a series of cheap pamphlets, designed to circulate 'Religious and Useful Knowledge as an antidote to the poison continually flowing thro' the channel of vulgar and licentious publications'? She persuaded a consortium of Evangelical printers and subscribers to fund the venture, and the first of her *Cheap Repository Tracts* was launched on 3 March 1795. These 'improving' tales were illustrated with woodcut engravings and written by a team led by More, much like the production of a weekly magazine. Thousands of copies were sold, and new editions printed for decades after-wards in England and America, recounting striking tales of 'Conversions, Holy Lives, Happy Deaths, Providential Deliverances, Judgments on the Breakers of Commandments, Stories of Good and Wicked Apprentices, Hardened Sinners, Pious Servants &c'. with titles such as *The Gin Shop; or, a Peep into a Prison* and *The Shepherd of Salisbury Plain*.

More's *Tracts* poured out of the presses until 1797, a two-year flood of short stories which although criticised by some for their moralising intent were also full of memorable characters – Hester Wilmot, denied a new dress by her feckless father; Black Giles, the Poacher; Betty Brown (whose name comes from one of Johnson's *Rambler* essays), the orange-seller from St Giles who falls victim to the wicked Mrs Sponge. More had grown up among country people, and at Cowslip Green and later Barley Wood, where she moved in 1801, she went back to live among them. If the religious bias was removed, they would still be powerful stories, deftly told – and they led Hannah on to write a full-scale, moralising novel.

Coelebs In Search of a Wife was published in 1808 by Thomas Cadell, whose continued support for More's work in spite of her changes in style and focus was a tribute to her talent as a writer. *Coelebs* is both highly original and deeply conservative. In a surprising reversal of the traditional plotline, More's novel has an eponymous hero, Charles Coelebs, who undergoes a difficult entrée into polite society as he looks for the perfect woman to marry.

Coelebs, of course, only admires women of a respectable character. He believes the present system of education for women 'is not very favourable to domestic happiness . . . For my own part, I call education, not that which smothers a woman with accomplishments, but that which tends to consolidate a firm and regular system of character; that which tends to form a friend, a companion, and a wife . . .'

More gives us a daunting revision of Mary Wollstonecraft's thoughts on the education of young women, but she also introduces her readers to the indomitable Miss Sparkes, whose vivacious personality shines much brighter than any of the other characters in the novel. Miss Sparkes complains that the 'plodding employments' of genteel women, 'cramp the genius, degrade the intellect, depress the spirits, debase the taste, and clip the wings of imagination'. Such self-willed independence of mind does not impress Coelebs, or the woman to whom he is attracted, the sensible but insufferably dull Miss Stanley. 'I thought I saw in Miss Sparkes's countenance a kind of civil contempt,' announces Miss Stanley, 'as if she would be glad to exchange the patient sickness and heroic death-bed for the renown of victory and the glory of a battle: and I suspected that she envied the fame of the challenge, and the spirit of the duel, more than those meek and passive virtues which we all agreed were peculiarly Christian and peculiarly feminine.'

'Meek and passive', 'peculiarly feminine'. Hannah advocated virtues for women which she herself never achieved, no matter how hard she tried. And although we are meant to agree with Lucilla Stanley and see the world through her eyes, Miss Sparkes is far too vivid a character for the reader not to suspect that More secretly had more in common with her point of view.

Coelebs was published without the name of its author on the title page, but Hannah left so many clues she was its author that it soon became public knowledge. The critics did not like it, but the novel was in tune with popular taste. Cadell had to print ten editions within six months, with another four editions in America as well as translations into French and German.

Hannah had created another literary triumph, and in spite of her wish to be cautious, conventional and conservative she had provided women with an appealing solution to their search for autonomy within the context of a world shattered by the events in France after 1789, and especially the guillotining of Louis XVI and Marie-Antoinette. Lucilla Stanley, the chief female character in the novel, is taught Latin by her father but she also excels in 'domestic knowledge'. She has enough education to attract Coelebs, but not too much to frighten him. Above all, her heart is fortified by her Christian faith so that her natural vanity is regulated by humility, and her desire for action is directed towards good works among the poor.

Action and education, with the satisfaction of virtue at the end of it. It was a recipe that fitted perfectly the atmosphere of the time, when women if they were to be successful without incrimination needed to be mindful of how they would appear to others.

More's success afforded her not a little satisfaction, and especially when she discovered that one of the fiercest critics of her book was the infamous Richard Cumberland who once vilified *Percy* as well as Charlotte Lennox's drama *The Sister*. Cumberland tried to claim that *Coelebs* was an anti-establishment novel, 'making *hell broth*'. Hannah proved her mettle yet once more, writing to a friend, 'Shall I not pity the poor man on the borders of fourscore, who *could* write such a criticism after having written a poem called *Calvary*? Alas! for poor human nature, that he has not forgiven, at the end of thirty years, that in my gay and youthful days a tragedy of mine was preferred to one of his . . .'

Yet in the end More did compromise her talent. In those 'gay and youthful days' she wrote with more spirit and less concern for her public image. By the 1790s she had begun referring, jokily, to her publications as 'dirty work' – a subconscious recognition, perhaps, that, by setting limits on what women should, and should not, do, she had sacrificed something of herself, an honesty about what she really, deep down, believed to be true.

Hannah More died, aged eighty-eight, on Saturday 7 September 1833. Her last words were 'Patty' (who had died before her in 1819) followed shortly after by a quiet exclamation, 'Joy!' She was buried in Barley Wood surrounded by the graves of her four sisters who had all predeceased her.

Few who attended her funeral would have believed that the elderly Mrs More had once walked backstage and consorted with actresses, or that her home in Barley Wood was financed by her earnings from her success in the theatres of London. In her life she advocated good works as the path to female virtue; advice which she exemplified in her zeal for education as the best way to relieve the poverty of those who lived in the villages close to her home. A Barley Wood school in Ceylon was named after her home in Somerset in honour of money she donated for its foundation, and her charity schools in Cheddar led to the Society for Promoting Female Education in the East, which sought to give education to girls trapped behind the zenana. Many of the later Victorian woman philanthropists were inspired by her example, including Elizabeth Fry and Clara Lucas Balfour, the wife of the future prime minister.

Hannah's wings were clipped by the antagonism of her male, and sometimes female, rivals, and by her own willingness to suppress her natural talent in the spirit of Christian duty. But the Sunday-school movement, initiated by Hannah and Patty, survived well into the twentieth century, providing rudimentary education as well as religious instruction for thousands of girls as well as boys. She would become one of the most influential of the *Nine Living Muses* painted by Richard Samuel in 1778, and a valiant hussar among the wits.

9

Resolutions?

Mary Wollstonecraft's afternoon with Samuel Johnson, their 'long conversation', is recorded by her husband, William Godwin, in his short account of his wife's life. He wrote it in haste, and great grief, just a few months after her tragic death in September 1797 – from puerperal fever contracted after childbirth. His *Memoirs of the Author of a 'Vindication of the Rights of Woman'* are a moving tribute to their brief marriage. Godwin adopted Johnson's biographical style as he described with touching frankness their growing fondness for each other:

> The partiality we conceived for each other, was in that mode, which I have always regarded as the purest and most refined style of love. It grew with equal advances in the mind of each. It would have been impossible for the most minute observer to have said who was before, and who was after. One sex did not take the priority which long-established custom has awarded it, nor the other overstep that delicacy which is so severely imposed. I am not conscious that either party can assume to have been the agent or the patient, the toil-spreader or the prey, in the affair.

There is, though, a political subtext to this intensely personal book. Godwin wanted to preserve Wollstonecraft's contribution to radical thinking and women's writing and to ensure that 'the treasures of her mind' and 'the virtues of her heart' were not forgotten. It's intriguing, then, that he took care to mention an encounter that took place many years before his marriage to Mary, and with a writer whose philosophy was so very different from his own, and from Wollstonecraft's too.

Godwin writes about that afternoon:

> It was [also] during her residence at Newington Green, that she was introduced to the acquaintance of Dr Johnson, who was at that time considered as in some sort the father of English literature. The doctor treated her with particular kindness and attention, had a long conversation with her, and desired her to repeat her visit often. This she firmly purposed to do; but the news of his last illness, and then of his death, intervened to prevent her making a second visit.

'A long conversation'? 'Particular kindness and attention'? Godwin insists that Johnson regarded Wollstonecraft with respect, almost you might say as an equal: 'The doctor treated her with particular kindness and attention . . .' He 'desired' that she should visit him again, and to 'repeat her visit often'. Wollstonecraft, in turn, 'firmly purposed' to call again, and would have done so had Johnson not died a few months later – on 13 December. Godwin appears to be repeating the very words that his wife used to describe the afternoon, as if her meeting with Johnson was something she talked about on several occasions.

Born on 3 March 1756, Godwin was two generations younger than Johnson and held very different views on how society should be organised and on how to live a moral life. Johnson was always remarkably benevolent to those in need, emptying his pockets for the vagrants and young children with no money for food and nowhere to sleep. But he never questioned the existing order, the established hierarchy. On the contrary, he based his moral views on the established order, whether at home, in the courts, or in political life.

Godwin, tinged with revolutionary fervour, despised 'the laws of this country and the mode of their execution'. His tense and thrilling novel *Caleb Williams* explores questions of justice and authority, and how both were abused by the present systems of domestic and public governance. Johnson would have been horrified by the book; and Godwin would have known this. In part he was writing against Johnson and his selective blindness to the entrenched hierarchies of his society. Yet, in his short memorial to his wife, Godwin ensures that her debt to Johnson was made permanent, in print, for anyone and everyone to read. He understood that in those shabby rooms in Bolt Court on that spring afternoon Mary had experienced one of those moments when a sudden shift in self-realisation takes place, almost from hearing a single phrase dropped into a long conversation.

Wollstonecraft's meeting with Johnson and his willingness to listen to what she had to say gave her the confidence to give up teaching and pursue her dream of writing for a living. His friends in London had included women such as Elizabeth Carter, Charlotte Lennox and Hannah More, who had all produced powerful intellectual works on philosophy, literature, history and politics. Carter and More succeeded in making enough money from their literary endeavours to be economically independent for the rest of their lives. Lennox was less fortunate, never quite making enough money from her work to secure her finances. None of them, though, relied on husbands to provide for them, and Johnson knew and appreciated this. Carter and More chose not to marry, preferring to preserve their mental space, their freedom to live at home according to their wishes. Lennox simply ignored her husband and lived according to her own wits. Johnson saw no reason why Wollstonecraft should not do the same.

Richard Samuel's 1778 painting *The Nine Living Muses of Great Britain* captured Carter, More and Lennox at the peak of their success, alongside other women who had succeeded in history, art, music and poetry. If he had painted it a few years later he would have had to include Wollstonecraft, whose original and far-seeing ideas galvanised the movement for change by questioning the established order, the presumptions behind the social hierarchy. Women were beginning to take advantage of the opportunities to use their creative talents and become professional writers, poets and artists. When Mary Wollstonecraft published her first book in 1787 her name as author was set in type across the title page; anonymity was unnecessary.

Yet there were still limitations on what women could do, especially if they did not belong to the topmost rank, either of talent or class. It's no accident that Wollstonecraft's first book was entitled *Thoughts on the Education of Daughters*. She understood that education was the key to women becoming more independent. She had observed, while working as a governess and a lady's companion, that many women were complicit in the trivialising of their own lives and of the lives of those who were dependent on them.

Because they had been given so little 'useful' education, their minds were filled with nothing, and they perpetuated this imbalance between the sexes by filling their daughters' lives with nonsense, with trivial obsessions about dress, domestic skills, and the right way to dance a quadrille. Their lack of understanding, of training for the mind, meant they were also not capable of caring for the well-being of those who had the misfortune to work for them as maids, nurses and governesses.

'Most women, and men too, have no character at all,' she once wrote, appropriating Alexander Pope's assertion that most women have no character at all and adding her own transformative gloss. Taking Rousseau as her guide, she insisted that education was of vital importance to *both* men and women because our characters can only develop from what we put into our minds. 'Just opinions and virtuous passions appear by starts . . . it is then in our power, this way, to strengthen our good dispositions, and in some measure to establish a character, which will not depend on every accidental impulse.' To think well you need to be taught well.

By the standards of Mary Wollstonecraft, Johnson's mother gave to her son perhaps the most valuable lesson of all. She expected him each week as a very young boy to memorise the collect of the day, which not only ensured that her son was best able to make use of his prodigious intellect by training his memory, but also familiarised him early on with some of the most rigorous and effective writing in the English language, in the *Book of Common Prayer* and the King James version of the Bible.

Too many mothers, though, exacerbated the frailties of their sex, declared Wollstonecraft: 'Indolence, and a thoughtless disregard of every thing, except the present indulgence, make many mothers, who may have momentary starts of tenderness, neglect their children.' Women connived in their own oppression, she argued, controversially, by failing in their duties to their children. Women were prevented from being properly useful not just by their lack of learning, she argued. 'No employment of the mind is a sufficient excuse for neglecting domestic duties, and I cannot conceive that they are incompatible.'

Wollstonecraft was prepared to criticise other women for their negligence, their foolishness, their willingness to exercise authority over other women less fortunate. She argued for women's rights at home and in society and for a revolution in the way women were educated, but she also appreciated that women, too, had duties to perform, as mothers and as the guardians of the next generation. There needs to be a balance, she demonstrated as a mother herself, between domestic duty and individual fulfilment. Education should be taken into the nursery, and the needs of children should be appreciated by both fathers and mothers.

Wollstonecraft was far too intelligent and far-seeing not to perceive that female difficulties often arise from causes that were far more complex than mere oppression. She had observed, as a governess herself, 'In the nursery, too . . . [children] not only hear nonsense, but that nonsense retailed out in such silly, affected tones as must disgust; yet these are the tones which the child first imitates, and its innocent playful manner renders them tolerable, if not pleasing; but afterwards they are not easily got the better of—nay, many women always retain the pretty prattle of the nursery, and do not forget to lisp, when they have learnt to languish.'

Young women who lisped and languished their way through life were often featured by Johnson in his *Rambler* and *Idler* essays. Perhaps surprisingly, Wollstonecraft, whose *Vindication of the Rights of Woman* asserts feminist views on the need for equality between the sexes, knew Johnson's essays well enough to quote from them by heart. In *The Female Reader*, her anthology of 'didactic and moral pieces', stories, allegories, poems and 'reflections on religious objects' which she compiled in 1789 'to imprint some useful lessons on the mind', and in particular on the minds of teenage girls, she listed two of Johnson's *Rambler* essays, Nos 130 and 133. Johnson here writes as 'Victoria', a society beauty.

My mother, says Victoria, brought me up to believe that no happiness or advantage could be expected 'but from beauty'. 'She snatched away my book because a young lady in the neighbourhood had made her eyes red with reading by a candle; but she would scarcely suffer me to eat lest I should spoil my shape . . .' Victoria is warned that 'nothing so much hindered the advancement of women as literature and wit, which generally frightened away those who could make the best settlements . . .' But all her mother's wiles cannot prevent Victoria from succumbing, in her nineteenth and crucial year (for her entrance into society), to smallpox. From being at the centre of attention at every assembly, Victoria is now neglected and even insulted.

'It is perhaps not in the power of a man whose attention has been divided by a diversity of pursuits,' says Victoria (or rather Johnson), 'and who has not been accustomed to derive from others much of his happiness, to image to himself such helpless destitution, such dismal inanity.' And it's the women of her acquaintance who give me the hardest time, complains Victoria, whispering behind her back, suggesting emollients, washes and creams that will 'smooth the skin', harassing her whenever she ventures out, 'with all the stratagems of well-bred malignity'.

Wollstonecraft did not regard this portrait of female folly and cruelty as insulting to women. She admired Johnson's imaginative forays into the dull and often miserable lives of young ladies deprived of a useful education and compelled to idle away their empty days in decorative embroidery and jam-making.

One of her early projects, a philosophical novel entitled 'The Cave of Fancy', was inspired by Johnson's *The History of Rasselas, The Prince of Abyssinia*. Johnson's young prince escapes from the Happy Valley of his childhood on an eighteenth-century equivalent of a gap year to find out about the world beyond the protected domains of the kingdom he will inherit. He takes instruction from sages, hermits, astronomers in his search for answers to life's chief riddles – 'the knowledge of nature' and 'the changes of the human mind as they are modified by various institutions and accidental influences of climate or custom'.

Wollstonecraft transforms Prince Rasselas into an anonymous young woman. Her heroine, Everywoman, pursues instruction, just like Rasselas, from an ancient philosopher who has taken himself away from the business of life to a hermit's cave, the Cave of Fancy.

Johnson begins:

> Ye who listen with credulity to the whispers of fancy, and pursue with eagerness the phantoms of hope; who expect that age will perform the promises of youth, and that the deficiencies of the present day will be supplied by the morrow; attend to the history of Rasselas prince of Abissinia.

Wollstonecraft, either by subconscious accident or by deliberate design, opens her 'Cave of Fancy' with an almost identical flourish:

> Ye who expect constancy where every thing is changing, and peace in the midst of tumult, attend to the voice of experience, and mark in

time the footsteps of disappointment; or life will be lost in desultory wishes, and death arrive before the dawn of wisdom.

She never published the novel, abandoning it after just three chapters, possibly because she realised she was too closely following Johnson's style and language. She had yet to find her own voice.

After Johnson's death on 13 December 1784, the bookshops and circulating libraries were soon flooded with biographies, books of anecdotes and the post-humous publication of his private prayers and meditations – anything that would cash in on his celebrity before he was replaced by the next popular talent. In 1788 the sermons which he had written for his clergyman friends to preach were collected and published, including the sermon he wrote for the funeral of his wife, Tetty, in March 1752, which was never delivered. Wollstonecraft was asked to review the collection by her editor and publisher, Joseph Johnson. He was no relation to Dr Johnson. On the contrary, he was a man of very different social, religious and political principles; a Dissenter, who refused to acknowledge the authority of the Chuch of England or swear allegiance to the monarch.

In April 1788, Wollstonecraft wrote to Joseph Johnson, 'If you do not like the manner in which I reviewed Dr J.'s s—— on his wife, be it known unto you—I *will* not do it any other way.' She suspected that her editor would be surprised to read of her respect for Dr J.'s religious convictions. 'I felt some pleasure,' she told him, 'in paying a just tribute of respect to the memory of a man—who, spite of his faults, I have an affection for—I say *have*, for I believe he is somewhere—*where* my soul has been gadding perhaps.'

Wollstonecraft felt a connection with Johnson, an affinity that touched the heart of what matters. She used the opportunity to pay tribute to Johnson's influence on her writing in the *Analytical Review* in August 1788:

> We read this sermon deliberately, and paused at some passages to reflect, with a kind of gloomy satisfaction, that the heart which dictated those pathetic effusions of real anguish now ceased to throb, and that the mind we had often received instruction from, was no longer disquieted by vain fears.

'The mind we had often received instruction from . . .'

Some years later she wrote again to Joseph Johnson, having read Boswell's *Life of Samuel Johnson*: 'I am not the only character deserving of respect, that has had to struggle with various sorrows—while inferior minds have enjoyed local fame and present comfort.—Dr Johnson's cares almost drove him mad.'

In her *Vindication of the Rights of Woman*, which she published in 1792 in response to the debates about equality and justice stimulated by events across the Channel in revolutionary France, Wollstonecraft begins by repeating the views she had earlier expressed in *Thoughts on the Education of Daughters*. 'Women,' she writes, 'must be considered as only the wanton solace of men when they become so weak in mind and body, that they cannot exert themselves, unless to pursue some frivolous fashion.' Women are the weaker sex, she admits, but this is because they have been denied access to education and opportunities to be useful. She then refers to Johnson, even though her experiences have led her to a very different philosophical and social standpoint:

> What can be a more melancholy sight to a thinking mind, than to look into the numerous carriages that drive helter-skelter about this metropolis in a morning, full of pale-faced creatures who are flying from themselves. I have often wished with Dr Johnson, to place some of them in a little shop with half a dozen children looking up to their languid countenances for support. I am much mistaken, if some latent vigour would not soon give health and spirit to their eyes, and some lines drawn by the exercise of reason on the blank cheeks, which before were only undulated by dimples, might restore lost dignity to the character, or rather enable it to attain the true dignity of its nature.

Wollstonecraft was prepared to acknowledge what she had learnt from Johnson, even though her solutions to the social problems they both discerned were very different.

Godwin's book about his late wife was entitled *Memoirs of the Author of a 'Vindication of the Rights of Woman'* as if he was extolling the life of a writer and political thinker. But by accident of feeling he produced the kind of character study which Johnson initiated in his *Life of Richard Savage*, and then developed in the short biographies collected in his *Lives of the English Poets*. These vivid sketches are filled with telling details, drawn from personal reminiscence and recollection. What value, asks Johnson, is there in a biography that does not investigate the private and domestic spheres of the individual just as much as the public realm?

Unfortunately for Mary's future reputation, Godwin took Johnson's recommendations too literally. Writing in the intimate, revelatory style recommended by Johnson, Godwin confided in his readers, giving them not just the painful details of his wife's moment of death, but also the extraordinary emotional turbulence she experienced before meeting Godwin. Of her death, he writes precisely, as if the details were etched on his heart, 'At six o'clock on Sunday morning, September the tenth Mr Carlisle [the physician] called me from my bed to which I had retired at one, in conformity to my request, that I might not be left to receive all at once the intelligence that she was no more. She expired at twenty minutes before eight.' We are intensely moved by what he writes; but at the same time shocked by his revelation of the intimate details.

Godwin exposed Mary to criticism by telling of her willingness to be seduced by the American adventurer Gilbert Imlay, of how she fell pregnant before she married Imlay, of her refusal to believe Imlay was betraying her, and of her attempts to kill herself, not once but twice, by throwing herself into the Thames from Putney Bridge. He doesn't dramatise these episodes, or ask for pity for his wife, but he outraged the readers of the *Memoirs*, and Wollstonecraft's reputation never really recovered, or at least not until the feminist revival of the 1970s. She became better known as the dramatic heroine of a very human tragedy than for what she wrote.

If Wollstonecraft had called on Johnson after her tempestuous years of love and marriage on the Continent, he, too, would probably have been reluctant to oblige her with tea and conversation. He would not have wished to spend an afternoon with a woman of such radical views, who was willing to embrace many of the social reforms advocated by the French. Wollstonecraft rejected all forms of authority, knowing too well that human frailty often corrupted the institutions of marriage, church and state. Johnson was too much the spokesman of an earlier generation not to believe that such institutions were vital to the stability of society. He grew up in a world that still remembered the ravages of civil war. But in 1784, when Wollstonecraft was young and desperate to prove herself, and Johnson was feeling his age and in need of company, they found in each other an unexpected consanguinity of spirit.

*

John Opie's portrait of Wollstonecraft from 1790–1 shows her dishevelled, in plain clothes, with pages in hand and a quill and inkpot at the ready. He portrays a woman who is a professional writer, and yet who is comfortable with having her picture painted in the plain, workaday clothes of home life. It's very much in the style of Frances Reynolds's earlier portrait of her friend Hannah More, a direct, naturalistic portrayal but also an assertion of Wollstonecraft's profession as a writer. Wollstonecraft benefited from the efforts of the bluestockings who had gone before her.

Looking again at the contradictions which shaped their lives, we may be able to discern the conflicting impulses that determine our own endeavours. How far away the idea of a 'neutral being', able to observe dispassionately the pros and cons of gender, appears to be. The conflict between home life and professional personality is still a fraught question for women. When Elizabeth Carter was praised for making such good puddings, was she pleased, or annoyed that she was being patronised? Were her endeavours to improve her domestic skills an attempt by her to compensate for the hours she spent as a scholar? Will it always be necessary for women to prove that they can be both homemakers and muses, wives and wits?

Johnson was too much a man of his time not to be a little wary of women of talent, as witnessed by his suspicion of Elizabeth Carter and Hannah More. Women he wanted to be equal, but not too equal. They should also be patterns of piety and models of purity. His affection for the sublimated Hill Boothby was in large part because of his hope, and desire, that her firm faith might have a beneficial effect on him. He did, though, also encourage his female friends to make best use of their minds, their talents. He enjoyed rallying to their cause, both in private, as in his letters to Charlotte Lennox and to his dear Renny, and in public, in his essays empathising with many of the difficulties faced solely by women and not usually discussed by men. Yet he neglected his mother, abandoned his wife Tetty for months at a time, and castigated Hester Thrale when she decided to follow the dictates of her heart after years of self-sacrifice to a man she had never loved.

Nothing is straightforward between men and women as they seek personal fulfilment, nor ever will be. 'Powerful men and the war of the sexes,' reads the headline as I write this, while the Playboy Club, with its bunny-girl waitresses, is reopening in London, and the Mothers' Union boasts a man as its chief executive. But if we take another look at Johnson and his circle, and especially at the wits and wives in his company of friends, we may uncover new interpretations of his world and the women who inhabited it. We may also be surprised by what we learn about ourselves through observing their attempts to reconcile domestic obligation and social expectation with professional and personal ambition. Perhaps, too, the thread that connects Johnson with Wollstonecraft through the span of a century is their ability to engage so directly with both men and women, no dissembling, no pretension. What they shared was a gift for friendship, and, to quote William Godwin, 'an unconquerable greatness of soul'.

Acknowledgements

My biggest debt in the writing of this book is to Fanny Burney, whose friendship with Dr Johnson gave me insights into his character I had not previously suspected. But it was my English teacher, Mrs Kaufman, and the enlightened examination board which set *Rasselas* as an A-level text, who first inspired my love of Johnson and his world. Without the generous scholarship and patient friendship of Jenny Uglow at Chatto & Windus, this book would never have materialised. Becky Hardie has valiantly seen the book through the press. My agent, Clare Alexander, has been remarkably astute and always encouraging, especially in defence of Johnson and his women. I would also like to thank the late Kate Jones, whose enthusiasm for the book and for the idea of friendship between the sexes in the eighteenth century ensured that I kept going at a crucial stage.

The Society of Authors has always been helpful, offering advice and granting me two awards to help with the research. The Arts Council of England gave me a Literature Award in 2006, their interest in the project enabling me to continue. The Royal Literary Fund, and especially Steve Cook and David Swinburne, have supported my writing life, by giving me the opportunity to work as a Fellow, tutoring students.

The staff of the British Library, the London Library, the Beinecke Library, the Huntington Library, Canterbury Cathedral, Deal Library, Lambeth Palace, the archive at the National Portrait Gallery, the London Metropolitan Archives and at the record offices of Birmingham, Derbyshire, Lichfield and

Acknowledgements

Westminster have all been unfailingly helpful. I must also thank especially the curators of the Samuel Johnson Birthplace Museum in Lichfield and Dr Johnson's House in London who have put up with innumerable queries and visits.

To Elisabeth Anderson, my editor at the *Spectator*, and my former colleagues on the magazine, I owe much thanks for putting up with so many conversations about the women and their lives. Elisabeth, in particular, has endured more than most in hearing the oft-repeated moan, 'It'll never be done.' Michael Heath has created a brilliant cover.

So many friends and scholars have helped me in suggesting ideas and confirming thoughts that no list will encompass all they have so generously given me. I should, though, make special mention of Graham Nicholls who read the chapters on Sarah Johnson and Tetty Johnson at an early stage. With Natasha McEnroe, former curator at Dr Johnson's House in London, I have shared many cups of tea in her office at the House. The late David Nokes generously commissioned me to research a small part of his biography on Johnson, and to him I owe many lively conversations. To Catherine Dille, Richard Edgcumbe, Elizabeth Eger, Karin Fernald, Bill Fraser, Nancy Johnson, Freya Johnston, Ian Kelly, Annette Kobak, Fiona Ritchie, Peter Sabor, Philip Smallwood, Gordon Turnbull, Sophie Vasset, Tara Ghoshal Wallace, and the members of the Johnson Society of London, the Johnsonians, and the Burney Society, I owe the gift of friendship in *salon* style, exchanging ideas, thoughts, worries, failures, successes and above all hope. Norbert Schürer most kindly gave me access to his forthcoming edition of Charlotte Lennox's letters, and to him, and to Susan Carlile, I am very grateful.

Mary Harron and Jill Florent both read early versions of some of the chapters at a stage when I was stuck. Their willingness to spend time with Johnson's women convinced me that I must continue. Christine Cameron, Vivien Cripps, Jean Gibson, Miriam Gross, Alison Lyon, Jane Lyons, Jane Mays, Heather Neill, Michael Prodger, Aileen Reid, Prue Skinner, Charles Spencer and Lucy Vickery have graciously allowed the eighteenth century to dominate our conversations.

To my mother, sister and niece, I owe the gift of female solidarity. But the biggest debt is to Michael, whose friendship began as this book began and who has since spent far too many hours in the company of Johnson's women.

List of Illustrations

1. Detail from Thomas Rowlandson's *Madame Weischel Singing at Vauxhall Gardens*, engraving by R. Pollard, aquatinted probably by F. Jukes. © V&A Images / Victoria and Albert Museum, London.
2. *Mrs Samuel Johnson* by Maria Verelst (1680–1744). With kind permission of the Hyde Collection at the Houghton Library, Harvard University (*2003JM-8).
3. *Dr Samuel Johnson* (1775), attributed to Frances Reynolds. © Albright Knox Art Gallery / Art Resource, NY / Scala, Florence.
4. *Elizabeth Carter as Minerva* (1735–41) by John Fayram. © National Portrait Gallery, London (NPG L242).
5. *Elizabeth Carter* (c. 1765) by Katharine Read. With kind permission of Dr Johnson's House Trust, London.
6. *Pencil sketch of Dr Johnson* by Paul Sandby (attribution unconfirmed). With kind permission of the Canterbury Auction Galleries, 40 Station Road West, Canterbury, Kent.
7. Frontispiece to *The Lady's Museum* (1760). © The British Library Board (C.175.n.15).
8, 9. *Portraits in the Characters of the Muses in the Temple of Apollo (The Nine Living Muses of Great Britain)* by Richard Samuel (1778). © National Portrait Gallery, London (NPG 4905).
10. Miniature portrait of *Hester Thrale* (1773) by Richard Cosway. © Harry Ransom Humanities Research Center, The University of

245

Texas at Austin (Carlton Lake Art Collection, 70.34).

11. *Mrs Thrale and Her Daughter Hester ('Queeney')* (1781) by Sir Joshua Reynolds. Gift of Lord Beaverbrook, The Beaverbrook Art Gallery, Fredericton, New Brunswick, Canada.

12. *Portrait of Hannah More* (c.1780) by Frances Reynolds. © Bristol City Museum and Art Gallery, UK (BAG165797)/The Bridgeman Art Library.

13. *Self-portrait of Frances Reynolds with her sister Mary.* © Private Collection.

14. *Dr Samuel Johnson* (1783), probably by Frances Reynolds. © Haverford College Quaker & Special Collections, Haverford, PA (HC09-4061).

15. *Mary Wollstonecraft (Mrs William Godwin)*(1790–91) by John Opie. © Tate, London (N01167).

16. *Breaking Up of the Blue Stocking Club* (c. 1815) by Thomas Rowlandson. © The Trustees of the British Museum (00126518001).

Chapter Notes

Chapter 1: Intimations

Many scholars to whom I am indebted have begun investigating the connections between Dr Johnson and the women in his friendship circle, especially Sylvia Harcstark Myers and her book *The Bluestocking Circle: Women, friendship and the life of the mind in eighteenth-century England* (Clarendon Press, Oxford, 1990) and Isobel Grundy, whose essay 'Samuel Johnson as Patron of Women' appeared in *The Age of Johnson: A scholarly annual*, volume 1 (AMS Press, New York) in 1987. Eithne Henson, in her essay 'Johnson and the Condition of Women' in *The Cambridge Companion to Samuel Johnson*, edited by Greg Clingham (Cambridge University Press, Cambridge, 1997), shows how often Johnson adopts the female voice in his *Rambler* and *Idler* essays. Kathleen Nulton Kemmerer wrote a book on Johnson's attempt to place himself as '*A Neutral Being Between the Sexes*': *Samuel Johnson's sexual politics* (Bucknell University Press, Lewisburg, PA, 1998). Norma Clarke's *Dr Johnson's Women* (Hambledon & London, London, 2000) brought together for the first time essays on the women writers in Dr Johnson's circle, drawing attention to their literary connections. See also her book *The Rise and Fall of the Woman of Letters* (Pimlico, London, 2004).

More recently, Elizabeth Eger celebrated the emergence of the bluestocking writers in her *Bluestockings: Women of reason from Enlightenment to Romanticism* (Palgrave Macmillan, 2010). Betty Schellenberg broke new ground with *The*

Professionalisation of Women Writers in Eighteenth-Century Britain (Cambridge University Press, Cambridge 2005). Harriet Guest writes about 'Bluestocking Feminism' in *Reconsidering the Bluestockings*, edited by Nicole Pohl and Betty Schellenberg (Huntington Library, San Marino, CA, 2003).

A curious forerunner of this recent scholarship can be found in W. H. Craig's *Doctor Johnson and the Fair Sex: A study in contrasts* from 1895 (Sampson Low, Marston & Co., London), which begins with that oft-quoted sentence from Johnson, 'If I had no duties, and no reference to futurity, I would spend my life driving briskly in a post-chaise with a pretty woman', and contains chapters entitled, 'Dr Johnson as a Squire of Dames', 'Dr Johnson as a Suitor', 'Dr Johnson on Dress and Deportment' and 'Dr Johnson on Marriage and the Relations of the Sexes'. Not quite the tone of current scholarship, but revealing of its time.

James Basker first drew my attention to the connections between Mary Wollstonecraft's journalism and Dr Johnson's *Rambler* essays in his chapter, 'Radical Affinities: Mary Wollstonecraft and Samuel Johnson', in *Tradition in Transition: Women writers, marginal texts and the eighteenth-century canon*, edited by Alvaro Ribeiro, SJ and James G. Basker (Clarendon Press, Oxford, 1996). Other essays by James Basker on Johnson's relationships with women include 'Myth Upon Myth: Johnson, gender and the misogyny question' in *The Age of Johnson: A scholarly annual*, edited by Paul J. Korshin, volume 8 (AMS, New York, 1997) and 'Multicultural Perspectives: Johnson, race and gender', in *Johnson Re-Visioned: Looking before and after*, edited by Philip Smallwood (Bucknell University Press, Lewisburg, PA, 2001).

The *Brilliant Women* exhibition at the National Portrait Gallery in 2008, and in particular the work of the co-curator Elizabeth Eger, gave us many insights into the changing opportunities for women writers and artists during Johnson's life. The catalogue, *Brilliant Women: 18th-century bluestockings*, edited by Elizabeth Eger and Lucy Peltz (National Portrait Gallery, London, 2008), is a beautifully illustrated and informative account of their lives and achievements, showing how these women took advantage of the publishing boom to develop careers as poets, novelists, biographers and historians. But at the close of the century they for the most part withdrew from the professional arena back to the drawing room after changes in the social and political climate, provoked by events across the Channel, made such public performance much more difficult to sustain.

William Godwin's memoir of his wife, Mary Wollstonecraft, was first published in March 1798 as *Memoirs of the Author of a 'Vindication of the Rights of Woman'* (J. Johnson, London). Janet Todd and Marilyn Butler's edition of *The Works of Mary Wollstonecraft* in seven volumes (Willliam Pickering, London, 1989) makes easily available all of Wollstonecraft's published writings, including *Thoughts on the Education of Daughters* (1787) and all of her book reviews in the *Analytical Review*. Wollstonecraft's *Vindication of the Rights of Woman* is available in paperback (Penguin Classic, Harmondsworth, 1983). Her letters have been edited by Janet Todd as *The Collected Letters of Mary Wollstonecraft* (London, Allen Lane, 2003). Other letters were included in Ralph Wardle's *Collected Letters of Mary Wollstonecraft* (Cornell University Press, Ithaca, NY, 1979). Wollstonecraft's *Letters Written During a Short Residence in Sweden, Norway and Denmark*, with an introduction by Sylva Norman (Centaur Press, Fontwell, 1970), are a valuable insight into her character, and a wonderful read.

Claire Tomalin's biography of Wollstonecraft, although published in 1974 before the re-evaluation of both Johnson and Wollstonecraft began, is still my favourite biography because of the empathy with which she brings her subject to life. Tomalin attaches no significance to Wollstonecraft's afternoon with Johnson; on the contrary, she argues that Wollstonecraft turned against Johnson's moral teachings as she matured as a thinker and essayist. I have tried to suggest in this book that there were sometimes surprising affinities between Johnson and Wollstonecraft, arising from their shared willingness to acknowledge human frailty, their appreciation of both intellectual and domestic life, and their passionate desire to alleviate suffering.

Janet Todd's *Mary Wollstonecraft: A revolutionary life* (Weidenfeld & Nicolson, London, 2000) is a richly detailed portrait from the point of view of a literary professor. The most recent study by Lyndall Gordon, *Mary Wollstonecraft: A new genus* (Little, Brown, London, 2005), is intriguingly different but does not give us such a deeply textured view of Wollstonecraft.

The richest source of information about Johnson's life remains James Boswell's *Life of Samuel Johnson, LLD*, first published in March 1795 and available in an unabridged Oxford World's Classics paperback edition (edited in great and useful detail by R. W. Chapman, with an insightful introduction by Pat Rogers). The success of Boswell's book meant that Sir John Hawkins's *The Life of Samuel Johnson, LLD* of 1787 has been almost forgotten, but

Hawkins was a contemporary of Johnson and his book (now available in an edition annotated by OM Brack Jr: University of Georgia Press, Athens and London, 2009) contains information not known to Boswell.

Johnson's collected letters have been published in several editions. R. W. Chapman's edition is still useful because he gives us letters both to and from Johnson and Hester Thrale (Clarendon Press, Oxford, 1952) but Bruce Redford's four-volume edition is the most up to date, with letters newly transcribed and edited (Clarendon Press, Oxford, 1992–4).

Johnson's *Rambler* and *Idler* essays have been published in a modern, annotated edition by the Yale University Press as part of their ongoing project, *The Yale Edition of the Works of Samuel Johnson* (volume 2, edited by W. J. Bate, John M. Bullitt and L. F. Powell, and volumes 3–5, edited by W. J. Bate and Albrecht B. Strauss, Yale University Press, New Haven, CT, 1958). Also worth reading are the *Prayers and Meditations*, edited originally by George Strahan in 1785 (T. Cadell, London) and available in Volume 1 of *The Yale Edition of the Works of Samuel Johnson*, edited by E. L. McAdam Jr with Donald and Mary Hyde (Yale University Press, New Haven, CT, 1958), which also contains the text of Johnson's early diaries, the *Annals* (first published in 1805 by Richard Wright, a surgeon in Lichfield and proprietor of the museum of antiquities and natural curiosities). *The History of Rasselas, Prince of Abyssinia* can be read in the original 1759 edition at the British Library, but has been republished many times, most recently as an Oxford World's Classics paperback, edited by Thomas Keymer (Oxford University Press, Oxford, 2009).

Of the many one-volume collections of excerpts from Johnson's works, I prefer Mona Wilson's edition for the Reynard Library (Rupert Hart-Davis, London, 1969). She includes a number of *Rambler* essays that deal with women's issues, plus *The Life of Richard Savage* and a selection from *The Lives of the Poets*, the preface to the *Dictionary* with Johnson's frank and touching admission of how much the task has cost him, ending with the superbly moving poem 'On the Death of Dr Robert Levet'.

In this chapter, I have quoted from Johnson's *Rambler* essays No. 39, No. 51, No. 60 and No. 107; from *Idler* No. 23 and *Adventurer* No. 115.

Johnson's life and character are constantly being re-visioned by succeeding generations. G. K. Chesterton wrote an illuminating and original character-study of Johnson, which is published as the introduction to Alice Meynell's selection of essays, *Samuel Johnson* (Herbert & Daniel, London, 1911). Of the most recent biographies, I would recommend Robert DeMaria Jr, *The Life of Samuel Johnson* (Oxford University Press, Oxford, 1993) and David Nokes, *Samuel Johnson: A life* (Faber, London, 2009). James Clifford's two-volume biography (he died having just completed the second of a proposed three-volume study) is full of insights and very readable. Volume 1 is published as *Young Sam Johnson* and Volume 2 as *Dictionary Johnson: Samuel Johnson's middle years* (McGraw-Hill, New York, 1955, 1979). OM Brack Jr and Robert E. Kelley have compiled a useful volume on *The Early Biographies of Samuel Johnson* (University of Iowa Press, Iowa City, 1974). As soon as Johnson died, publishers wishing to cash in on his 'celebrity' flooded the book market with biographies, usually very short and incomplete, and filled with his pithy epigrams and conversational soundbites gathered from those who knew him.

Richard Holmes's study of Johnson's friendship with the unfortunate but brilliant poet Richard Savage, *Dr Johnson & Mr Savage* (Hodder & Stoughton, London, 1993) gives us a vivid picture of Johnson's peripatetic life in London before the publication of the *Dictionary*. Lyle Larsen's *Dr Johnson's Household* (Archon Books, Hamden, CT, 1985) is the first modern account of the people who lived with Johnson after the death of his wife Tetty. Michael Bundock has taken this work further by looking in detail at the life of Johnson's black servant, Francis Barber, published in the *New Rambler* (2003–4) as 'From Slave to Heir: The strange journey of Francis Barber'.

Other sources for this chapter and for the book include:

The Burney Collection of Newspapers from the eighteenth century, compiled by Frances Burney's brother Charles and formerly available only on microfiche at the British Library but which can now be accessed online via any library. Go to: www.jisc-collections.ac.uk/catalogue/burney?keywords =burney+collection.

Johnsonian Gleanings, the twelve volumes of genealogy, biography and facts about Johnson, collected, written up and privately published by Aleyn Lyell Reade (1909–52), is an invaluable source of information on Johnson, his family and his friends, although some of the material in the earlier volumes was later corrected by Reade so double-checking between the volumes is vital.

The Samuel Johnson Encyclopedia, edited by Pat Rogers (Greenwood Press, Westport, CT, 1996).

Samuel Johnson's Dictionary: Selections from the 1755 work that defined the English language, edited by Jack Lynch (Atlantic Books, London, 2004).

Anecdotes of the Late Samuel Johnson, LLD, *during the last twenty years of his life*, by Hester Lynch Piozzi (T. Cadell, London, 1786), now available in a modern edition edited by Arthur Sherbo (Oxford University Press, Oxford, 1974).

Thraliana: The diary of Mrs Hester Lynch Thrale (Later Mrs Piozzi), *1776–1809*, edited by Katharine C. Balderston (two volumes, Clarendon Press, Oxford, 1951).

The Early Journals and Letters of Fanny Burney, 1768–91, edited by Lars Troide, Stewart Cooke and Betty Rizzo, volumes 3 and 4 (Oxford University Press, Oxford, 1988–2003).

The Bas Bleu: A conversation by Hannah More (published by Horace Walpole at his Strawberry Hill press in 1786).

A Series of Letters between Mrs Elizabeth Carter and Miss Catherine Talbot, from the year 1741 to 1770 (four volumes, which include Elizabeth's letters to her friend Elizabeth Vesey, F. C. and J. Rivington, London, 1809) and *Letters from Mrs Elizabeth Carter to Mrs Montagu, between the years 1755 and 1800, chiefly upon literary and moral subjects* (three volumes, F. C. and J. Rivington, London, 1817) edited by Elizabeth Carter's nephew, Montagu Pennington.

Chapter 2: Here's a Brave Mother

Graham Nicholls, former curator of the Samuel Johnson Birthplace Museum in Lichfield, read this chapter in an earlier form. He alerted me to the strange comments in the *Thraliana* about Michael Johnson and his relationship with his elder son. I am also indebted to members of the Johnson Society of London for many discussions about Johnson, as a writer and a moralist, and as a most complicated and contradictory personality.

The American scholar Walter Jackson Bate produced a tour de force of Johnsonian scholarship in his 1977 biography *Samuel Johnson* (Harcourt Brace Jovanovich, New Haven, CT). Jackson Bate takes a radically different view of Johnson, which was incredibly useful at the time although its psychoanalytical approach now seems outdated. Still, it's a biography that should be read by anyone seeking to understand Johnson's relations with his family, not necessarily to agree with Jackson Bate but just because he takes us into new areas of thought.

Johnson's own early accounts of his life were first published in 1805 by

Richard Wright. Unfortunately, that manuscript is now lost, and when George Birkbeck Hill republished the *Annals* in 1897 as part of his two-volume *Johnsonian Miscellanies* he could not check back with the original text. The *Johnsonian Miscellanies* (Clarendon Press, Oxford, 1897) are still of immense value because they include many previously unknown short studies of Johnson with scrupulous and detailed notes.

Johnson's religious beliefs are very much of their time and are difficult for us to fathom. Some of the texts he would have read as an impressionable child include:

The Saints Everlasting Rest: or, a Treatise of the Blessed State of the Saints in their enjoyment of God in Glory . . . Written by the Author for his own use, in the time of his languishing, when God took him off from all Publik Imployment; and afterwards Preached in his weekly Lecture: And now published by Richard Baxter, Teacher of the Church of Kederminster in Worcestershire (printed by Rob. White, for Thomas Underhill and Francis Tyton, to be sold at the Blue Anchor and Bible in St Paul's Churchyard, near the little North door, and at the Three Daggers in Fleet Street, near the Inner Temple gate, 1650).

The Whole Duty of Man: Laid down In a plain and familiar Way, for the Use of all, but especially the meanest Reader . . . With Private Devotions for several Occasions (printed for Robert Pawlet, at the Sign of the Bible in Chancery Lane, near Fleet Street, 1675).

An Essay upon Miracles, by William Fleetwood (C. Harper, London, 1701).
The Book of Common Prayer, 1549, revised and added to in 1662.

Dr Jane Steen, Canon Chancellor and Theologian of Southwark Cathedral, spoke to the Johnson Society of London on 'Samuel Johnson's Anglicanism and the Art of Translation', now published in *The New Rambler* (2007–8).

Peter Laslett's *The World We Have Lost* (Methuen, London, 1965) was very influential when I was a student. It still has much to tell us about the kind of thought world inhabited by Johnson's mother. Other useful books about life in Christian England in the late seventeenth century include:

Peter Clark and Paul Slack's *English Towns in Transition 1500–1700* (Oxford University Press, Oxford, 1976); David L. Edwards's *Christian England, Volume Two: From the Reformation to the eighteenth century* (Collins, London, 1983); and, perhaps the most vividly written, David Underdown's *Fire from Heaven: Life in an English town in the seventeenth century* (HarperCollins, London, 1992).

Raymond Crawfurd's *The King's Evil* (Clarendon Press, Oxford, 1911) is a useful source for an explanation of the royal 'touching' ceremony.

Aleyn Lyell Reade's *Johnsonian Gleanings* (privately printed, 1909–52), provides much valuable information about Sarah Johnson's upbringing as the daughter of Cornelius Ford. (Lyell Reade was a distant relative of the Johnsons with an amateur interest in genealogy.)

Hester Thrale's *Anecdotes of the Late Samuel Johnson LLD* were written by her in haste and entirely from memory while she was living in Italy with her new husband, Gabriel Piozzi (T. Cadell, London, 1786). They are available in a modern edition, edited by Arthur Sherbo (Oxford University Press, Oxford, 1974). Her diaries were not published until Katharine C. Balderston's two-volume edition of Hester Thrale's *Thraliana* first appeared in 1941 (revised second edition, Clarendon Press, Oxford, 1951). Balderston's painstaking scholarship made available for the first time the intimate details of the Thrale household, adding great colour and drama to our picture of Johnson's life with the family at the brewery in Southwark and at their country estate, Streatham Park.

Mary Wollstonecraft published her *Thoughts on the Education of Daughters* in 1787 (J. Johnson, London). She devotes this, her first book, to what she sees as the most urgent task, not just to improve the lot of women but more importantly to address the health of society, by ensuring that one half of the population are properly prepared for life as mothers, wives, daughters *and* professionals.

Johnson's struggle to create the *Dictionary* from his signing of the contract in 1746 until its publication in 1755 was given colourful and illuminating life in the 'Celebrating Johnson's Dictionary, 1755–2005' conference at Pembroke College, Oxford, in August 2005. I am particularly indebted to Jack Lynch, whose abridged version makes the flavour, the style and the range of the *Dictionary* easily available in one volume: *Samuel Johnson's Dictionary: Selections from the 1755 work that defined the English language* (Atlantic Books, London, 2004). I am also grateful to Anne McDermott for her authoritative paper, 'How Johnson's Dictionary Was Made', and to Graham Nicholls and Catherine Dille for their insights into Johnson at this period.

Of the many sources for descriptions of life in London in the eighteenth century, the following are the most useful:

M. Dorothy George's *London Life in the Eighteenth Century* (Penguin,

Harmondsworth, 1992) was first published in 1925 and is now outdated. But it is still a marvellous read.

Richard B. Schwartz's *Daily Life in Johnson's London* (University of Wisconsin Press, Madison, WI, 1983) is a short but densely packed compendium.

Liza Picard's *Dr Johnson's London: Life in London 1740–1770* (Weidenfeld & Nicolson, London, 2000) is less reliable than her book on *Restoration London* and takes a rather old-fashioned view of Johnson but it is packed full of detail and threaded through with a love of London that Johnson would have appreciated.

Two more modern evocations of the London that Johnson would have known are *Walking the Streets of Eighteenth-Century London*, a collection of essays inspired by John Gay's *Trivia* of 1716 and edited by Clare Brant and Susan E. Whyman (Oxford University Press, Oxford, 2007) and Emily Cockayne's *Hubbub: Filth, noise & stench in England, 1600–1770* (Yale University Press, New Haven, CT, 2007).

The London Encyclopaedia, edited by Ben Weinreb and Christopher Hibbert (revised edition, Macmillan, London, 1993), is a vast resource in one handy volume for all the significant buildings and streets of London.

The A to Z of Georgian London (with introductory notes by Ralph Hyde, London Topographical Society, London, 1982) is a facsimile of John Rocque's map of 1746 and a brilliant way to understand the walks that Johnson loved to take across the City, through the Law Courts and over the river to the brewery in Dead Man's Place, Southwark.

Finally, a summary of Johnson's own works consulted in this chapter:

The Rambler, No. 45, Tuesday 21 August 1750; No. 95, Tuesday 12 February 1751.

The Dictionary of the English Language, 1755.

The Idler, No. 41, Saturday 27 January 1759.

The History of Rasselas, Prince of Abyssinia (R. & J. Dodsley, London, 1759).

Prayers and Meditations, edited originally by George Strahan in 1785 (T. Cadell, London) and now available in Volume 1 of *The Yale Edition of the Works of Samuel Johnson*, edited by E. L. McAdam Jr with Donald and Mary Hyde (Yale University Press, New Haven, CT, 1958)

The Letters of Samuel Johnson, collected and edited by R. W. Chapman (Clarendon Press, Oxford, 1952).

Chapter 3: Love and Death

This chapter is dedicated to David Nokes. We did not agree on Tetty's character, or Johnson's fondness for her, but I have benefited greatly from his understanding of Johnson's literary life, and I value my memories of our conversations about eighteenth-century literature.

I must also thank Catherine Dille, Elizabeth Eger, Judith Hawley, Nancy Johnson, Freya Johnston, Christine Rees and Fiona Ritchie for sharing with me their scholarly knowledge of the period. Simon Chaplin, Curator of the Hunterian Museum, generously researched John Ranby and Tetty's doctors.

Aleyn Lyell Reade's twelve-volume *Johnsonian Gleanings* (privately printed, 1909–52) provides much detailed information on the history of Tetty's family and also of her first husband Henry Porter's origins. Several volumes deal with the Jervis and Porter families, but it is worth cross-checking between the volumes for the corrections which Reade made over the years as he updated his research.

Among the clutch of biographies of Johnson that appeared very soon after his death is William Shaw's *Memoirs of the Life and Writings of the late Dr Samuel Johnson*, the first comprehensive account, based on his conversations with many of those who had known Johnson, including Mrs Desmoulins. From Mrs Desmoulins he heard about Johnson's late-night visits to her room during Tetty's illnesses; a story that many other biographers did not repeat but about which gossip continued for many years. A modern edition of Shaw's book is available, edited by Arthur Sherbo (Oxford University Press, Oxford, 1974). Gordon Turnbull's article, 'Not a Woman in Sight', in the *Times Literary Supplement*, 18 and 25 December 2009, introduces new evidence concerning the Desmoulins family and Johnson's household in his last weeks.

Sir John Hawkins is the only major biographer to have known Johnson while he was married, and his reflections on the marriage are stilted but revealing. His biography takes up the first volume of his edition of *The Works of Samuel Johnson, LLD* (J. Buckland, J. Rivington and sons, T. Payne and sons, T. Longman, T. Cadell, E. Newbery, Leigh and Sotheby, J. Murray and others, London, 1787). A new edition of Hawkins's *The Life of Samuel Johnson, LLD*, edited by OM Brack Jr is now available (University of Georgia Press, Athens and London, 2009).

Hester Thrale was fascinated by Johnson's relationship with his wife, but she can only repeat gossip and the opinions of others, being too young to have known Tetty herself. She writes about Tetty in her *Anecdotes of the Late Samuel Johnson, LLD* (available in an edition edited by Arthur Sherbo, Oxford University Press, Oxford, 1974).

Anna Seward, also, never knew Tetty and can only repeat the gossip she heard as an observant child. She was no defender of Tetty. Her letters contain intriguing snippets about the Johnsons' marriage, which were still circulating in Lichfield almost fifty years later: *Letters of Anna Seward, written between the years 1784 and 1807* (edited by Archibald Constable in six volumes, Edinburgh, 1811).

Modern essays on Tetty's life with Johnson include:

Gay W. Brack's 'Tetty and Samuel Johnson: The romance and the reality', published in *The Age of Johnson: A scholarly annual*, edited by Paul J. Korshin, volume 5 (AMS, New York, 1992). Mary Hyde's 'Tetty and Johnson', *Transactions of the Johnson Society, Lichfield* (December 1957). Mary Hyde was an ardent supporter of Tetty, perhaps inspired by the portrait which she owned and which gives us such a vivid impression of how Tetty must have appeared to Johnson: serene, capable and above all experienced.

Margaret Lane's essay 'Dr Johnson in his Relations with Women', also for *Transactions of the Johnson Society, Lichfield* (December 1971), is an insightful portrait. Roy W. Menninger's 'Johnson's Psychic Turmoil and the Women in his Life', in *The Age of Johnson: A scholarly annual*, edited by Paul J. Korshin, volume 5 (AMS, New York, 1992), is written from the viewpoint of a psychiatrist. Phyllis Rowell was the curator of Dr Johnson's House in London and her article for the *New Rambler*, 'The Women in Johnson's Life' (London, January 1964), has all the insights of someone who knew the house where he once lived with Tetty.

But perhaps the best and most inspiring essay on Tetty is by Alice Meynell. An experienced biographer, who herself wrote a study of Johnson, her short tribute to 'Mrs Johnson' in her collected essays, *Essays of Today and Yesterday* (Harrap, London, 1926), is a passionate defence of Tetty's reputation. It was Tetty, she argues, who protected Johnson from his 'black dog'.

Of the modern biographers of Johnson, very few provide detailed portraits of the marriage, as if embarrassed by the idea of Johnson's sexuality. David Nokes in *Samuel Johnson: A life* (Faber, London, 2009) is the most recent exception and gives a vivid account of the marriage (though from a different perspective than that taken in this chapter). Walter Jackson Bate's *Samuel Johnson* (Harcourt Brace Jovanovich, New Haven, CT, 1977), James Clifford's *Young Sam Johnson* and *Dictionary Johnson:*

Samuel Johnson's middle years (McGraw-Hill, New York, 1955, 1979) and Margaret Lane's *Samuel Johnson and His World* (Hamish Hamilton, London, 1975) also take an interest in Tetty. James Clifford unearthed many letters not previously published, including *Lucy Porter to Dr Johnson: Her only known letter* (Johnsonians, New Haven, CT, 1979).

Bertrand H. Bronson takes an unusual approach in his collection of essays, *Johnson Agonistes & Other Essays* (Cambridge University Press, Cambridge, 1946), looking in particular at Johnson's tragedy, *Irene*. He suggests that Johnson based the character of Aspasia on Tetty and that Johnson read to her the manuscript as it was being written. She also encouraged him in his endeavour to have it staged at Drury Lane.

Fiona Ritchie gave an illuminating talk on Hannah Pritchard, the actress who played Irene in Johnson's tragedy, published in the *New Rambler* (2005–6) as 'Hannah Pritchard: Johnson's Irene'.

Edward Cave began publishing the *Gentleman's Magazine* in January 1731, the first of its kind, providing its readers with information, gossip, foreign news, poetry and reviews of the latest plays and books. It's a hugely important source for anyone wishing to understand life in Georgian London. The 'deaths' column is a compelling record of the fragility (and violence) of life in the city, with brief accounts of violent murders or of young girls burnt to death in minutes after dancing too close to a candle. Johnson's first published piece in the magazine was a poem in Latin in March 1738. His poem in English 'To Eliza Plucking Laurel in Mr Pope's Gardens' appeared a few months later in August.

Issues of the *Gentleman's Magazine* can now be read, and searched, online via the Bodleian Library's project, the Internet Library of Early Journals, at: www.bodley.ox.ac.uk/ilej/.

Mary Wollstonecraft's *Vindication of the Rights of Woman* was published in 1792 (J. Johnson, London), a sequel to her *A Vindication of the Rights of Men* (J. Johnson, London, 1790), both written as an antidote to the conservative reaction to the French Revolution.

Johnson's works consulted in this chapter are:

London: A poem. In imitation of the Third Satire of Juvenal (R. Dodsley, London, 1738).

An Account of the Life of Richard Savage, first published in 1744 (Edward Cave, London).

Irene: A Tragedy (R. Dodsley, London, 1749).

The Rambler, No. 60, Saturday 13 October 1750.

The Rambler, No. 68, Saturday 10 November 1750.

The Rambler, No. 208, Saturday 14 March 1752 – the last issue.

The Dictionary of the English Language, 1755.

The History of Rasselas, Prince of Abyssinia (R. & J. Dodsley, London, 1759).

A Sermon written by the late Samuel Johnson LLD for the Funeral of his Wife, published by the Rev. Samuel Hayes, AM, usher of Westminster School (London, 1788). This is also printed in the volume dedicated to Johnson's sermons in *The Yale Edition of the Works of Samuel Johnson*, volume 14, edited by Jean Hagstrum and James Gray (Yale University Press, New Haven, CT, 1978).

Johnson wrote many prayers in memory of Tetty. When these were published as the *Prayers and Meditations* he won many new admirers, especially among women readers. They were edited originally by George Strahan in 1785 (T. Cadell, London) and are now available in volume 1 of *The Yale Edition of the Works of Samuel Johnson*, edited by E. L. McAdam Jr with Donald and Mary Hyde (Yale University Press, New Haven, CT, 1958). Aleyn Lyell Reade discovered some letters relating to Johnson's female readers, including Mrs Nicholas of Chichester, who were won over by the fondness with which Johnson remembers Tetty in his *Prayers and Meditations*: 'A New Admirer for Dr Johnson', The *London Mercury* (ed. J. C. Squire), xxi (November 1929 to April 1930).

The Letters of Samuel Johnson, collected and edited by R. W. Chapman (three volumes, Clarendon Press, Oxford, 1952), and especially Johnson's letter to 'Dearest Tetty', dated Thursday 31 January 1740. The letter in which he writes so movingly about grief was sent to Thomas Warton and is dated Saturday 21 December 1754. In it, Johnson tells his friend that Mr Dodsley, the publisher, has lost his wife and then adds, 'I hope he will not suffer so much as I yet suffer for the loss of mine . . . I have ever since seemed to myself broken off from mankind a kind of solitary wanderer in the wild of life . . .'

Chapter 4: An Equal Mind

This chapter, in particular, has benefited hugely from the work of Elizabeth Eger and Lucy Peltz, published in the catalogue of the *Brilliant Women* exhibition (National Portrait Gallery, London, 2008). Clare Barlow, who assisted in the research for that exhibition, discovered the portrait of Carter as the goddess Minerva. She also gave an insightful talk on Elizabeth Carter to the Johnson Society of London. I must also thank the librarians at Canterbury Cathedral, Deal Library in Kent, Lambeth Palace and the Huntington Library in San Marino, California, for access to Elizabeth Carter's letters and papers connected with her life in Deal.

Roger Lonsdale did much to resurrect the reputation of Carter and her fellow poets in his edition, *Eighteenth-century Women Poets* (Oxford University Press, Oxford, 1990). Judith Hawley edited the volume dedicated to the works of Elizabeth Carter in *Bluestocking Feminism: Writings of the Bluestocking Circle, 1738–85*, volume 2 (Pickering & Chatto, London, 1999), which includes an enlightening introductory essay. Harriet Guest's essay on 'Bluestocking Feminism' in *Reconsidering the Bluestockings*, edited by Nicole Pohl and Betty Schellenberg (Huntington Library, San Marino, CA, 2003), places Elizabeth Carter in context as an influential figure.

An early fan of Carter's work was Alice C. C. Gaussen whose *A Woman of Wit and Wisdom: A memoir of Elizabeth Carter, one of the 'Bas Bleu' society* appeared in 1906 (Smith, Elder & Co., London). Virginia Woolf's tribute to Elizabeth Carter appears in *A Room of One's Own* (Hogarth Press, London, 1929), a precis of women's writing through the ages, or rather an exposé of the difficulties faced by women writers as they struggle to find time, mental space, or the opportunity to publish.

Carolyn D. Williams wrote a valuable essay on Carter, 'Poetry, Pudding and Epictetus: The consistency of Elizabeth Carter', published in *Tradition in Transition: Women writers, marginal texts and the eighteenth-century canon*, edited by Alvaro Ribeiro, SJ and James G. Basker (Clarendon Press, Oxford, 1996). She also gave a talk to the Johnson Society of London, 'Elizabeth Carter and Catherine Talbot: Rational piety in the *Rambler*', published in the *New Rambler* (2000–1).

Brigitte Sprenger Holtkamp's 'Miss Epictetus, or the Learned Eliza: A literary biography of Elizabeth Carter' (unpublished PhD Thesis, University of London, 1996) alerted me to Virginia Woolf's praise of Elizabeth Carter, and to much else in Elizabeth's letters to Catherine Talbot and Elizabeth Vesey.

An anonymous *Sketch of the Character of Mrs Elizabeth Carter, who died in London, on February the 19th, 1806, in the eighty-ninth year of her age* (Kelso, A. Ballantyne, 1806) includes details not found in the memoir compiled by her nephew, the Revd Montagu Pennington, and published a year later in 1807. His two-volume *Memoirs of the Life of Mrs Elizabeth Carter, with a new edition of her Poems, some of which have never appeared before; to which are added some Miscellaneous Essays in Prose, together with her Notes on the Bible, and Answers to Objections concerning the Christian Religion* (F. C. and J. Rivington, London) is a useful source, but Pennington was a scrupulous editor, dedicated to preserving his aunt in his own image. He then destroyed all the papers he had used, making it impossible for us now to discover how much he obscured or left out.

Pennington, christened Montagu after his godmother Elizabeth Montagu, also collected and edited his aunt's letters: *A Series of Letters between Mrs Elizabeth Carter and Miss Catherine Talbot, from the year 1741 to 1770* (four volumes, which include Elizabeth's letters to her friend Elizabeth Vesey, F. C. and J. Rivington, London, 1809) and *Letters from Mrs Elizabeth Carter to Mrs Montagu, between the years 1755 and 1800, chiefly upon literary and moral subjects* (three volumes, F. C. and J. Rivington, London, 1817). Once again, Pennington destroyed all the letters he had used, so we cannot find out what he deleted or compressed to suit his own editorial intentions.

The letters between Elizabeth and Thomas Birch are quoted by Edward Rucke in his essay, 'Birch, Johnson and Elizabeth Carter: An episode 1738–9', *PMLA*, lxiii, 5, i (December 1958).

The letters which Elizabeth sent to Richardson, reprimanding him for publishing her 'Ode to Wisdom' without her consent, can be read in the *Monthly Magazine, or British Register*, 33, i (London, 1812).

The first mention of Johnson's now famous quote about Elizabeth, puddings and Epictetus is in Sir John Hawkins's 'Apophthegms, Sentiments, Opinions and Occasional Reflections', published in volume 11 of his edition of *The Works of Samuel Johnson, LLD* (J. Buckland, J. Rivington and sons, T. Payne and sons, T. Longman, T. Cadell, E. Newbery, Leigh and Sotheby, J. Murray and others, London, 1787). Hawkins writes, 'Upon hearing a lady of his acquaintance commended for her learning, he said—A man is in general better pleased when he has a good dinner upon his table, than when his wife talks Greek. My old friend, Mrs Carter, said he, could make a pudding, as well as translate Epictetus from the Greek, and work a handkerchief as well as compose a poem.'

Hawkins adds, intriguingly, 'He thought she was too reserved in conversation upon subjects she was so eminently able to converse upon, which was occasioned by her modesty and fear of giving offence.'

Hawkins also includes Johnson's curious 'Meditation of a Pudding' in his biography of Johnson, published as volume 1 of *The Works of Samuel Johnson, LLD*. 'Let us seriously reflect on what a pudding is composed of,' Johnson wrote, as quoted by Hawkins. 'It is composed of flour that once waved in the golden grain, and drank the dews of the morning—of milk pressed from the swelling udder by the gentle hand of the beauteous milk-maid, whose beauty and innocence might have recommended a worse draught; who, whilst she stroked the udder, indulged no ambitious thoughts of dwelling in palaces, and formed no schemes for the destruction of her fellow-creatures—milk which is drawn from the cow, that useful animal, that eats the grass of the field, and supplies us with that which made the greatest part of the food of that age, which the poets have agreed to call golden.'

Johnson was making fun of the popularity of poems about mundane subjects, overinflating the everyday. But its inclusion by Hawkins in his biography raises doubts about Johnson's intentions when he praised Carter for her gifts as a pudding-maker. Is Johnson here betraying a hint of misogyny or simply reflecting the attitudes of his time?

A new edition of Hawkins's biography is now available, edited by OM Brack Jr (University of Georgia Press, Athens and London, 2009).

Elizabeth Carter's published volumes are:

Poems upon Particular Occasions (E. Cave, London, 1738).

Poems on Several Occasions, dedicated to the Earl of Bath and signed Eliz. Carter (John Rivington, London, 1762).

All the Works of Epictetus, Which are now Extant; consisting of His Discourses, preserved by Arrian, in four books, The Enchiridion, and Fragments, translated from the original Greek by Elizabeth Carter (J. and F. Rivington, London, 1768).

Her early contributions to the *Gentleman's Magazine* are available online at: www.bodley.ox.ac.uk/ilej/.

Carter contributed two essays to Johnson's *Rambler*: No. 44, Saturday 18 August 1750 (in which Elizabeth debates the opposing virtues of 'Religion' and 'Superstition') and No. 100, Saturday 2 March 1751 (sent in by Elizabeth as an attempt to 'write a cheerful paper to the Rambler').

Mary Wollstonecraft includes one of Elizabeth's poems, 'Written at

Midnight during a Thunder-storm', in her *The Female Reader*, a collection of pieces in prose and verse 'for the improvement of young women', published in 1788 (J. Johnson, London) and now available in Janet Todd and Marilyn Butler's edition of *The Works of Mary Wollstonecraft* (William Pickering, London, 1989).

Catherine Talbot never published what she wrote but after her death Elizabeth Carter arranged for her religious meditations to be printed. *Reflections on the Seven Days of the Week* (John and Francis Rivington, London, 1770) was such an immediate success that Carter then published Talbot's *Essays on Various Subjects* (John and Francis Rivington, London, 1772), followed by a collected edition, *The Works of Catherine Talbot* (John and Francis Rivington, London, 1772).

Johnson's early poems are now published in volume 6 of *The Yale Edition of the Works of Samuel Johnnson*, edited by E. L. McAdam Jr and George Milne (Yale University Press, New Haven, CT, 1964).

The memorial to Elizabeth, erected by her nephew Montagu Pennington, in St George's Chapel in Deal, reads:

> Sacred to the Memory of Mrs Elizabeth Carter, a Native and Inhabitant of this Town, where her Benevolence and Virtue will be long remembered. She was eldest Daughter of the Revd Nicolas Carter, DD, for upwards of 50 years Perpetual Curate of this Chapel, by Margaret, Sole Daughter and Heiress of Richard Swayne of Bere in the County of Dorset Esq. In deep Learning, Genius, Extensive Knowledge She was equalled by few, in Piety, and the practice of every Christian duty Excelled by none. She was born Dec 16th 1717 and died Feb 19th 1806 in London and was interred there in the burial Ground of Grosvenor Chapel. This memorial is erected by her nephew, the Revd M. Pennington.

Other known portraits of Elizabeth Carter are a three-quarter-length by Joseph Highmore, which shows her as a young woman (although it is claimed that it was painted *after* the success of *Epictetus* in 1758 when she would have been over forty). There is also a portrait of her in old age, in a mob cap and looking almost Victorian, painted by Sir Thomas Lawrence and now in the National Portrait Gallery. The Highmore portrait now hangs in the town hall at Deal.

Chapter 5: Miss Sainthill and the Female Quixote

An earlier version of this chapter was published in the *New Rambler* (2005–6).

Much of my work on Charlotte Lennox depends on conversations with Susan Carlile and especially on Norbert Schürer's forthcoming edition of Lennox's letters. Fiona Ritchie discussed with me her understanding of Lennox's importance as a Shakespeare scholar, generously showing me her chapter on Lennox, 'Women's Criticism of Shakespeare in the Age of Johnson', for her forthcoming study of the role of women writers in resurrecting Shakespeare's tragedies in the mid-eighteenth century. I am also grateful to Jane Darcy for sharing with me her insights into Hill Boothby's life in Derbyshire, and to the late Kate Jones for our discussions on friendship, which helped to shape my ideas for this book.

The quotations from Charlotte Lennox's letters are taken from Norbert Schürer's forthcoming edition of Lennox's correspondence (72 letters), which updates the series of Lennox letters published by Duncan Isles in the *Harvard Library Bulletin*, xviii (October 1970), xv (1971), xx (1971) and xxx (1972); and also the article by Eric C. Walker, 'Charlotte Lennox and the Collier Sisters: Two new Johnson letters', in *Studies in Philology*, 95:3 (Summer 1998). I am very grateful to Norbert for permission to quote from them in my chapter. Susan Carlile's 'Charlotte Lennox's Birth Date and Place', in *Notes and Queries*, new series 51:4 (December 2004), helps to clarify the confusions surrounding Lennox's birthplace and early years.

The only published full-length biography of Lennox is Miriam R. Small's 1935 study *Charlotte Ramsay Lennox: An eighteenth century lady of letters* (republished by Archon Books in 1969 in their series *Yale Studies in English*, volume 85). This is a useful if not very lively record of Lennox's life and work, adapted from a PhD thesis.

The story about Charlotte sitting on Johnson's knee and eating pastries comes from an anonymous short biography of her in the *Lady's Monthly Museum* (June 1813).

Charlotte Lennox's works remained out of print for most of the nineteenth and twentieth centuries but are gradually now being republished, beginning with *The Female Quixote* (1752), now available as an Oxford World's Classic, edited by Margaret Dalziel, with an introduction by Margaret Anne Doody (Oxford University Press, Oxford, 1989). This edition also includes an appendix by the Lennox scholar, Duncan Isles, 'Johnson, Richardson, and *The Female Quixote*', which discusses in great detail Lennox's debt to Johnson and to Richardson and the question of whether or not Johnson actually wrote the penultimate chapter of her novel. Doody asserts in her introduction that the chapter is Lennox's and hers alone. OM Brack Jr and Susan Carlile have also debated this difficult question in their article 'Samuel Johnson's Contributions to Charlotte Lennox's *The Female Quixote*', in the *Yale University Library Gazette* (April 2003). They conclude, based on literary and typographical evidence, that the chapter belongs to Lennox.

Other works by Lennox now easily available are:

The Life of Harriot Stuart, written by herself (1751), edited by Susan Kubica Howard (Broadview Editions, Buffalo, NY, 2005).

Sophia (first published in serial form between March 1760 and February 1761 as *The History of Harriot and Sophia*, and republished as *Sophia* in 1762), edited by Norbert Schürer (Broadview Editions, Buffalo, NY, 2008).

Euphemia (1790), edited by Susan Kubica Howard (Broadview Editions, Buffalo, NY, 2008).

Other major works not so far published in a modern edition are:

Poems on Several Occasions, Written by a Young Lady (printed for and sold by S. Paterson, at Shakespear's Head, opposite Durham-yard in the Strand, London, 1748).

Shakespear Illustrated; or the Novels and Histories on which the Plays of Shakespear are Founded, Collected and Translated from the Original Authors with Critical Remarks (two volumes, A. Millar, London, 1753). A third volume was added in 1754.

Memoirs of Maximilian de Bethune, Duke of Sully, translated from the French (three volumes, A. Millar and R. and J. Dodsley, London, 1756). Two additional volumes were published in 1757 and new editions kept appearing until 1856, which has an historical introduction attributed to Sir Walter Scott.

The Memoirs of the Countess of Berci, taken from the French by the author of *The Female Quixote* (two volumes, A. Millar, London, 1756).

Philander: a dramatic pastoral, by the author of *The Female Quixote* (A. Millar, London, 1757).

Henrietta, by the author of *The Female Quixote* (two volumes, A. Millar, 1758).

The Greek Theatre of Father Brumoy, translated from the French (three volumes, Messrs Millar, Vaillant, etc, London, 1759).

The Lady's Museum, by the Author of *The Female Quixote*, March 1760 to February 1761 (J. Newbery, London). This is worth chasing up in the British Library (catalogue no. C.175.n.15).

The Sister: A comedy, by Mrs Charlotte Lennox (J. Dodsley and T. Davies, London, 1769).

Old City Manners: A comedy (altered from the original *Eastward Hoe*, by Ben Jonson), (T. Becket, London, 1775).

John Hawkins's *Life of Samuel Johnson, LLD* (J. Buckland, London, 1787) is dull, but has useful insights because Hawkins knew Johnson as a much younger man. Only in Hawkins can we find an account of the evening celebrating the publication of Charlotte Lennox's first novel. There's a new edition, edited by OM Brack Jr (University of Georgia Press, Athens and London, 2009). Hawkins's daughter Laetitia Matilda Hawkins published her own anecdotes of the people she met through her father's wide circle of acquaintance in her *Memoirs*, which were republished in an edited version by Francis H. Skrine: *Gossip about Dr Johnson and Others* (Nash and Grayson, London, 1926).

The infamous incident in 1778 when Charlotte Lennox was accused of assaulting her maid can be followed in the session rolls of the Middlesex Quarter Sessions now held in the London Metropolitan Archives (references: MJ/SP/1778/10/029 and MJ/SR/3358 and 3359).

Fanny Burney's early diaries have been published in a modern edition, edited by Lars Troide, Stewart Cooke, Betty Rizzo, Peter Sabor, et al: *The Early Journals and Letters of Fanny Burney, 1769–91*, volumes 1–4 so far published (Clarendon Press, Oxford, 1988–).

The Letters of David Garrick have been edited by David M. Little and George M. Kahrl (Oxford University Press, Oxford, 1963).

Betty Schellenberg talks about Lennox's grasp of the publishing business and her professional dealings with the most important printers in London in *The Professionalisation of Women Writers in Eighteenth-Century Britain* (Cambridge University Press, Cambridge 2005).

The key source for Hill Boothby's friendship with Johnson is the edition of their letters, first published by Richard Wright, surgeon and proprietor of the museum of antiquities, natural and artificial curiosities at Lichfield (who acquired the letters from Francis Barber, Johnson's servant and heir), and printed by Richard Phillips (London, 1805) in *An Account of the Life of Dr Samuel Johnson, from his Birth to his Eleventh Year, Written by Himself. To*

which are added Original Letters to Dr Samuel Johnson, by Miss Hill Boothby.
Unfortunately, the manuscript copy has since been lost.

Chester F. Chapin's chapter 'Johnson's Correspondence with Hill Boothby' in his book, *The Religious Thought of Samuel Johnson* (University of Michigan Press, Ann Arbor, MI, 1968) draws attention to Hill Boothby's influence on Johnson.

Papers belonging to the Fitzherbert family of Tissington Hall, including Mary Fitzherbert's will, which places her children in the care of Hill Boothby (and grants her 'negro servant' 'enough money to purchase and obtain his freedom as a naturalised subject in England'), can be seen at the Derbyshire Record Office in Matlock (239m/ F8237; F8240; F6503; F113; F105; F6525–6548).

Other sources used in this chapter include:

Bruce Redford's edition of the letters: *The Letters of Samuel Johnson* (four volumes, Clarendon Press, Oxford, 1992–4).

The Spiritual Quixote; or, The Summer's Ramble of Mr Geoffrey Wildgoose: A comic romance by Richard Graves was published in three volumes by J. Dodsley (London, 1773).

Donald and Mary Hyde first drew attention to Hill Boothby as a possible wife for Johnson in 'Dr Johnson's Second Wife', which they published in *New Light on Dr Johnson: Essays on the occasion of his 250th birthday*, edited by Frederick W. Hilles (Yale University Press, New Haven, CT, 1959). Adam Sisman has also written on Johnson's second wife in his book, *Boswell's Presumptuous Task: The making of the Life of Johnson* (Hamish Hamilton, London, 2000), and again in 'Dr Johnson's Second Wife', *Transactions of the Johnson Society, Lichfield* (2002).

The Adventurer, published (by John Payne) on Thursdays and Saturdays from 7 November 1752 to 9 March 1754, was the brainchild of John Hawkesworth and written by a team which included Hawkesworth himself, Joseph Warton of Oxford and Hester Chapone. Johnson began contributing sometime after March 1753 and probably supplied about one quarter of the 140 essays. They are reprinted in volume 2 of *The Yale Edition of the Works of Samuel Johnson*, edited by W. J. Bate, John M. Bullitt and L. F. Powell (Yale University Press, New Haven, CT, 1963).

The Rambler, No. 39, Tuesday 31 July 1750, highlights the plight of women, who 'whether they embrace marriage, or determine upon a single life, are exposed, in consequence of their choice, to sickness, misery, and death'. *The*

Yale Edition of the Works of Samuel Johnson, volume 3, edited by W. J. Bate and Albrecht B. Strauss (Yale University Press, New Haven, CT, 1969).

The Rambler, No. 18, Saturday 19 May 1750, discusses the pros and cons of marriage.

Chapter 6: A Stifled Sigh

'A Stifled Sigh' owes much to Natasha McEnroe, former Curator of Dr Johnson's House in Gough Square, to whom I am thankful for all our insightful conversations concerning Hester Thrale and her curious relationship with her children.

Johnson's relationship with Hester Thrale was fictionalised by Beryl Bainbridge as *According to Queeney* (Little, Brown, London, 2001), which gives us tantalising glimpses of their intense friendship as seen through the eyes of Hester's highly intelligent eldest child, Queeney. Bainbridge was inspired by the surviving correspondence between Johnson and Queeney, published by the Marquis of Lansdowne as *The Queeney Letters, being letters addressed to Hester Maria Thrale by Doctor Johnson, Fanny Burney and Mrs Thrale-Piozzi* (Cassell & Co., London, 1934).

The primary sources for this chapter belong to Hester Thrale herself:

Anecdotes of the Late Samuel Johnson, LLD, during the last twenty years of his life, by Hester Lynch Piozzi (T. Cadell, London, 1786), now available in a modern edition edited by Arthur Sherbo (Oxford University Press, Oxford, 1974).

Letters to and from the Late Samuel Johnson LLD, to which are added some Poems never before Printed. Published from the original MSS in her possession (two volumes, A. Strahan and T. Cadell, London, 1788).

Thraliana: The diary of Mrs Hester Lynch Thrale (Later Mrs Piozzi), 1776–1809, edited by Katharine C. Balderston (two volumes, Clarendon Press, Oxford, 1951).

Katharine Balderston's earlier essay 'Johnson's Vile Melancholy' created a huge stir in Johnsonian studies because of the way it highlighted certain strange and unexplained aspects of his relationship with Hester Thrale: the key, the padlock, the letters in French. The essay was published in *The Age of Johnson: Essays presented to Chauncey Brewster Tinker*, edited by Frederick W. Hilles (Yale University Press, New Haven, CT, 1949).

James Clifford's 1941 biography *Hester Lynch Piozzi (Mrs Thrale)* (Clarendon

Press, Oxford) was published before Katharine Balderston's enlightening scholarship but was the first modern biography and an excellent read. (A paperback version of the second edition has an illuminating introduction by Margaret Anne Doody: Clarendon Press, Oxford, 1987.)

Mary Hyde's *The Thrales of Streatham Park* is a detailed family study, written with the benefit of immediate access to the huge collection of Johnson manuscripts collected by her husband, Donald Hyde, and especially Hester Thrale's 'The Children's Book', begun by her on Queeney's birthday, 17 September 1766 and continued to the end of 1778 (Harvard University Press, Cambridge, MA, 1977).

William McCarthy's literary portrait of 1985, *Hester Thrale Piozzi: Portrait of a literary woman* (University of North Carolina Press, Chapel Hill, NC) updates James Clifford's study.

Ian MacIntyre's *Hester: The remarkable life of Dr Johnson's 'Dear Mistress'* (Constable, London, 2008) is an easy and colourful read, if a bit old-fashioned.

Lee Morgan's *Dr Johnson's 'Own Dear Master'* (University Press of America, Maryland, 1998) is a rare example of a study of Henry Thrale.

Lyle Larsen's *Dr Johnson's Household* (Archon, Hamden, CT, 1985) sheds light on the life Johnson was living when not at Streatham, providing a valuable backdrop to the letters and intimacies of their friendship.

Jenny Uglow's *Hogarth: A life and a world* (Faber, London, 1997) has details of the portrait, *The Lady's Last Stake*, for which Hester may have sat as a pert sixteen-year-old.

Hester Thrale and Johnson wrote many letters to each other. R. W. Chapman's three-volume edition for the Clarendon Press, Oxford, 1952, gives us letters both to and from Johnson and Hester Thrale. Bruce Redford's four-volume edition is more up to date (Clarendon Press, Oxford, 1992–4).

Edward and Lillian Bloom's six-volume edition of *The Piozzi Letters: Correspondence of Hester Lynch Piozzi (formerly Mrs Thrale)*(University of Delaware Press, Newark, DE, 1989–2002) tells the story of Hester's second marriage to Gabriel Piozzi.

Many of the letters Hester wrote while she was married to Henry Thrale remain unpublished, and can only be read at the John Rylands Library in Manchester or the Huntington Library in San Marino, California.

R. W. Chapman wrote several articles exploring the stories that lie behind many of the letters:

'Did Johnson Destroy Mrs Thrale's Letters?' *Notes and Queries*, clxxxv (28 August 1943).

'Piozzi on Thrale', *Notes and Queries*, clxxxv (23 October 1943).

'Mrs Piozzi's Omissions from Johnson's Letters to the Thrales', *Review of English Studies*, xxii (January 1946).

'Mrs Thrale's Letters to Johnson Published by Mrs Piozzi in 1788', *Review of English Studies*, xxiv (January 1948).

A. M. Broadley's *Doctor Johnson and Mrs Thrale* (John Lane, London, 1910) prints many original letters between them.

In his book, *The Converse of the Pen: Acts of intimacy in the eighteenth-century familiar letter* (University of Chicago Press, Chicago, 1986), Bruce Redford devotes one chapter to 'Samuel Johnson and Mrs Thrale'.

Fanny Burney's account of her visits to Streatham Park and acquaintance with both Johnson and Hester Thrale have been edited in a modern version by the Burney Centre at McGill University: *The Early Journals and Letters of Fanny Burney, 1768–91*, edited by Lars Troide, Stewart Cooke and Betty Rizzo, volumes 3 and 4 (Oxford University Press, Oxford, 1988–2003). Her sister Charlotte's diaries have not been published, but can be read in manuscript in the Berg Collection at the New York Public Library and the Barrett Collection at the British Library.

Johnson's 'Life of Pope' is just one of the *Lives of the Poets* which he published individually from 1777 to 1781 and then collected in a ten-volume edition as *Prefaces Biographical and Critical to the Works of the English Poets*, organised by a consortium of printers that included Thomas Cadell, Thomas Davies and William Strahan. The Victorian scholar, George Birkbeck Hill, prepared an annotated three-volume edition, *Lives of the Poets* (Clarendon Press, Oxford, 1905). Roger Lonsdale's four-volume edition for Oxford University Press (Oxford, 2006) is now the definitive source.

Boswell's relationship with Hester Thrale was fraught with jealousy. His *Life* is not always to be trusted when it comes to Johnson's life with the Thrale family. Mary Hyde's *The Impossible Friendship: Boswell and Mrs Thrale* (Chatto & Windus, London, 1972) looks at the rivalry as each sought to outdo the other in claiming 'intimate' knowledge of Johnson.

Johnson's *Rambler* essay on biography is No. 60, Saturday 13 October 1750: 'All joy or sorrow for the happiness or calamities of others is produced by an act of the imagination, that realises the event however fictitious, or approximates it however remote, by placing us, for a time, in the condition of him whose fortune we contemplate; so that we feel, while the deception lasts, whatever motions would be excited by the same good or evil happening to ourselves . . .'

After Johnson's death Hester published not just her *Anecdotes* and her edition of their letters, but also a volume of travel writing taken from her experiences on the Continent and two volumes of original (in all its senses) scholarship:

Observations and Reflections Made in the Course of a Journey through France, Italy and Germany (two volumes, A. Strahan and T. Cadell, London, 1789).

British Synonymy; or an Attempt at Regulating the Choice of Words in Familiar Conversation (two volumes, G. G. and J. Robinson, London, 1794).

Retrospection: or a Review of the Most Striking and Important Events, Characters, Situations, and their Consequences, which the Last Eighteen Hundred Years Have Presented to the View of Mankind (two volumes, John Stockdale, London, 1801).

None of them has been reprinted.

Chapter 7: 'Renny Dear'

Michael Copland-Griffiths (a descendant of Theophila 'Offie' Gwatkin, née Palmer, Frances Reynolds's niece) and his wife Larysa very kindly invited me to visit their home to read Frances Reynolds's unpublished commonplace book. I am very grateful to them for their hospitality.

I am also indebted to the scholarship of Martin Postle, Richard Wendorf, Helen Ashmore and Robert Folkenflik and to the researches of Richard Aylmer (who publishes the *Reynolds Newsletter*, densely packed with family history). Howard Weinbrot introduced me to a possible self-portrait of Frances Reynolds and gave me his insights into her skills as an artist. At the Pembroke College Tercentenary Conference in September 2009, the librarian of Trinity College, Oxford, very kindly showed us a portrait of Johnson as a young man, which may or may not be by Frances Reynolds. It seems unlikely: Johnson is seen as a handsome, well-proportioned young man. The portrait is very forgiving. Most probably it is a Victorian reimagining.

Frances Reynolds's portrait of Hannah More dominated the *Brilliant Women* exhibition at the National Portrait Gallery in the summer of 2008 because of its lack of display. Its simplicity drew the eye, inviting us to get to know this woman with the warm and homely face and deep, thoughtful expression. The exhibition catalogue *Brilliant Women: 18th-century Bluestockings*, edited by Elizabeth Eger and Lucy Peltz (National Portrait Gallery, London, 2008) has high-quality reproductions of the portraits and most instructive essays on the importance of these women to scholarship.

Germaine Greer in her study *The Obstacle Race: The fortunes of women painters and their work* (Secker & Warburg, London, 1979) first made the suggestion that Frances might have been a better artist than her brother. But many years earlier, in 1876, Ellen C. Clayton had recognised Frances's gifts by including her in her compendium of *English Female Artists* (two volumes, Tinsley Brothers, London).

Richard Wendorf's unusual and elegant study of *Sir Joshua Reynolds: The painter in society* (Harvard University Press, Cambridge, MA, 1996) looks in chapter 2 at the 'Other Voices' in Sir Joshua's life, including a sympathetic portrait of Frances, detailing her troubled relationship with Joshua.

Other useful studies of Frances's art and correspondence include:

Richard Wendorf and Charles Ryskamp's 'A Blue-Stocking Friendship: The letters of Elizabeth Montagu and Frances Reynolds in the Princeton Collection', *Princeton University Library Chronicle*, 41 (1979–80).

Richard Wendorf's *Frances Reynolds and Samuel Johnson* (A Keepsake to mark the 286th birthday of Samuel Johnson and the 49th annual dinner of The Johnsonians: The Houghton Library, Harvard University, Cambridge, MA, 1995).

Helen Ashmore's '"Do Not, My Love, Burn your Papers": Samuel Johnson and Frances Reynolds: a new document' in *The Age of Johnson*, volume 10 (AMS Press, New York, 1999).

Martin Postle's essay 'Johnson, Joshua Reynolds and "Renny Dear"' in the *New Rambler* (2004–5).

The second volume of James Clifford's biography of Johnson, *Dictionary Johnson: Samuel Johnson's middle years*, contains valuable insights into his relationships with the Reynoldses, and especially Frances (McGraw-Hill, New York, 1979). Derek Hudson, *Sir Joshua Reynolds: A personal study* (Geoffrey Bles, London, 1958) gives us details of life in the Reynoldses' household. Ian McIntyre's detailed biography *Joshua Reynolds: The life and times of the first President of the Royal Academy* (Allen Lane, London, 2003) is a useful source of information.

John Ingamells and John Edgcumbe have edited *The Letters of Sir Joshua Reynolds* (Yale University Press, London, 2001). Sir Joshua's *Discourses on Art*, which were first published in 1797, have been edited by Robert R. Wark (second edition, Yale University Press, London, 1975).

Frances Reynolds's *An Enquiry Concerning the Principles of Taste, and of the*

272

Origin of Our Ideas of Beauty, etc., which Johnson advised her not to publish, was eventually privately printed in 1785 after his death, as if Frances knew she was being misguided but could not help herself, so determined was she to prove that she also could write on art. It was republished in 1951, with an introduction by James L. Clifford (The Augustan Reprint Society, Los Angeles, CA).

Frances's previously unpublished 'Recollections of Dr Johnson' were included by George Birkbeck Hill in his two-volume edition of anecdotes and reflections by Johnson's friends and contemporaries, *Johnsonian Miscellanies* (Clarendon Press, Oxford, 1897).

R. W. Chapman's edition of Johnson's letters (three volumes, Clarendon Press, Oxford, 1952) adds notes from the letters that Frances wrote to Johnson.

Fanny Burney's *The Witlings* was never performed in her lifetime but has been given several staged readings in recent years. The text is available in two editions: Clayton J. Delery's *The Witlings* (Colleagues Press, East Lansing, MI, 1995) and in volume 1 of Peter Sabor's *The Complete Plays of Frances Burney* (two volumes, William Pickering, London, 1995).

See Joyce Hemlow's edition of *The Journals and Letters of Fanny Burney (Madame d'Arblay)*, *1791–1840* (twelve volumes, Clarendon Press, Oxford, 1972–84) for references to both Frances and Sir Joshua. And also *The Early Journals and Letters of Fanny Burney*, *1768–91*, edited by Lars Troide, Stewart Cooke and Betty Rizzo, volumes 3 and 4 (Oxford University Press, Oxford, 1988–2003).

Hester Thrale's *Thraliana* can be read in the edition, now out of print, by Katharine C. Balderston (two volumes, Clarendon Press, Oxford, 1951). Her *Anecdotes of the Late Samuel Johnson, LLD, during the last twenty years of his life, by Hester Lynch Piozzi* (T. Cadell, London, 1786) are available in a modern edition, edited by Arthur Sherbo (Oxford University Press, Oxford, 1974).

Frances Reynolds's correspondence with her friend Charlotte Lennox is included in Norbert Schürer's forthcoming edition of Lennox's correspondence.

The information on Francis Barber is derived from many discussions with Michael Bundock and from his article in the *New Rambler* (2003–4): 'From Slave to Heir: The strange journey of Francis Barber'.

Mary Wollstonecraft's *Vindication of the Rights of Woman* was published in 1792 (J. Johnson, London), and is now available in several modern editions such as the Penguin Classics, with an introduction by Miriam Brody (Penguin, London, 1983).

Ellis Cornelia Knight wrote an autobiography which has been edited by Roger Fulford and published as *The Autobiography of Miss Knight* (William Kimber, London, 1960).

John Croker's 1832 edition of Boswell's *Life of Johnson* includes the poem, 'I therefore pray thee, Renny dear . . .'

A list of Frances Reynolds's portraits (suggested, but not necessarily confirmed) would include:

Johnson as a young man, owned by Trinity College, Oxford. Probably not by Frances Reynolds, although it was said to be by her in a catalogue for an exhibition of historical portraits in Oxford in 1906.

Johnson reading, from about 1775, a slightly altered copy of Sir Joshua's Streatham portrait, formerly owned by the Courage brewery, which took over Barclay, Perkins & Co., the successor to the Anchor brewery owned by Henry Thrale, and now in the Albright-Knox Gallery, Buffalo, New York.

Johnson as an old man, the 'grimly ghost' portrait from 1783, now owned by Haverford College, Pennsylvania.

Anna Williams, now exhibited at Dr Johnson's House in Gough Square, London, painted after the cataract operation conducted in the House which left Ms Williams blinded in both eyes.

Elizabeth Montagu, 1778, a sitting reported on by Boswell. 'Don't make me fifteen,' Elizabeth instructed Frances.

Hannah More, 1780, showing Hannah as a professional writer after her success with *Percy*.

John Hoole, 1783, used as the frontispiece for his translation of *Orlando Furioso* and praised by Elizabeth Montagu as a 'perfect resemblance to him; you have conveyed into his eye the celestial fire which glows in his translations'.

Other portraits said to be by Frances are of James Harris, the critic and philosopher, and James Beattie, the Scottish poet, and his wife.

Known portraits of Frances:

As a young woman of about 17, by her brother Sir Joshua, now owned by Plymouth City Art Gallery and Museum.

Self-portrait with her sister Mary, in private ownership.

Chapter 8: The Taming of a Female Wit

Hannah More's crucial role among the bluestockings as a playwright and educator has largely (and most unfairly) been forgotten, with just the occasional attempt to resurrect her life history, most recently and admirably by Anne Stott with her 2003 biography *Hannah More: The first Victorian* (Oxford University Press, Oxford). Stott writes with great enthusiasm and verve and her book leaves you feeling that you really know More and have been with her on her long journey from the obscurity of a Devon schoolhouse to the heights of fame in London and back to rural retirement at Barley Wood. Stott also takes us inside 'the work', attempting to resolve its contradictions and difficulties for the twenty-first-century reader.

I was inspired to write this chapter by a rehearsed reading of Hannah More's tragedy *Percy*, produced by Susan Crofts and directed by Eileen Pollock at what was the London Theatre Museum in Covent Garden (18 June 2000). It was possible to see from this thoughtful reading why the play had been such a success; the dramatic tension and verse had Shakespearean power, and left me wanting to know more about the woman who had written it, and why she is now such a neglected playwright. *Percy* should be read in conjunction with Johnson's tragedy *Irene*, if only to discover the superiority of More's dramatic intuition.

The conference organised by Marion Wynne-Davies at Chawton House Library and the University of Surrey in September 2008, *Her Make is Perfect*, highlighted the difficulties of women playwrights when negotiating the transition from writing in private, in the closet, to stage-managing a performance. Elizabeth Kuti's paper in particular dealt with 'Hannah More and the Theatre of Virtue'.

Ian McIntyre's biography of *Garrick* (Allen Lane, London, 1999) is a useful source on Hannah More's friendship with the Garricks; as is George Winchester Stone Jr and George M. Kahrl's *David Garrick: A critical biography* (Southern Illinois University Press, Carbondale, IL, 1979). I have also referred to *The Letters of David Garrick*, edited by David M. Little and George M. Kahrl (Oxford University Press, Oxford, 1963).

Hannah More's reputation as a writer can be judged by three facts:

On her death, fifty years after her major success with *Percy*, publishers rushed to produce editions of her memoirs and correspondence; volumes that were reprinted and reissued several times. William Roberts's *Memoirs of the Life and Correspondence of Mrs Hannah More* appeared in four volumes (R. B. Seeley and W. Burnside, London, 1834).

Long before her death, an edition of More's 'complete works' was brought out by her publisher Thomas Cadell as early as 1801, in eight bulky volumes:

The Works of Hannah More, including several pieces never before published (T. Cadell and W. Davies, London).

Finally, the Johnson scholar R. Brimley Johnson edited a new, more concise volume of her correspondence in 1925, ninety years after her death: *The Letters of Hannah More* (John Lane, London).

Hannah More never published her thoughts on Johnson, nor did she ever write on her true mentor, David Garrick. But G. Birkbeck Hill did include a brief chapter of 'Anecdotes by Hannah More' in his *Johnsonian Miscellanies* (two volumes, Clarendon Press, Oxford, 1892).

Of Hannah's huge number of works, here is a selection:

The Search After Happiness (2nd edn, printed and sold by S. Farley in Castle Green, Bristol. Sold also by T. Cadell, Bookseller in Wine Street, Bristol; T. Cadell, Bookseller in the Strand, London, 1773).

The Bas Bleu; A conversation (published by Horace Walpole at his Strawberry Hill press in 1786). A section of the poem (and other works by More) is included in Roger Lonsdale's *Eighteenth-century Women Poets* (Oxford University Press, Oxford, 1989, and also available in paperback).

Slavery: A poem (T. Cadell in the Strand, London, 1788).

Strictures on the Modern System of Female Education (1799, included in *The Works of Hannah More*, eight volumes, T. Cadell and W. Davies, London, 1801).

Coelebs In Search of a Wife, comprehending observations on domestic habits and manners, religion and morals (two volumes, T. Cadell and W. Davies, London, 1808).

Cheap Repository Tracts, in several collected editions beginning in 1797 and ending in 1819, which are worth dipping into if only to discover quite how pious Hannah became; never, though, losing her gift for vivid fluency.

The 'unauthorised' biography which peddled inaccurate rumours about Hannah was written probably by William Shaw (who also wrote a biography of Johnson), and was provoked by her controversy with the curates of Blagdon: *The Life of Hannah More, with a critical review of her writings, by the Rev. Sir Archibald MacSarcasm, Bart* (T. Hurst, Bristol, 1802).

Johnson's essay in which he conjures up the 'Female Army' is *Idler*, No. 5, Saturday 13 May 1758: 'It were to be wished that some man, whose experience and authority might enforce regard, would propose that our encampments for the present year should comprise an equal number of men and women, who should march and fight in mingled bodies. If proper colonels were once appointed, and the drums ordered to beat for female volunteers, our regiments would soon be filled without the reproach or cruelty of an impress. Of these heroines, some might serve on foot, under the denomination of the "Female Buffs", and some on horseback, with the title "Lady Hussars".'

Other sources used in this chapter include the new scholarly edition of *The Early Journals and Letters of Fanny Burney, 1769–91*, edited by Lars Troide, Stewart M. Cooke, Peter Sabor et al (four volumes so far published, Clarendon Press, Oxford, 1988–). Katharine C. Balderston's edition of Hester Thrale's *Thraliana* (two volumes, Clarendon Press, Oxford, 1951). Hester Thrale's *Anecdotes of the Late Samuel Johnson* in the modern edition by Arthur Sherbo (Oxford University Press, Oxford, 1974).

Ellen Donkin's *Getting into the Act: Women playwrights in London, 1776–1829* (Routledge, London, 1995) is a valuable guide to the difficulties faced by women writers for the stage in late eighteenth-century London and follows not just Hannah's career but those of her 'rivals', such as Hannah Cowley.

Ann Yearsley's volumes of poetry, *Poems on Several Occasions* and *Poems on Various Subjects* (London, 1785 and 1787), have long been out of print.

Chapter 9: Resolutions?

William Godwin's memoir of his wife was first published in March 1798 as *Memoirs of the Author of a 'Vindication of the Rights of Woman'* (J. Johnson, London). Godwin would never have agreed with Johnson's politics, or his moral code, but he must surely have been inspired by Johnson's strictures on biography outlined in the *Rambler*, and especially No. 68 (Saturday 10 November 1750), in which Johnson declares, 'The most authentick witnesses of any man's character are those who know him in his own family.' It's also intriguing to read Godwin's memoir in conjunction with Johnson's *Life of Richard Savage* from 1744. Godwin's extraordinary novel *Caleb Williams* is available as a Penguin Classic (Penguin, London, 1988). After reading it, the critic William Hazlitt declared, 'No one ever began *Caleb Williams* that did not read it through. No one that ever read it could possibly forget it.'

I am indebted to Nancy Johnson for her readings of Godwin and for introducing me to *Caleb Williams*. Also for her understanding of the social and intellectual changes wrought by the events in France during the Revolution.

The seventh volume of Janet Todd's edition of *The Works of Mary Wollstonecraft* (Willliam Pickering, London, 1989) includes all her reviews for the *Analytical Review*. Wollstonecraft's *Vindication of the Rights of Woman* is now easily available as a Penguin Classic (with an introduction by Miriam Brody, 1983), and her novel *Maria; or the wrongs of woman* is published by W. W. Norton (New York and London, 1975). Todd's edition enables us to read the volumes that would be otherwise unavailable because long out of print, including *Thoughts on the Education of Daughters*, *The Female Reader*, and the unfinished fragment of 'The Cave of Fancy'. Janet Todd has also edited *The Collected Letters of Mary Wollstonecraft* (London, Allen Lane, 2003).

Johnson's sermon on the death of Tetty was first published as a separate pamphlet in 1788: *A Sermon written by the late Samuel Johnson LLD for the Funeral of his Wife* (The Rev. Samuel Hayes, AM, usher of Westminster School, London). It's more easily available in volume 14 of *The Yale Edition of the Works of Samuel Johnson*, edited by Jean Hagstrum and James Gray (Yale University Press, New Haven, CT, 1978).

I also referred in this chapter to *Rambler* No. 60 (on biography), No. 130 and No. 133.

The catalogue to the *Brilliant Women* exhibition at the National Portrait Gallery, edited by Elizabeth Eger and Lucy Peltz (National Portrait Gallery, London, 2008), contains a fine discussion of Richard Samuel's portrait *The Nine Living Muses*, resurrecting the painting, which had been in storage for many years, and its extraordinary statement of women's place in the arts in the mid-eighteenth century.

Index

Addison, Joseph 133
Allen, Edmund (printer) 126, 145, 192
Analytical Review 238
Andrewes, Lancelot 31
Anne, Queen 27, 28–9
Anti-Jacobin 207
Ariosto, *Orlando Furioso* 188, 189
Aristotle 182
  Poetics 93
Ascham, Roger 36
Austen, Jane 107, 121, 152
  Northanger Abbey 107

Bacon, Francis 36
Barbauld, Anna Laetitia (blue-stocking; 1743–1825) 8, 94
Barber, Francis 'Frank' (Johnson's manservant; c.1742–1801) 2, 192, 219
Baretti, Giuseppe ('Streatham Worthy') 50
Barry, James (artist) 172
Baxter, Richard, *The Saints Everlasting Rest* 20

Béthune, Maximilian de, Duke of Sully 119–20
Birch, Thomas (antiquarian scholar) 56, 73–4, 75, 77–9, 90, 117
  General Dictionary; Historical and Critical 73
Birmingham (home of the Porter family) 32–3, 42, 43
Birmingham Journal 38, 43, 52
Blaney, Elizabeth (friend of Michael Johnson; d.1694) 22
bluestockings 8–10, 13, 81, 89, 92, 97, 209, 216, 219, 220–22, 241
Book of Common Prayer 31, 67
Boothby, Sir Brooke 129
Boothby, Hill (1708–56) 13, 241
  description and character 111–13
  epistolary relationship with Johnson 113–16, 129–31
  illness and death 116, 128–30
  looks after orphaned children 112, 116
  receives a copy of the *Dictionary* 115

Boscawen, Frances (bluestocking; 1719–1805) 8, 81, 208, 209, 216

Boswell, James, *Life of Samuel Johnson* 3, 13, 14, 29, 36, 39, 41, 45, 46, 47–8, 97, 113, 134, 146, 179, 184, 197, 217–18, 238

Boyse, Samuel (poet) 82

Brighton (or Brighthelmston) 133, 151, 155, 164

Bristol (home to the More sisters) 202, 203

Bristol Journal 202

British Museum 29

Bromley, Kent, Tetty's grave 65–6, 114

Burke, Edmund 184

Burney, Dr Charles (musicologist) 5, 184

Burney, Charles, newspaper collection 251

Burney, Charlotte 151

Burney, Frances 'Fanny' (1752–1840) 6, 103,
  comments on Charlotte Lennox meeting Richardson 104
  comments on David Garrick 209
  comments on Frances Reynolds 183
  comments on Hannah More 217, 218, 222, 228
  comments on Hester Thrale 139–40, 151, 166
  comments on Johnson 147, 194–5, 196
  comments on 'Nonsenses' at Streatham Park 147–8
  fails to see her first play performed 213–14
  father denies her opportunity to learn Latin and Greek 5
  friendship with Johnson 6, 97, 155, 217, 218

Cecilia 152
The Witlings 175–6, 214

Cadell, Thomas (publisher) 208, 222, 223, 228

Carmichael, Poll (dates and fate unknown) 4, 145, 146

Carter, Elizabeth (1717–1806) 97, 103, 110, 119, 209, 216, 234
  birds, freedom and wild weather 80–1
  birth and family background 69–71
  buys a house in Deal 96
  comments on Lennox's poetry 99–100
  comments on slavery 191–2
  contributions to magazines 68, 71–7, 88–9
  correspondence with Catherine Talbot 8, 9, 10, 80, 84, 88–9, 92, 100
  description and character 68–9, 76, 84–5, 93, 95
  illnesses and death 83–4, 95
  insulted by Johnson 218
  letters published and destroyed 78–80, 83–4, 92–4
  poems concerning 55–6, 74, 79, 81–2
  portraits of 8, 82, 94–5, 96, 201
  praises More's *The Bas Bleu* 222
  as pudding-maker and domestic manager 69, 83, 241
  relationship with Thomas Birch 77–8
  religious ardour 75
  reputation, marriage and freedom 79–81
  as scholar and intellectual 6, 9–10, 13, 68–9, 70, 71–5, 81, 84, 89, 95, 203
  told of More's education scheme 225–6

withdrawal from London and Grub
Street 78–9, 81–3, 87
All the Works of Epictetus 89–92, 96
Body–Mind dialogue 85–6
An Ode to Melancholy 78
'Ode to Wisdom' 86–7, 90
'On the Death of Mrs Rowe' 76–7
'Poem Upon the Stars' 75
Poems on Several Occasions 94
Poems upon Particular Occasions 76
Carter, Nicholas (Elizabeth's father)
70, 71, 72, 74, 81, 202
Catherine the Great 91
Cave, Edward 'Sylvanus Urban'
(1691–1754) 51, 55, 56, 57, 59,
60, 61, 71, 72, 73, 74–5, 76, 81,
115, 117
Cervantes, Miguel de, *Don Quixote*
107
Ceylon 230
Chambers, Catherine 'Kitty' (Sarah
Johnson's servant; 1708–67) 38
Chambers, William (architect) 187
Chapone, Hester (née Mulso, blue-
stocking; 1727–1801) 267
Charles II 19, 27
Chaucer, Geoffrey 36
Cholmondeley, Mary (bluestocking;
1729–1811) 15
Chops (dog) 28
Cicero 79
Clayton, Ellen, *English Female Artists*
182
Clive, Catherine 'Kitty' (actress;
1711–85) 215, 217
Colman, George (dramatist and
theatre manager) 103
Congreve, Richard (from Lichfield)
16, 50
Congreve, William, *The Mourning
Bride* 98
copyright 100, 120
Cotterell, Admiral 179

Covent Garden Journal 107
Covent Garden Theatre 127, 175,
205, 212, 213
Cowley, Hannah (playwright; 1743–
1809) 220
Cranmer, Thomas 31
Critical Review 91–2, 168
Cumberland, Richard (playwright)
127, 230

Deal, Kent (home to Elizabeth
Carter) 69–70, 78, 79, 93, 96,
223, 225
Defoe, Daniel 22
Desmoulins, Mrs (of Johnson's house-
hold; b.1716) 41, 63, 145, 146
Devil Tavern, London 101
Dodsley brothers (publishers) 103
Drury Lane Theatre 46, 54–5, 175,
207, 210, 213

Edial school 52
Eliot, George, *Scenes of Clerical Life*
223
Elphinston, James (schoolmaster) 18,
115
Epictetus 83, 89–92

Farley, Sarah (Quaker printer) 203
Fayram, John (artist) 82, 201
Fielding, Henry 106–7, 175
Fitzherbert, Mary (friend of Hill
Boothby; d.1753) 112
Five-Mile Act (1665) 19
Fleetwood, Charles (theatre manager)
53
Fleetwood, William, Bishop of Ely,
An Essay upon Miracles 20
Floyer, Sir John (physician; 1649–
1734) 27, 29
Foote, Samuel (actor-dramatist) 98
Ford, Cornelius (Sarah Johnson's
father; 1632–1709) 19–20

Ford, Cornelius (Johnson's cousin; 1694–31) 35–6
Ford, Sarah *see* Johnson, Sarah
Fry, Elizabeth 231

Gabell, Revd Henry Dyson (corresponds with Mary Wollstonecraft) 10
Garrick, David (1717–79) 32, 218
attends Johnson's school at Edial 52
befriends Hannah More 207, 208, 209–15, 216, 218–19, 223
champions women playwrights 220
correspondence with Lennox 103, 127
description and 'sketch' of Tetty 45–6
determined to become an actor 53
farewell performances 210–11
has rooms at the Adelphi 188, 208–9
illness and death 97, 207, 210, 219
portraits of 182
as Shakespearean actor 124, 210
stages *Irene* by Johnson 54–5
stages *Old City Manners* by Lennox 127
Garrick, Eva-Marie (bluestocking; 1724–1822) 6, 97, 188, 218
Garrick, Peter 53
General Advertiser 98
Gentleman's Magazine
acknowledgement of women as authors 205
advertisement for Edial school in 52
book reviews 102–3
Carter's contributions 68, 71–4, 75, 76–7, 79, 82, 86–7
as inspiration for the *Lady's Museum* 117
Johnson's contributions 13, 55–6, 59–60, 115

launching of 51
Lennox's contributions 99–100
George III 17, 90
Godwin, William (1756–1836) 6
marries Mary Wollstonecraft 232
Caleb Williams 233
Memoirs of the Author of a 'Vindication of the Rights of Woman' 232–4, 239–40
Goldsmith, Oliver 103
Graves, Richard, *The Spiritual Quixote* 112, 130
Greene, Richard (surgeon and apothecary) 18
Greer, Germaine, *The Obstacle Race* 174
Griffith, Elizabeth (bluestocking; 1727–93) 8
Gwatkin, Mrs (friend to Hannah More) 209
Gwatkin, Robert (husband of 'Offie') 209

Harris, Thomas (theatre manager) 213, 219–20
Hawkesworth, John (essayist; 1720–73) 65
Hawkins, Sir John (lawyer and writer; 1719–89) 101–2, 126, 145–6
Hawkins, Laetitia Matilda (author of *Gossip about Dr Johnson and Others*; 1759–1835) 101, 126, 127
Hector, Edmund (Johnson's schoolfriend) 16, 38, 43
Hector, George (Edmund's father) 23
Herrick, Robert 31
Hill, George Birkbeck, *Johnsonian Miscellanies* 194
Hogarth, William (1697–1764) 175
'A Modern Midnight Conversation' 35

The Lady's Last Stake 139
Homer 35
Hoole, John (translator) 188–9
Hopkins, Gerard Manley 163
Horace 68
Hudson, Thomas (portrait painter;
      1701–79) 174
Hume, David 29, 30
Hunter, John (anatomist) 219
Hunter, William (John's brother) 219

Ivy Lane Club 100–2

Jervis family 42
Johnson, Elizabeth 'Tetty' Jervis
      (1689–1752) 16
   birth and family background 42
   children of 42, 48, 64, 165
   death of Henry Porter 44–5
   description and character 12–13,
      45–7, 49, 52
   encourages Johnson to go to
      London 53
   first meeting with Johnson 43–4
   funeral and burial 62–3, 65–6, 238
   illness and death 12, 13, 55, 58,
      61–2, 106, 109, 111, 113, 131,
      145, 192
   marriage to Harry Porter 42–3
   marriage to Johnson 12, 40–2,
      47–50, 51, 53, 56, 62–4, 66–7
   miserable life in London 55, 56–60,
      112
   moves to Gough Street 60–1
   opens Edial school with Johnson
      52, 203
   portrait of 46–7
Johnson, Joseph (radical publisher)
      238
Johnson, Michael (Johnson's father;
      1656–1731) 12, 19, 21–3, 29,
      33–4, 36–7, 38
Johnson, Nathaniel (Johnson's

brother; 1712–37) 19, 28, 32,
      34–5, 38, 51
Johnson, Samuel (1709–84)
   attitude towards women 3–4, 5, 7,
      11, 116, 201, 237, 241–2
   birth and infancy 23–5
   'black dog' experiences 10, 138,
      163, 198–9, 239
   breadth of conversation 6
   comment on friendship 10–11
   comment on Pope 12
   comments on marriage 21, 22
   comments and views on Piozzi and
      his marriage to Hester Thrale
      151, 159–61, 165
   concern for Tetty's health 58–9
   considers possible second marriage
      113–14
   contributions to the *Gentleman's
      Magazine* 13, 55–6, 59–60, 115
   creates new kind of biography 87,
      239–40
   description and character 12, 43–4,
      132–3, 151, 161, 170–1, 194–9
   education of 31, 36–9
   epistolary relationship with Hill
      Boothby 113–16, 129–31
   exceptional abilities of 31–2
   adopts the role of female confi-
      dante 111, 131, 180
   financial situation 17, 53, 55, 56,
      59–60, 61–2
   his first play staged by Garrick in
      London 53–5
   household arrangements after
      Tetty's death 145–7
   illness and death of 192, 218–19,
      238
   interest in medicine and chemistry
      129, 136
   love of London 56–7, 187
   marriage to his 'dear Tetty' 12, 40–2,
      47–50, 51, 53, 56, 62–4, 66–7

meeting with Mary Wollstonecraft 1–2, 5–6, 232, 233–4, 240

moves to Gough Square 60–1

newspaper reports of his affair with Hester Thrale 153–4

opens Edial school with Tetty 52, 203

passion for letter-writing 10, 136–7

portraits of 172, 173, 180, 189, 194, 196, 199

reaction to Tetty's illness and death 61–3, 64–6

relationship with Charlotte Lennox 97–8, 102, 103–4, 106, 109–11, 124–5, 127–8, 131, 147, 155, 218, 241

relationship with Elizabeth Carter 55–6, 69, 74, 83, 88–9

relationship with Frances Reynolds 172, 179–80, 185, 195–9, 209, 241

relationship with Hannah More 200, 201, 217–18, 219

relationship with Hester Thrale 132–4, 136–8, 144–5, 150–1, 159–64, 167–71, 199

relationship with his father 33–5

relationship with his mother 14–19, 31, 39

relationship with the Thrale children 154–7, 165

religious convictions 21, 30, 112–13, 198–9

stays with relations 33, 35, 36

strange episode of the letters in French 161–4

suffers from scrofula 25–31

understanding of the domestic situation 2–3, 11–12

voracious appetite and lack of table manners 12, 33, 129, 147

wordgames and rhyme-making competitions 136, 147–8

Adventurer essays 114–15

Annals 22, 24, 25, 28

Dictionary of the English Language 2, 14, 15, 16, 17, 26–7, 30, 32, 35, 36, 44, 51, 60, 61, 63, 66, 72, 90, 103, 115, 124, 130, 132, 167

Harleian Miscellany 167

The History of Rasselas, Prince of Abyssinia 3, 5, 21, 66, 203, 237

Idler essays 18, 35, 69, 117, 132, 201, 228, 236

Irene 53–5, 64

Life of Pope 137

Life of Richard Savage 60, 87, 239

Lives of the English Poets 12, 30, 32, 162, 239

London: A poem 57

Prayers and Meditations 66

Rambler essays 4, 12, 21, 32, 35, 41, 66, 69, 87–9, 109, 115, 116, 120, 132, 236

Taxation No Tyranny 192

'To Eliza Plucking Laurel in Mr Pope's Gardens' 55–6, 74

Johnson, Sarah (née Ford; 1669–1759)

birth and family background 19–20

birth of her sons 23–4

carries on her husband's business 38–9, 57

death 14, 18, 21

description and character 12, 13, 14–15, 18, 31

devotional reading 20–1

education of Samuel 31–3

illness of Samuel 25–9

marriage 21, 22–3

memorial stone and epitaph 18–19

relationship with her son 14–19, 31, 39

sends Samuel to a wet-nurse 24–5

shops for souvenirs in London 30–1

uses her inheritance to send
Samuel to Oxford 37
Jonson, Ben 31
Eastward Hoe 127
Juvenal 35, 57

Kauffmann, Angelica (artist; 1741–
1807) 8, 94, 179
Kenwood House, Hampstead 144
Keppel, Commodore Augustus 177
Knight, Ellis Cornelia (writer) 182

*The Ladies' New and Polite Pocket
Memorandum Book* 94–5
Lady's Museum magazine 117–18
Lennox, Alexander (Charlotte's
husband; d.1797) 103–4, 119,
120–1, 128
Lennox, Charlotte (1729/30–1804) 7,
8, 13, 62, 145, 234
alienation from other women
writers 109–10
appearance in court 126–7
becomes an actress 98
birth and family background 98
children of 116
creates an illustrated magazine
117–18
death and burial 128
description and character 98, 103,
104–5, 119, 126, 127–8
as gifted and prolific writer 98–100,
102–3, 106–9, 116–17
ill-health 116
as innovator and inspiration to
others 117, 118–19
marriage 103–4, 119–21
night of triumph 100–2
portraits of 103, 119
as pudding-maker 124
relationship with Johnson 97–8,
102, 103–4, 106, 109–11, 124–5,
127–8, 131, 147, 155, 218, 241

shares rooms with Frances Reynolds
186
'Art of Coquetry' 99–100, 118
Euphemia 121–4
The Female Quixote 62, 98, 104–9,
112, 117
The Greek Theatre of Father Brumoy
117
Henrietta 127
The History of Harriot and Sophia
117, 118, 121
*The Life of Harriot Stuart, Written
by Herself* 100, 102–3, 107
Memoirs of Maximilian de Béthune
119–20
Old City Manners 127, 186
*Poems on Several Occasions, Written
by a Young Lady* 99
Shakespear Illustrated 103, 124–6
The Sister 127, 205, 230
Lennox, George Louis (Charlotte's
son; b.1770) 116, 128
Lennox, Harriet Holles (Charlotte's
daughter; b.1765) 116, 126, 127–8
Levet, Robert (of Johnson's house-
hold; 1705–82) 145–6
Licensing Act (1737) 175
Lichfield Cathedral Library 36
Lichfield Grammar School 32, 37
Linley, Elizabeth (singer and
Sheridan's wife; 1754–92) 8
Literary Club 6, 7, 40, 209
Literary Magazine 120
Little Theatre, Haymarket 98
Lobo, Father Jerome, *Voyage to
Abyssinia* 38–9
London
Adelphi, Strand 188–9, 208, 209,
211
Bolt Court 2, 5, 145–6, 189, 234
British Museum 29
Covent Garden Theatre 127, 175,
205, 212, 213

Dead Man's Place 133
Devil Tavern 101
Drury Lane Theatre 46, 54–5, 175, 207, 210, 213
Goodman's Fields, Whitechapel 53
Gough Square 60–1, 62, 64, 89, 103, 106, 129, 145, 192, 194
Grub Street 72, 81, 87, 119
Leicester Fields 181, 182, 184, 185, 187, 189
Little Britain, St Paul's 28
Little Theatre, Haymarket 98
Old Slaughter's Coffee House, St Martin's Lane 175
Opera House, Haymarket 175
Pantheon 216
Ranelagh Gardens 1
St John's Gate 72–4, 77
St James's Palace 28
Southwark 17, 135, 144, 150, 153, 162
Three Chickens, Cheapside 28
Tothill Fields, Westminster 65
Vauxhall Gardens 245
Wine Office Court 103
London Packet 132

Macaulay, Catherine (bluestocking; 1731–91) 8
Macrobius 36
Malahide Castle, Ireland 113
Malone, Edmond 177, 184
Marklew, John 24
Metastasio, Pietro 203
Millar, Andrew (printer) 103, 104–5, 119
milliners 175–6
Montagu, Elizabeth (bluestocking; 1720–1800) 8, 9, 70, 81, 92, 94, 119, 133, 190, 193, 200, 209, 216
Montagu, Lady Mary Wortley (writer; 1689–1762) 74

Monthly Review 92, 102
More, Elizabeth 'Betty' (sister of Hannah) 202
More, Hannah (1745–1833) 6, 7, 8–9, 97, 103, 234
  adopts the cause of Ann Yearsley 222–3
  anti-slavery campaigner 191, 224–5
  birth and family background 201–2
  conflict between ambition and virtue 200, 205, 215, 216, 218, 219, 220, 222
  death of 230
  defends herself in an ecclesiastical court 227
  description and character 202, 205, 206, 207, 216–18, 230
  engaged and abandoned 205–7
  life in London 200–1, 216–17
  lives at Cowslip Green, Somerset 222, 223–4, 228
  meets and becomes a 'pupil' of Garrick 209–15
  portraits of 173, 193, 200, 206, 241
  as pupil then teacher at her sisters' school in Bristol 202–3
  relationship with Johnson 200, 201, 217–18, 219
  zeal for education 225–31
  The Bas Bleu (The Bluestockings) 7–8, 9, 220–2
  Cheap Repository Tracts 228
  Coelebs In Search of a Wife 228–30
  The Fatal Falsehood 219–20
  The Inflexible Captive 207–8
  Percy 13, 212–16, 220, 222, 230
  Sacred Dramas 223
  The Search After Happiness 203–5, 212
  Slavery: A Poem 224–5
  Strictures on the Modern System of Female Education 202–3, 226
  Village Politics 227–8

More, Jacob (father to the More sisters) 201–2
More, Martha 'Patty' (sister of Hannah) 202, 208, 226, 230, 231
More, Mary (sister of Hannah) 202, 203
More, Sarah (sister of Hannah) 200, 202, 207, 208
Morning Post 153, 168
Mothers' Union 241
Mozart, *Clemenza di Tito* 203
Murphy, Arthur (playwright) 133

Neild, Mary (of Derby; b.1663) 22
Newbery, John (publisher) 61
Newton, Isaac 73, 175
Newton, Revd John (anti-slavery campaigner) 223, 225
Nicholson, John (owner of Chops) 28
North, Anne Speke, Lady 215
North, Frederick, Lord (prime minister:1770–82) 215

Old Slaughter's Coffee House, St Martin's Lane 175
Oliver, Dr (inventor of the Bath Oliver) 134
Opera House, Haymarket 175
Opie, John (artist) 241
Ovid 35
Oxenden, Sir George (friend of the Carter family) 70, 74

Palmer, Theophila 'Offie' (niece of Frances and Joshua Reynolds; 1757–1848) 186, 209
Pantheon, London 216
Payne, John (publisher) 103
Pembroke College, Oxford 37–8, 39
Pennington, Montagu (Elizabeth Carter's nephew and editor) 78, 92

Petrarch 35
Piozzi, Gabriel (1740–1809) 151–4, 159–61, 164–6
Piozzi, Hester Lynch Thrale *see* Thrale, Hester
Plato 82, 182
Playboy Club, London 241
Pliny 9
Plymouth, Devon 175, 176, 178
Plympton, Devon 173, 175, 207
Pope, Alexander 12, 35, 56, 74, 76, 137
 Essay on Man 73
Porter, Elizabeth *see* Johnson, Elizabeth 'Tetty' Jervis
Porter family 42–3
Porter, Henry 'Harry' (d.1734) 40, 42, 43, 44–5, 47
Porter, Jervis (Tetty's son; b.1716) 42, 48, 61, 64
Porter, Joseph (Tetty's son; b.1724) 42, 48, 49, 61, 64
Porter, Lucy (Tetty's daughter, b.1715) 16, 42, 43–4, 46, 48, 49, 57, 61, 64, 165
Priestley, Joseph, *The History and Present State of Electricity* 221

Ramsay, Allan (artist) 175, 193
Ranby, John (sergeant-surgeon), *The Method of Treating Gun-shot Wounds* 58
Reynolds, Elizabeth (Frances's sister; b.1721) 173, 174, 175
Reynolds, Frances 'Renny' (1729–1807) 11, 13, 168, 200
 artistic talent 172–3, 174, 178, 179, 180–1, 182, 186, 193–4, 206, 217, 241
 attempts to live at Wick House 187–8
 becomes a milliner 175–6, 178
 birth and family background 173–4

comments on sex and race 191–2
death of 185
description and character 172, 175, 176, 181, 182, 183–4, 186, 190
friendship with Johnson 172, 179–80, 185, 195–9, 209, 241
keeps house for her brother Joshua 178–9, 184
leaves London for Paris 184–5, 186
love, but no marriage 184–5, 187
peripatetic life 188–9
portraits of 175, 176
relationship with her brother Joshua 174, 178–9, 182, 187, 188
retires to Devon 186–7
shares rooms with Charlotte Lennox 186
shows Johnson More's poem *The Bas Bleu* 222
An Enquiry Concerning the Principles of Taste, and of the Origin of Our Ideas of Beauty etc. 189–93
'Recollections of Johnson' 194, 195–7, 198–9
Reynolds, Sir Joshua (1723–92) 11, 103, 168, 216
birth and family background 173–4
death of his sister Theophila 173
difficult relationship with his sister Frances 174, 178–9, 182, 187–8, 188
'employs' Frances as his house-keeper in London 178–9, 184
gift for friendship 174–5, 176–7, 184
gives chaotic dinner parties at Leicester Fields 184, 200
as good businessman 174, 181–2
invites his niece Theophila ('Offie') to take over from Frances as housekeeper 186
lectures and writings 189
looks after his unmarried sisters 175

single-mindedness and dedication 172–3, 174
the 'Streatham Worthies' 138
travels in Italy 177–8
Discourses 189
A View from Richmond Hill 187
A Young Black 192
Reynolds, Mary 'Molly' (Frances's sister; b.1716) 173–4, 175, 176
A Devonshire Dialogue 174
Reynolds, Revd Samuel (Frances's father) 173, 175
Reynolds, Theophila (Frances's mother) 173, 175
Richardson, Samuel 88, 90, 104–5, 106
Clarissa 10, 86–7, 103
Rowlandson, Thomas 13
Royal Academy 179, 184, 189
Royal Literary Fund 128
Royal Society of Arts 172
Rugby School 42, 51

St James's Chronicle 142
St James's Palace 28
St Michael's Church, Lichfield 18
St Oswald's, Ashbourne (Derbyshire) 128
St Peter and St Paul, Bromley (Kent) 65–6, 113
St Werburgh's, Derby 47
Salusbury, John (father to Hester Thrale) 139, 142
Salusbury, Sir Thomas (uncle to Hester Thrale) 140, 141, 143
Samuel, Richard (artist; fl.1770–86), *The Nine Living Muses* 8, 94–5, 119, 179, 200, 212, 231, 234
Savage, Richard (poet; d.1743) 56, 60
School of Anatomy, London 219
scrofula (the 'King's Evil') 25–9
Secker, Thomas, Archbishop of Canterbury 91, 93

Seneca 35, 182
Seward, Anna (the 'Swan of
    Lichfield'; 1742–1809) 22, 49
Seward, Sarah (Anna's sister; d.1764)
    49
Shakespeare 7, 31, 32, 98, 103,
    124–6, 138, 209, 210, 216
  Hamlet 125
  Henry V 15
  Measure for Measure 125
  A Midsummer Night's Dream 14
  Much Ado About Nothing 9–10
  The Winter's Tale 125
Shaw, William (biographer of
    Johnson; 1749–1831) 63
Sheridan, Richard (playwright,
    husband of Elizabeth Linley) 213
  The School for Scandal 216
Shipton, John (surgeon; 1680–1748)
    58
Siddons, Sarah (actress; 1755–1831)
    182
*Sketch of the Character of Mrs Elizabeth
    Carter* 95
slavery 191–2, 224–5
Smollett, Tobias, *Launcelot Greaves*
    118
  'The Progress of the Arts and
    Sciences under the Reign of
    George II' 118–19
Society for Promoting Female
    Education 230–1
South Sea Bubble (1720) 70–1
Stanhope, Philip, Earl of Chesterfield
    35
Stationers' Company 7
Stillingfleet, Benjamin (the first blue-
    stocking; 1702–71) 8
Stonhouse, Revd James (friend of the
    More family) 206–7, 209
Strahan, William (printer) 103, 106
Strawberry Hill, Twickenham 220
Streatfeild, Sophy (Greek scholar and

society beauty; 1754–1835)
    147–8
Streatham Park 137–8, 142–3, 146–9,
    151, 152, 171, 186
Sunday-school movement 226–7, 231
Swift, Jonathan 22
  Gulliver's Travels 60
Swynfen, Dr (father to Mrs
    Desmoulins) 63

Talbot, Catherine (bluestocking;
    1721–70), correspondence with
    Elizabeth Carter 8, 9, 10, 80, 81,
    84, 88–9, 92, 93, 100
  *Reflections on the Seven Days of the
    Week* 93
Taylor, the Revd John (Johnson's
    schoolfriend) 61, 62–3, 65, 112
Thirty-Nine Articles of the Church
    of England 19
Thrale, Anna (d.1770) 158
Thrale, Cecilia (b.1777) 144, 159,
    164, 166
Thrale, Frances Anna (d.1775) 144,
    158
Thrale, Frances (d.1765) 158
Thrale, Henry 'Harry' (d.1776) 158–9
Thrale, Henrietta (d.1783) 151, 159
Thrale, Henry (1728–1781) 152, 162,
    186
  brewery attacked 153
  commissions Reynolds to paint
    fourteen portraits 138
  concerned at Johnson's eating
    habits 145, 146
  considered inferior and insignificant
    compared with Hester 134
  constructs summerhouse and labo-
    ratory for Johnson 144–5
  creates library at Streatham Park
    137–8
  description and character of 140,
    141, 143

dinners with Johnson and friends 104, 133, 137

illness and death 148–50

known as the 'Southwark Macaroni' 142, 164

marriage to Hester 140–3, 164, 170

shock at death of his son Harry 159

Thrale, Hester (née Salusbury; 1741–1821) 4, 5, 104, 180, 186, 209

anecdotes of Johnson 17–18, 33–4, 45–6, 48

asks Johnson about Tetty 47

birth and family background 138–9

births and deaths of her children 134, 143–4, 158–9

comments on Hannah More 201, 217

comments on Reynolds and his sister 178–9, 187, 198

description and character of 132, 134, 136, 139–40, 144, 150–1

friendship with Johnson 132–4, 136–8, 144–5, 150–1, 159–64, 167–71, 199

illness and death of her husband 149–50

Johnson's relationship with her children 154–7

life at Streatham Park 143, 146–9

literary career 142, 167–9, 170

marriage to Henry Thrale 140–3, 164, 170

marriage to Piozzi 151–4, 159–61, 164–6, 241

newspaper reports of her affair with Johnson 153–4

portraits of 138, 139

relationship with her children 157–9

strange episode of the letters in French 161–4

told of More's poem *The Bas Bleu* 222

Anecdotes of the Late Dr Samuel Johnson, during the last twenty years of his life 17–18, 33–4, 45–6, 48, 161, 167, 170, 194, 217

British Synonymy 168

'Imagination's Search after Happiness' 142

Observations and Reflections Made in the Course of a Journey through France, Italy and Germany 167–8

Retrospection 168

Thraliana 34, 134–6, 147, 151, 154–5, 161, 170, 178–9

Thrale, Hester Maria 'Queeney' (b.1764) 137, 151, 154, 155–7, 158, 159, 164–6

Thrale, Lucy Elizabeth (d.1773) 158

Thrale, Penelope (d.1772) 158

Thrale, Ralph (d.1775) 144, 158

Thrale, Sophia (b.1771) 164

Thrale, Susannah (b.1770) 164

Three Chickens, Cheapside 28

Tissington Hall, Derbyshire 112, 113, 115, 116, 129

Titian 177

Turner, William (affianced to Hannah More) 205–7

Tyndale, William 31

Verelst, Marie (artist; 1680–1744) 46–7

Veronese, Paolo, *The Marriage of Cana* 177

Vesey, Elizabeth (bluestocking; 1715–91) 8, 9, 81, 92, 220

Virgil 35

Walpole, Horace 98, 103, 168, 220

Warren, Thomas (newspaper proprietor) 38, 43

The Whole Duty of Man (1657) 20, 24

Wick House, Richmond Hill (Surrey) 187–8

Wilberforce, William 224, 225
Williams, Anna (of Johnson's household; 1706–83) 89, 145, 146, 193–4, 195
Woffington, Peg (actress sister of Mary Cholmondeley; 1720–60) 15
Wollstonecraft, Mary (1759–97) 8, 229
  argues for women's rights and duties 4, 235–6
  comment on 'fine ladies' 176
  death of 232, 240
  description and character 2, 240, 241
  familiarity with Johnson's works 3, 10–11, 236, 237
  influenced by Johnson 4, 5, 237, 239
  meeting with Johnson 1–2, 5–6, 232, 233–4, 240
  portrait of 241
  reviews publications on Johnson 238–9
  sets up a school with her sisters 203
  unimpressed by Charlotte Lennox's novel *Euphemia* 121
  works as governess and lady's companion 234–5
  'The Cave of Fancy' 237–8
  The Female Reader 236
  Maria; or The Wrongs of Woman 121
  Thoughts on the Education of Daughters 5, 24, 118, 234–5, 239
  Vindication of the Rights of Woman 2, 54, 176, 239
Woodhouse, James (poet) 133
Woolf, Virginia, *A Room of One's Own* 95
Wright, Joseph (artist, of Derby) 129

Yearsley, Ann ('milkmaid' and poet; 1752–1806), *Poems on Several Occasions* 222–3